THE GOOD COM:

Has China become just another capitalist country in a socialist cloak? Will the Chinese Communist Party's rule survive the next ten years of modernization and globalization? Frank N. Pieke investigates these conundrums in this fascinating account of how government officials are trained for placement in the Chinese Communist Party. Through in-depth interviews and a survey of staff members and aspiring trainees, he shows that while the Chinese Communist Party has undergone a radical transformation since the revolutionary years under Mao, it is still incumbent upon cadres, who are selected through a highly rigorous process, to be ideologically and politically committed to the party. It is the lessons learned through their teachers that shape the political and economic decisions they will make in power. The book offers unique insights into the structure and the ideological culture of the Chinese government, and how it has reinvented itself over the last three decades as a neo-socialist state.

FRANK N. PIEKE is a Lecturer in Modern Politics and the Society of China at the University of Oxford, and is a Fellow of St Cross College. His previous publications include *The Ordinary and the Extraordinary: An Anthropological Study of Chinese Reform and the 1989 People's Movement in Beijing* (1996) and he was the first co-author of *Transnational Chinese: Fujianese Migrants in Europe* (2004).

THE GOOD COMMUNIST

Elite Training and State Building in Today's China

FRANK N. PIEKE

University of Oxford

CAMBRIDGE UNIVERSITY PRESS

CAMBRIDGE
UNIVERSITY PRESS

University Printing House, Cambridge CB2 8BS, United Kingdom

Cambridge University Press is part of the University of Cambridge.

It furthers the University's mission by disseminating knowledge in the pursuit of education, learning and research at the highest international levels of excellence.

www.cambridge.org
Information on this title: www.cambridge.org/9781107547698

© Frank N. Pieke 2009

This publication is in copyright. Subject to statutory exception and to the provisions of relevant collective licensing agreements, no reproduction of any part may take place without the written permission of Cambridge University Press.

First published 2009
First paperback edition 2015

A catalogue record for this publication is available from the British Library

ISBN 978-0-521-19990-2 Hardback
ISBN 978-1-107-54769-8 Paperback

Cambridge University Press has no responsibility for the persistence or accuracy of URLs for external or third-party internet websites referred to in this publication, and does not guarantee that any content on such websites is, or will remain, accurate or appropriate.

Contents

List of illustrations		*page* vi
Preface		vii
1	Socialism, capitalism and the anthropology of neo-socialist rule	1
2	Cadres, cadre training and party schools	26
3	Cadre training and education in the twenty-first century	56
4	Life and work at party schools	81
5	Marketization and centralization of cadre education and training	114
6	Cadre training, cadre careers and the changing composition of China's political elite	141
7	Conclusions: cadre training and the future of party rule	180
Appendix 1	*List of interviewees*	196
Appendix 2	*Student questionnaire survey*	201
Appendix 3	*Glossary of Chinese terms*	206
References		210
Index		222

Illustrations

PHOTOGRAPHS

Photo 1.1 Professor Duan Eryu and the author in front of the entrance of the Yunnan Provincial Party School	*page* 22
Photo 4.1 Inside the Yunnan Provincial Party School	82
Photo 4.2 Student dormitory at the Yunnan Provincial Party School	83
Photo 4.3 Getting ready for lunch at the Yunnan Provincial Party School	84
Photo 5.1 Entrance of the Qujing Party School	134
Photo 5.2 Classroom at the party school of Honghe Prefecture	135

FIGURES

Figure 6.1 Odds of rank mobility by gender, age and education	152
Figure 6.2 Crossover of units by age and gender	155

MAPS

Map 1 The People's Republic of China	viii
Map 2 Yunnan Province	ix

Preface

The fieldwork, survey and documentary research carried out in China between 2004 and 2007 would not have been possible without the help and cooperation of the many scholars, students and administrators in Yunnan and Beijing who freely gave their time to answer the many questions I put to them. My most important debt is to Professor Duan Eryu, who was my official counterpart at the Yunnan Provincial Party School. He had the courage and foresight to accommodate the outrageous request from a foreign anthropologist to be allowed into the inner sanctum of the Chinese Communist Party. He not only arranged my fieldwork at the provincial and sub-provincial schools in Yunnan featuring in this book, but also became my most important informant and, in time, a personal friend. In facilitating other parts of the project, I would like to thank Zhao Baige, Fan Jianhua, Zhang Lihua, Shen Yuan, Liu Xirui, Xiang Biao, Yang He and several others who should remain anonymous. Excellent research assistance was given by Li Yongkang in Yunnan, Wu Qiquan and Zhang Huayang in Beijing and Meera Balarajan in Oxford.

In the course of writing the manuscript, I have burdened several friends with the thankless task of reading drafts of papers, chapters or even the whole manuscript. Chris Hann, Sun Xiangdong, Susan Greenhalgh, Bill Hurst, Brian McVeigh and an anonymous reviewer for Cambridge University Press are in no way responsible for any of the mistakes or omissions that remain, but should certainly be given much credit for whatever qualities the finished product has.

Fieldwork research for the project was funded by the Economic and Social Research Council (grant no. RES-000-22-0727) and the Nuffield Foundation (grant no. SGS/01020/G). Their support is gratefully acknowledged.

FRANK PIEKE
Oxford

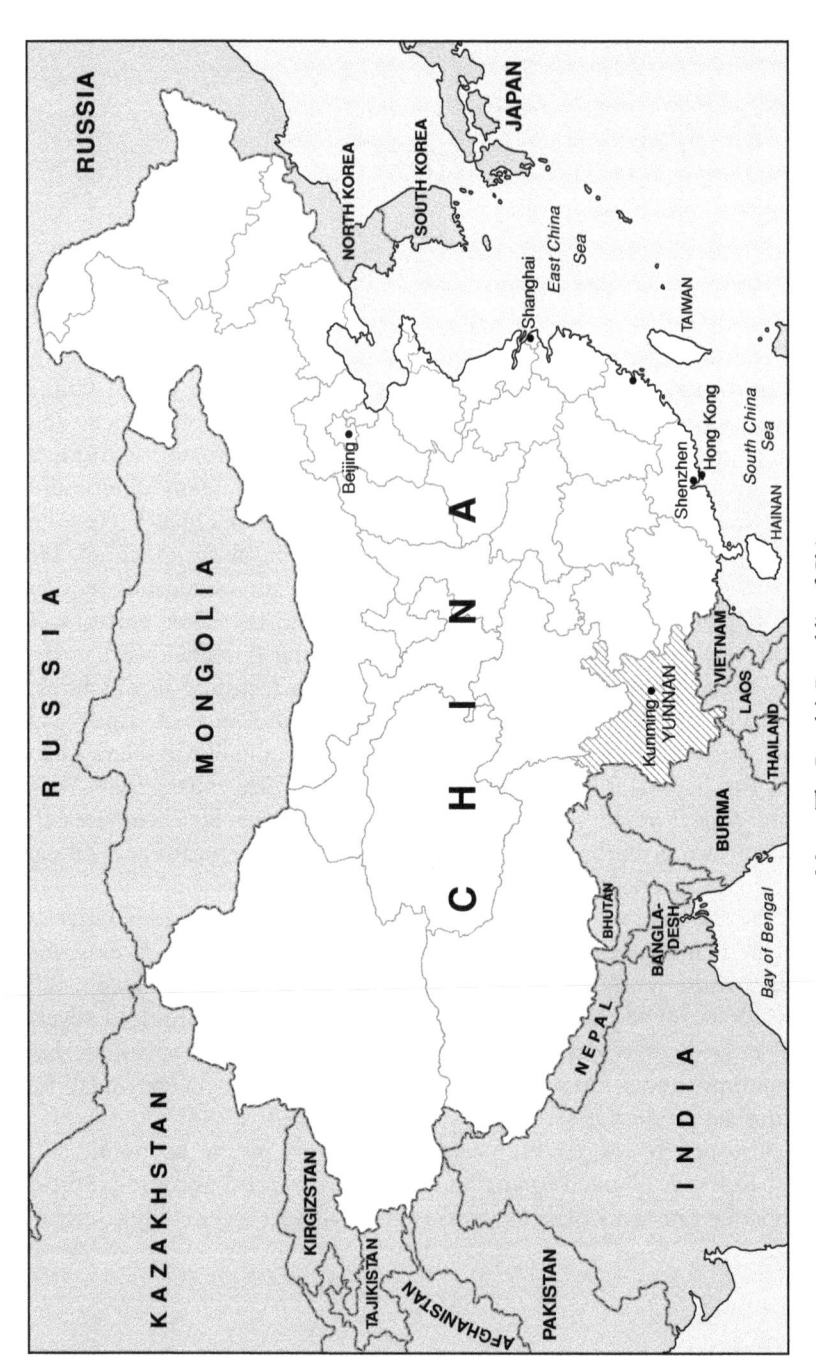

Map 1 The People's Republic of China

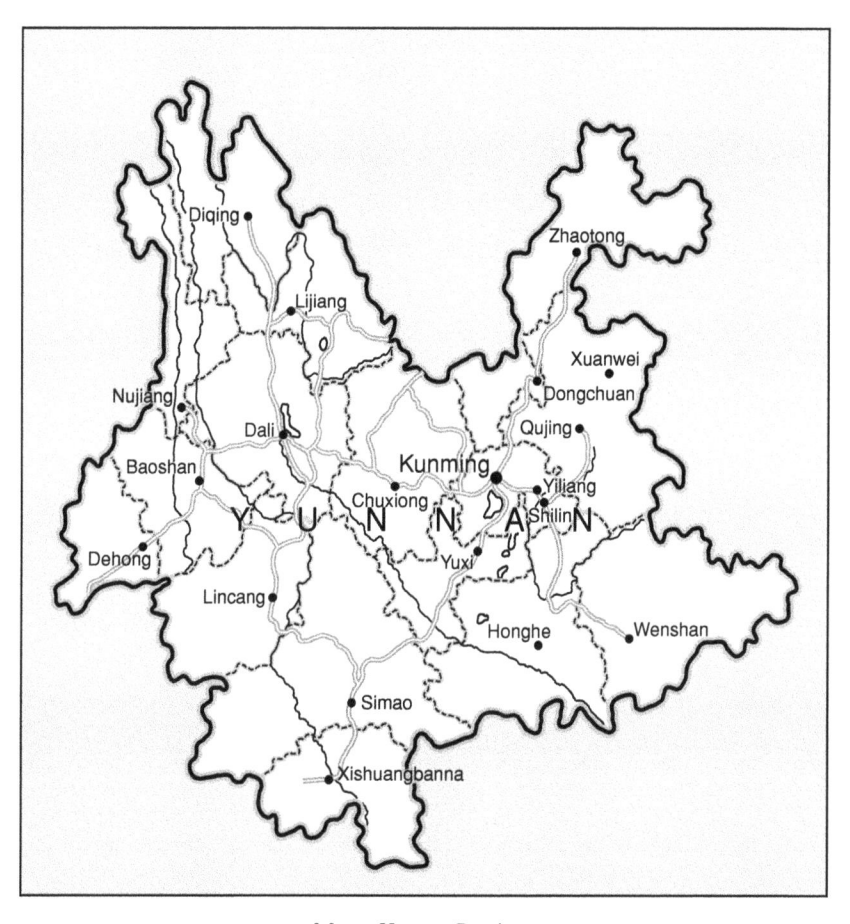

Map 2 Yunnan Province

CHAPTER I

Socialism, capitalism and the anthropology of neo-socialist rule

Putting the Chinese Communist Party's reinvention of the party-state at the centre of the epochal transformation of China into a global superpower, this study homes in on the education and training of cadres (administrators and politicians), a crucial but almost completely overlooked aspect of the Chinese party-state. Cadre training is an entry into the often opaque and mysterious world of the people in China who staff the party-state and rule the country, a way of understanding the Communist Party's enduring and growing power inside and outside China without having to risk an investigation in the often secret and highly sensitive specifics of the exercise of that power itself. Cadre training also highlights the fact that China's contemporary administration is Mao Zedong's worst nightmare become real. Gone forever are first-hand revolutionary experience and direct involvement in the life and work of China's toiling masses. Instead, cadres have become a ruling elite who worship book learning and formal educational qualifications. As the embodiment and chief instrument of the party's leading role in society, cadres are to be leaders, managers, moral exemplars and faithful servants of the party at the same time. The learning, discipline and privilege that cadre training provides is a key transformational experience in the construction of cadres' unique personhood, a sense of self that straddles the boundaries between strong individuality, total submission to the party's will, elitist exclusivity and faceless anonymity. Before the reforms, cadre training had always been the principal means to instil ideological uniformity and commitment to the party, but since the early nineties it has increasingly been tasked with much more. Nowadays, training also aspires to equip cadres with the managerial skills, professional knowledge and broad understanding of China and the world that the party considers necessary for the people who will have to lead the country to full modernity and global prominence.

In this book I draw on my ethnography of China's cadre corps for a critique of the commonly held view (both inside and outside China) that socialism in China is dead in all but name. At the most general level, this view is based on the notion that socialism and capitalism are mutually exclusive and antagonistic social formations, despite their common roots in the western modernizing project.[1] The basis of the assumed antagonistic relationship of socialism and capitalism lies in the holistic status that they are given. Although this in turn traces its origin to Marxist theory, the assumption of the inevitable clash between socialism and capitalism has long since been shared by socialist and bourgeois thinking alike. Socialism and capitalism are thought to be all-inclusive social formations, comprising a specific organization of the economy, politics, social relations and culture. Through revolution, warfare or evolution, the exploited masses will rise against their masters and socialism will eradicate capitalism. Alternatively, capitalism will supplant socialism as a new middle class and propertied bourgeoisie created by market reform demand democracy.[2] One variant of the latter idea that is particularly relevant to this book is that capitalism might not necessarily bring full-blown democracy, but at least will turn China into a non-socialist technocracy (White 1998: 500).

However, as living ideologies and realities, socialism and liberalism can and have been intertwined, or, as Raman and West put it, 'actually existing socialism and actually existing capitalism were never so distinct, and never independent of each other' (Raman and West 2009: 5). If we no longer assume that, for instance, a capitalist market economy must bring other aspects of 'bourgeois' society like democracy and human rights as well, there is nothing irreconcilable between, for instance, a capitalist economy and a socialist form of government. We will then be able to see that the evolution away from the state socialism and revolutionary voluntarism of the Maoist era and the growth of a market economy do not necessarily spell doom for a locally meaningful understanding of socialism as a form of governance, i.e. the exercise of political authority and the use of institutional resources to coordinate and control activities in society that include, but are not limited to, the work of government. Obviously, this in great measure depends on how one defines socialism. In particular, such an analysis sits uneasily with externally defined criteria that determine what the essential components

---

[1] On the latter point, see Buck Morsse 2000.
[2] See Tsai (2007) for an extensive critique and empirically grounded refutation of this argument. In chapter 4 of *The Transformation of Chinese Socialism*, Lin Chun thoughtfully discusses the larger issue of the Chinese fate of western liberalism and democracy, concluding that 'we must treat political democracy as something subordinated to the imperatives of human needs and human rights, public welfare and social justice, peace and ecology' (Chun 2006: 249).

of socialism ought to be (for instance, public ownership of the means of production, dictatorship of the proletariat, fairness and redistribution, democratic centralism). By contrast, this book does not evaluate or measure the degree of socialist purity of contemporary China. Likewise, I also do not wish to engage the debates in China itself about the nature and contemporary relevance of socialism, although I do, where necessary, of course discuss the recent elaborations on the party's official ideology.[3] Instead, I approach socialism ethnographically as it is lived and reproduced every day by the elite personnel, or *cadres*, that lead the institutions of governance: 'really existing reform socialism' from the perspective of those who govern rather than those who are governed. To cadres, the unique nature of socialist governance has always been linked with the dominance of the Chinese Communist Party (CCP), which has not seriously been challenged, despite the heavy blows that the party suffered during the 1989 student movement.

In the nineties, to myself and many other observers the turmoil and suppression of the 1989 protest movement and the long-term corrosive impact of market reform made a fundamental shift in China's political structure seem inevitable, leading either to a more democratic and pluralistic form of government, or else to the fragmentation or at the very least a radical decentralization of the state (Pieke 1996). There were several reasons for this. Perhaps the most legitimate one, at least in my own anthropological eyes, is the routine cynicism and contempt with which citizens of all socialist states treat the party, the state, its cadres and its ideology.[4] In Chinese studies after 1978 this was compounded by the embarrassment, or alternatively glee, over the follies of sixties and seventies fellow-travelling

---

[3] Not much of these debates is known outside China, or indeed in China itself outside the small circle of ideological professionals in party schools, universities and the party apparatus itself. For a clear and concise discussion of the Chinese Communist Party's recent ideological innovations, see 'Rebuilding the Party: The Ideological Dimension', chapter 6 in David Shambaugh's recent book on the Chinese Communist Party (Shambaugh 2008: 103–127). In his book *What Does China Think?* Mark Leonard discusses debates among some of China's New Left intellectuals that are directly or indirectly relevant to the meaning of socialism as a guiding ideology (Leonard 2008).

[4] It is quite hard, and methodologically not easy to defend, to say that the natives have got it wrong. However, as far as the natives are concerned I would argue that cynicism is not simply a rejection, but more a way of coping with the grim realities of 'really existing socialism'; it is, in fact, a curiously backhanded internalization of communist rule. A rejection of the ideology goes together with the acceptance of many of its practical manifestations, such as cradle-to-grave social security, state paternalism, the pervasiveness of party rule and the like. Currently in China, cynicism about the state and denunciations of the CCP and its corrupt cadres continue to be widespread, but – and this is where outsiders often get it wrong – it is only infrequently coupled with a fundamental rejection of the *status quo*.

that took the CCP's ideological messages largely at face value. It has now become a 'habit of the heart' among China scholars to reject Maoism and its successor ideologies (Deng Xiaoping Theory, the 'Three Represents', the 'harmonious society') as blatant lies that merely serve to coat the CCP's rule in a thin veneer of legitimacy, rather than as serious attempts to define socialism or the CCP's role and vision.

More generally, and in a neat reversal of scientific Marxist evolutionism, the military and diplomatic defeat of the Soviet Union in the Cold War was too often glossed as the ideological and historically inevitable victory of democracy and capitalism over dictatorship and socialism. Although somehow China had escaped the same destiny, at least temporarily, the attempts of the CCP to reinvent itself since 1989 seemed of little importance, the final spasms of a doomed and fundamentally flawed system. Instead, the main issues being debated in the field were how much the state had to negotiate with local elites in exercising power; to what extent special interests and personal relationships informed the behaviour of agents of the state; to what extent the unified state had become a loose configuration or federation of regional governments or local state corporations; or how state-led democratization, legal reform and administrative restructuring were giving civil society the space to operate in opposition to the state.[5]

Yet since the late nineties, it has become increasingly clear that the weakening of the Chinese party-state has not happened. Capitalizing on rapidly rising prosperity and continued economic growth, the party-state has reinvented itself, putting the rule of the CCP on an increasingly solid footing both materially and organizationally, and, increasingly, ideologically. Although the jury is still out on the long-term sustainability of the reinvention of the Chinese party-state, radical political change now seems unlikely. It seems that the reformers around Deng Xiaoping who assumed power in 1978 were right, and western, particularly American, proponents of the 'peaceful transformation' thesis were wrong: market reform and socialist governance are, for now at least, perfectly compatible and even support each other. As Dali Yang put it: 'while the Chinese state has played an important role in expanding the market, market expansion has, in turn, helped prepare the ground for the rationalization of the state' (Yang 2001: 19). In other words, the state has created the conditions for the market to flourish, while the growth of a market economy has made possible an ambitious state-building effort. The end of state strengthening is by no

---

[5] For an overview of these debates, see Baum and Shevchenko (1999).

means in sight, and potentially outstrips all earlier attempts to rationalize and strengthen the state in Chinese history.[6]

REFORM AND THE PARTY-STATE

In the last twenty-five years, the Chinese economy and society have developed at an extraordinary speed. Many issues and problems have emerged as a result, but on the whole the real miracle has been that China has maintained a remarkable stability and direction despite many fundamental changes. The reasons behind this are obviously diverse and defy quick generalizations, but governance is an important component. China's unique administrative structure, with a finely struck and negotiable balance between centralization and devolution, and between the selfish (and often corrupt) behaviour of officials and party discipline is at the heart of this success story. In post-Mao China, entrepreneurial success has been bred by different forms of state involvement in the market, ranging from 'local state corporations' to 'income generating' spin-off companies to symbiotic networks of officials and entrepreneurs to outright graft and corruption.[7] Parts of the state, in other words, have mutated to become a range of institutions that have enabled the market to grow. Despite mounting empirical evidence, it should be noted that this counterintuitive conclusion is by no means uncontested. Alternative analyses of the Chinese market economy tend to look at the lack of appropriate institutional guarantees as they are found in western capitalist countries, such as an independent legal system or the democratic election of officials, either concluding that the 'market transition' is still incomplete (Nee 1989; Nee and Su 1990; Nee 1996; Woo 1999), or else pointing to the predatory rent-seeking behaviour of officials simply as inhibitive to sustained economic development (Bernstein and Lü 2000; Lü 2000; Bernstein and Lü 2003).

China is indeed one of the most corrupt countries in the world, but it is quite another thing to say that corruption fatally undermines the CCP's

---

[6] A few scholars have begun to turn their attention to the growth and transformation of the state, and, increasingly, the Communist Party itself; see for instance Edin 2000; Blecher and Shue 2001; Dickson 2003; Shevchenko 2004; Walder 2004; Yang 2004. For a comparative study of three specific periods of state strengthening during the Qing dynasty, Republican China and the People's Republic, see Thornton (2007). I will have to add that Thornton herself does not seem to believe in the impact of the current state-building drive, instead emphasizing the corrupting influence of the market on the CCP's rule.

[7] On these institutional inventions, see for instance Oi 1992; Lin 1995; Pieke 1995; Walder 1995; Pieke 1996; Duckett 1998; Gore 1998; Lin and Ye 1998; Gore 1999; Oi 1999; Wank 1999; Remick 2004; Tsai 2007.

legitimacy and governmental capacity, or to claim that western democracy is a necessary cure for corruption. Illinois governor Blagojevich's botched attempt in 2008 to sell President-Elect Barack Obama's vacant seat in the US Senate has demonstrated again that mature democratic political systems, too, are capable of accommodating deeply entrenched corruption.[8] Analyses of the antagonism of state and market are predicated on the belief, as outlined at the start of this chapter, that there is a fundamental incompatibility between socialism and capitalism. Because of that, they tend to focus only on what China does not have rather than on what it does have, and fail to acknowledge that the mice of economic development and political stability can be caught by cats, and indeed even corrupt cats, of many different colours. There is little doubt that, particularly in the nineties, corruption in China was rampant, with cadres high and low using their official powers to rake in money from the booming market sector, both for private gain and to boost the income of the local governments and departments for which they were responsible. Similarly, there is also ample evidence from surveys that by the late nineties corruption had become the foremost societal problem in the eyes of the Chinese people. However, there is much less evidence that corruption necessarily undermined the state's capacity to rule. Anti-corruption campaigns aimed at individual culprits, for instance, in the eyes of the public put the central authorities on the side of the people, thus in fact strengthening the state's legitimacy (Hsu 2001; Yang 2004: 221–222). More broadly, particularly in the nineties, corruption was the grease in the wheels of a society that combined a rapidly growing market economy with what was, at the time, a still largely old-fashioned socialist state (Wank 1999).

As Shevchenko has persuasively argued, in this context of proliferating state-market arrangements the continued presence of the CCP at the heart of the system has provided the stability, direction and detachment from local, sectoral or individual interests that are crucial for the reform process to continue (Shevchenko 2004). In other words, the continued presence of the Chinese Communist Party is not the *problem* that the reforms have to overcome; quite the contrary, the CCP's blend of modernist adaptability and Leninist ideological and organizational principles is one of the main *causes* of twenty-five years of economic growth and social stability. At the core of the CCP's strategy lies not simply its ability to facilitate institutional invention at the interface of state and society. As Maria Edin observed,

[8] Evan Thomas, Suzanne Smalley and Richard Wolffe, 'Being Rod Blagojevich', *Newsweek* 22 December 2008, online at www.newsweek.com/id/174386 (checked on 8 January 2009).

equally, if not more, important is the party's willingness to reinvent itself (Edin 2003a: 4), while, at the same time, retaining core Leninist principles of governance that continue to guarantee its leading role over state and society.

As this new fusion of socialism and the market in China continues to develop, transform and adapt to new challenges, it becomes necessary that we go beyond the limits of the concept of *post*socialism dominating the study of the former Soviet bloc (Verdery 1996; Humphrey 1998; Burawoy and Verdery 1999; De Soto and Dudwick 2000; Hann 2002; Mandel and Humphrey 2002). To account for the resilience of socialist rule, China scholars now often use the term 'late socialism'. However, implicit in this term is the assumption that socialism has simply gained a stay of execution: sooner or later, the prefix 'late' suggests, the forces of history are sure to catch up with China. In my view, this not only undervalues the staying power of the CCP and the importance of the modernization and state-building effort in post-Mao China, but also seriously under-theorizes the novelty of what I propose to call the *neo-socialist* social, political and ideological institutions that have emerged.[9]

NEOLIBERALISM AND NEO-SOCIALISM

It has become quite common, mainly in the American literature, to characterize the Chinese reforms or aspects thereof as neoliberal and thus comparable to the backlash against the welfare state in many western countries (and especially the Anglo-Saxon world) since the late seventies. In his influential book on neoliberalism, David Harvey typifies the Chinese reform project as simply 'neoliberalism "with Chinese characteristics"' (Harvey 2005). Similarly, Gary Sigley concludes that China has witnessed what he calls the 'emergence of a hybrid socialist-neoliberal (or perhaps "neoleninist") form of political rationality' (Sigley 2006: 489). Susan Greenhalgh and Edwin Winckler observe that China's birth control policy has evolved from a Maoist–Stalinist approach in the eighties to a Leninist–neoliberal

---

[9] In earlier work, I developed the concept of 'capital socialism' (Pieke 1995; 1996); more commonly used nowadays is 'market socialism'. Both these terms focus on economic and social institutions and practices. In this book governance itself is central, hence 'neo-socialism'. Interestingly enough, my use of the term neo-socialism is rather similar to the earliest occurrence of the term postsocialism that I know of in an article by Arif Dirlik, in which he describes postsocialism not as something that simply comes after socialism, but as a 'condition of socialism' that 'represents a response to the experience of capitalism' with the reforms and opening up of China in the eighties (Dirlik 1989: 364).

approach since 2000 (Greenhalgh and Winckler 2005).[10] This characterization certainly has its uses, and I would not wish to simply dismiss it here. Neoliberalism highlights a distinct convergence or borrowing between China and capitalist countries in the strengthening of markets, the retreat of the state as welfare provider and the creation of 'responsible' individuals and families. It also helps better understand the strengthening of the state in other respects. Unlike classical liberalism, neoliberalism believes that a healthy market economy cannot be left to its own devices, but needs strong institutional guarantees for its growth and protection, guarantees that only a strong state can provide. Likewise, strong government needs the market (for instance through privatization or the contracting out of services) to keep it honest and effective. The problem is that neoliberalism is in the main a negatively charged term used to expose the self-serving and cynical application of liberalist notions by right-wing politicians and ideologues. This neoliberal language not only conflates, as traditional liberalism does, the economic freedom of unfettered market exchange and the political freedom of universal suffrage and multi-party democracy. In the hands of big business and big government neoliberalism can also be a blatant legitimizing tool in the exploitation and suppression of poor and powerless individuals, groups and even whole nations. As such, for many progressive intellectuals neoliberalism has become a convenient alternative to terms such as 'capitalism' and 'imperialism', that served a similar function in the sixties and seventies, but whose more direct Marxist roots have rendered them politically largely impotent in our post-Cold War world.

A strongly politically charged term, neoliberalism as an analytical concept has some distinct disadvantages wherever it is applied, but perhaps even more so in the Chinese context. Using the example of the discourse on 'quality' (*suzhi*) in China, Andy Kipnis has argued that simply presenting this discourse as a manifestation of neoliberalism ignores *suzhi*'s specific roots and connotations. Presenting 'quality' as neoliberal thus suggests similarities that aren't really there, for instance to the American right-wing discourse that 'blames the poor' for their own poverty (Kipnis 2007). I largely agree with Kipnis here. In the context of this book, it would be misleading to assume a simple equivalence between, say, Margaret Thatcher's privatization of government functions in the eighties and the marketization of cadre training in China in the 2000s, if only because of the fundamentally different political and ideological context. As we shall see, the Chinese reform of cadre training is part of a massive state-building effort based

---

[10] Other works that are frequently referred to in this regard include Anagnost (1997) and Ong (2006).

on a very un-Thatcherite faith in the power of a modern, centralized and well-resourced government in shaping society and the economy. Yet treating China's attempts at state building entirely *sui generis* would be equally incorrect. For several decades now, Chinese leaders, administrators, academics and businesspeople have mined western (and above all American) society, culture, politics and economy for clues, ideas and models – many of them 'neoliberal' – that may help make China a better place, and this book will give many examples of this effort. Following Nikolas Rose and Peter Miller, it might therefore be useful to distinguish between larger 'political rationalities' with specific genealogies in certain locations on which the exercise of power is conceptualized, and more limited governmental technologies that are easily borrowed and transposed (Rose and Miller 1992: 175). Although the Chinese reforms borrow many ideas and techniques of government from neoliberal thought and practice in the West, they are blended with indigenous socialist ideas and practices, producing a distinctively Chinese neo-socialist governmental discourse. From a Chinese perspective, the coming of neoliberalism thus resembles less the spread of a hegemonic western blanket than a process of selective borrowing and mixing, a 'creolization' process rather similar to other aspects of globalization (Hannerz 1987; 1992; 2000) in which Chinese actors moreover remain firmly in control.

Just as the 'neo' in neo-socialism suggests a rather loose connection well short of a direct equivalence with western neoliberalism, so does the 'socialism' of neo-socialism not refer to the state socialism of the collective period, which entailed a planned economy, collective or state ownership of the means of production, state or collective responsibility for citizens' welfare, and the mobilization and transformation of the entire society for the realization of the communist utopia. Under neo-socialism, the CCP's socialist mission is formulated as the engineering of an orderly process of socialist modernization and the engagement of economic globalization and the 'multi-polarization' (*duojihua*) of the community of nations (Hu Jintao 2003). An equally, if not more, important aspect of the socialism of neo-socialism is the perpetuation of the CCP's Leninist rule. Leninism (less its mobilizational and transformational aspects) continues to inform the core of the party's work: party leadership over all institutions of governance, and, within the party itself, the enforcement of democratic centralism and party discipline, and the requirement of an unqualified belief and adherence to the party's principles and ideology (Jowitt 1992).

Neo-socialism in China entails more than an old-fashioned Leninist party that puts neoliberal techniques to familiar uses. As I will show in this book, under neo-socialism, innovative neoliberal and home-grown governmental technologies cut right to the heart of the party-state itself, serving to support, modernize and strengthen the party's Leninist leading role in Chinese society. Crucial to the party's neo-socialist project has been a combination of centralization, strengthening and selective retreat of the state. Since 1994, the central state has broadened its tax base and control over local revenue.[11] This has enabled the state (particularly, but not exclusively the Centre) to take a whole raft of policy initiatives that in the early nineties still were utterly impossible, including a deliberate and selective process of streamlining, professionalizing, democratizing and centralizing the Chinese state apparatus. The party itself has sought to broaden its base in society by recruiting new members among China's new elites, including intellectuals and even private entrepreneurs (Dickson 2003; on China's new rich see Goodman 2008). The state has assumed the role of managing, facilitating and supervising society: 'while governments at both the central and the local level are clearly far less intrusive than before, micro-managing fewer areas of socioeconomic and cultural life, they have arguably become more adept at macro-management – in effect, governing less but governing more effectively' (Baum and Shevchenko 1999: 352).

A second characteristic of the neo-socialist strategy has been the selective, partial and gradual nature of the marketization of state or collective assets and functions. This ranges much wider than the well-known issue of the very slow pace of privatization of state-owned enterprises. Gradually, markets have been created for a vast range of commodities, resources and services, including labour, capital, insurance, housing, education, health care and land. In none of these cases has the state fully retreated from the markets its own policies have created, retaining a larger or smaller role for state agencies or state-owned enterprises as providers, regulators and quite often also as major stakeholders. Crucially, competitive markets also have been created for at least some functions that are at the very core of the party-state's Leninist legacy. One of the main findings of this book is how cadre training and education are no longer the unchallenged monopoly of party schools. A range of local, national and international providers,

---

[11] See Wong 2002. In a recent paper, Christine Wong argues that budgetary revenues began to rebound only in 1996, three years after the tax reforms of 1994 which are more conventionally taken as the point when the central state began to regain control. According to Wong, the main reason for the time lag between policy and effect was the impact of continued centre-to-local government tax rebates that allowed local governments to continue to maintain their spending levels (Wong 2007: 6).

mostly regular universities and schools, have entered this new, lucrative market. Likewise, cadre recruitment has been broadened with the open, competitive selection of first ordinary government personnel and later also leading officials.[12]

Third, the Chinese Communist Party invested considerable resources in ideologically redefining its place in Chinese society from a 'revolutionary party' to a 'ruling party', since 2000 formulated as the Party's 'Three Represents' (*sange daibiao*). No longer is the party the 'vanguard of the proletariat', but the representative of the fundamental interests of the broad mass of the population, advanced productive forces and advanced culture. This formulation can be read either very inclusively or very exclusively, depending on the issue of the day, but clearly the working class is no longer especially privileged. However, we should not treat such truths emanating from the party's ideological apparatus with more respect than they get in China itself. In the Maoist period, the party and the state in the final analysis were mere tools to achieve what really mattered: a communist utopia. In that situation, the question of faith in the ideology was deadly serious, often literally so. Under neo-socialist rule, the communist utopia has been replaced by a technocratic objective of a strong, peaceful and modern China that is almost synonymous with strong, effective and forward-looking government. With this, the specifics of the party's ideology have become much less of an issue: one could even say that any ideological construction that justifies continued party rule would be just as good as any other. Not only is faith in socialism equated with loyalty to the party-state and acceptance of its continued right to authoritarian rule. This also was the case during high Maoism. Much more seriously, means and end have swapped positions. Socialist ideology is no longer the end served by Communist Party rule, but the mere means by which party rule is perpetuated. Yet this does not mean that ideological innovation is therefore unimportant at the level of practical governance: recent elaborations such as the 'harmonious society' (*hexie shehui*) or 'taking people as the basis' (*yi ren wei ben*) signalled important policy shifts. The specific relevance of ideology in justifying the CCP's rule means that in this book we will investigate the deployment of ideology as part of the party-state's ongoing quest to reproduce and reinvent itself: ideology is treated not as the objective of rule but as an inseparable aspect of practical governance.

---

[12] In a sample constructed by Ian Seckington of 162 published biographies of county leaders, 57% had received training at a party school, 26% at a university, 6% overseas and less than 5% each at either a radio/TV college or an adult education college (Seckington 2007: 13).

THE PARTY-STATE AS SOCIETY

This book is intended as a study of the nature and repercussions of Chinese neo-socialist governmental practice. The strengthening and increasing sophistication of the neo-socialist Chinese party-state, both organizationally and ideologically, make it imperative that our understanding of Chinese society is explicitly informed by research of the party-state itself. However, such research should not fall into the trap of earlier 'statist' work that reified the state as a separate object external to society (Skocpol 1985). Research has to be sensitive to the multifaceted and often quite deliberately ambiguous interaction that takes place across the state–society interface. In order to understand what constitutes the state, we have to understand what happens in society and vice versa.

In its embedded view of the Chinese party-state, this book takes its cue from the recent literature on the state, power and governmentality in anthropology and sociology that has been directly or indirectly inspired by the work of Michel Foucault. Much of this literature concludes that we have to direct our attention away from the state in favour of a much broader 'problematics of government' (Rose and Miller 1992: 174). I agree that a simple focus on the power of the state often obscures more than it illuminates. The state is just one of many ways of governing society, each with its own specific modes of representation, strategies of legitimization of power, programmes of rule, governmental technologies and interlocking fields of interaction (Corrigan and Sayer 1985; Abrams 1988; Foucault 1991; Rose and Miller 1992; Gupta 1995; Trouillot 2001; Ferguson and Gupta 2002). However, there are two considerations that make this approach less than satisfactory. First, specifically in China the totalitarian aspirations of the collective period still loom large. Despite thirty years of reform, the institutions of the state continue to be involved almost wherever one looks. Partial and often conflicting processes of decentralization, centralization, marketization and regulation have created a complex and opaque web of institutions that involve a range of different state and private actors rather than autonomous institutions of civil society and economy. More than in western liberal democracies, the hand of the state in China weighs very heavily indeed and is formally or informally present in (almost) all governmental activities. The second consideration is more generally relevant: an undue focus on the production, use and distribution of power in the exercise of government. Like all other social institutions, the state is much more than what is does, i.e. a way that power is exercised in the government of society. As I will demonstrate in this book, the state is to the people who staff it also a lived-in reality: a way of life, a culture of being and a community of belonging. Understanding aspects of the state that do not directly revolve around the use of power and government, including more formal activities like cadre training and education, I argue, is not only important in its own right, but ultimately (and perhaps paradoxically) also indispensable to understanding how the state as a practical governing institution operates.

Empirically, this translates as what Joel Migdal has called an interdisciplinary anthropology of the state (Migdal 1994; 2001). This approach disaggregates the groups, individuals, levels and institutions that are discursively glossed and legitimized as 'the state'. Moreover, the state is not viewed as a finished product, but, like all other institutions, as an ongoing process of becoming, as forever incomplete efforts at reinvention and formation both by design and the attrition of countless intentional and unintentional daily actions (Shue 1988: 25–29). This 'state-in-society' approach conceptualizes the state less as a clearly delineable set of institutions than as an aspect that is present in many, if not all, institutions and practices in society. However, there also is another side to this coin. As I explained in an earlier publication (Pieke 2004), I would like to go a bit farther than Migdal and other proponents of the state-in-society approach. To me, thinking of the state as merely interacting with society reveals the remnants of a way of thinking that continues to be predicated on the idea of a state–society dichotomy, thereby implicitly assuming that the state is somehow qualitatively different from all other social institutions. Instead, we should think of the state *as* society: the state is not merely in society, the state is society. The state undeniably is a set of unique institutional arrangements, yet, as I explained above, it is also more mundanely a social environment in which people live. Interaction of real-life people in the context of state institutions produces forms of social action that are at the same time both highly specific and informed by patterns of behaviour existing in society beyond state institutions. Analytically, the anthropology of the state as society approaches the state ethnographically, just like any other community or institution. This perspective draws our attention to the specific ways of life and work within state institutions, patterns of sociality and consumption, and more generally the bodily and cultural practices that together constitute the distinctive life style of the agents of the state.

The anthropology of the state thus begs the question of culture in both of the two broad senses of the word: shared ways of making sense of the world ('collective representations') and shared patterns of behaviour that make it possible to live in a specific social and natural environment. Approaching the state as they would any other aspect of society, anthropologists are obviously aware that the state is also a rather special social environment, namely one that specializes in the exercise of power in ruling a territory and population. Even more than in other environments, the anthropology of the state has to be sensitive to what Abner Cohen long ago called man's 'two-dimensional' nature. Building on the work of earlier anthropologists who were partially outside the mainstream of British social anthropology, such as Gregory Bateson, Max Gluckman and Victor Turner, Cohen asserts that social life consists of both cultural (or 'symbolic' in the now nearly obsolete language of the seventies) action and power relationships. According to Cohen, the central problem of anthropology ought to be the relationship between these two: a concentration on only one results in mere description (Cohen 1974: 13). From this follows that power is not simply coercive or even just hegemonic. Power, as the ability to make people behave in a certain way, is always culturally constituted; indeed – and this is the ultimate conclusion that we can draw from Cohen's work – power and culture in the final analysis are just different sides of the same coin. To anthropologists, there is no 'raw' power. Power can only be culturally constituted, reproduced, exercised and challenged, just as cultural action always implies the exercise of power.

Bringing such general observations to the study of the state, some anthropologists (and other social scientists of a kindred spirit) have tended to focus on the more obviously cultural aspects of the exercise of state power: the ritual and pomp of ceremonies, the symbolism of state ideologies, the sacralization of leaders (Bellah 1967; Moore and Myerhoff 1977; Geertz 1980; Hobsbawm and Ranger 1983; Abélès 1988; Kertzer 1988). In the case of cadre training, too, ritual aspects are by no means absent, and I will show in this book that there is indeed considerable mileage in treating cadre training as a rite of passage (or rite of renewal) that establishes or confirms cadres' membership and allegiance to the party or the wider field of Chinese administration. However, cadre training is much more than a ritual; to begin with, certain aspects of training are better understood as a preparation for participation in the secular rituals of the party-state, including what Herzfeld called the 'commonplace rituals' of daily bureaucratic action (Herzfeld 1992: 37). In more general terms, we therefore have to conclude that the connections (and ultimate identity) of power and culture in the context of the state go far beyond ritual or ritualization. Again Abner Cohen in a later book entitled *The Politics of Elite Culture* has been a pioneer is this respect. What Cohen terms the 'dramaturgy of power' includes the cultivation of both a power cult and a cult of eliteness that render the exercise and possession of power mysterious and ambiguous, and, we could add, seem natural and legitimate. The importance of Cohen's approach to the ethnography of the Chinese party-state is that his focus on the mystique of power-as-culture enables us to see the exercise of power not as a separate quality, but as an aspect of the entire life and life style of a ruling group. Indeed, the exercise of power is part of everything that members of a ruling group do, from the food they eat (or choose not to eat) to the people they marry and socialize with, the neighbourhoods they live in, the patterns of consumption they can afford, the way they speak and write, the comportment of their bodies, and the schools and universities their children go to (Cohen 1981).

In the more than twenty-five years since Cohen wrote *The Politics of Elite Culture* anthropology has developed enormously. In particular, the impact of Foucauldian discursive 'constructivism' has impelled anthropologists to focus much more and much more explicitly on the web of connections between culture and power. Specifically, Foucault's observations on the 'governmentalization' of the state and other institutions of society – the exercise of power through the formation of governmental apparatuses and a complex of knowledges which have as their target not mere sovereignty and rule but the disciplining and surveillance of the population (Foucault 1991; see also 1977; 1978) – are directly relevant to the anthropology of contemporary China. Susan Greenhalgh's book on the genealogy of Chinese birth control (Greenhalgh 2008) and Matthew Kohrman's study on disability and the formation of the China Disabled Persons Federation (Kohrman 2005), for instance, have shown how specific discourses of science, suffering and modernity have been produced and brought to bear on forms of governmentality that are a potent mix of Leninism, Stalinism, neoliberalism and scientism. In this book we will take a further step. In the context of cadre training, we will see how the Chinese party-state has developed specific disciplinary, educational and surveillance techniques which are part of a larger strategy of governmentality that takes the party-state and its leaders themselves as its object. In the process, the party-state creates a highly specific power cult that turns bureaucratic administrators into an elite who embody the charisma of the party and its ideology. In the process, they have developed a specific cult of eliteness. From this perspective, the party and its ideology are not simply vehicles for the ruling elite's exercise of power, but are generative of this elite and its power cult. However, we shall also see that the ruling elite's power cult and cult of eliteness, in true Gramscian fashion, are only in part imposed by the central leadership of the party. The events, social networks, knowledge and habits that make up much of the daily practice of governance are also a product of the accumulated interaction of localized ruling elites, and formal training at party schools and elsewhere plays an important role in shaping these.

The reason for highlighting Cohen's contribution here is not only that his work is uncluttered by the excessive theorizing jargon that has come to Foucault-inspired anthropology since the early eighties. More importantly, Cohen shows with unusual clarity how his insight into the culture of power and the power of culture is to be realized ethnographically in a non-European context, and it is here that his work makes a direct and tangible contribution to my anthropology of the Chinese party-state. Like Cohen's study on Sierra Leone's ruling elite, this book views the Chinese party-state as it is being lived in by the people who populate it and shape the networks, communities of practice, ways of exercising power, institutions and administrative levels that collectively are called 'the state'.

Such a specifically ethnographic approach brings us back to our point of departure, namely the state as society. The state as society approach treats where and how the state exists as an empirical question: How do the people who work and live with the state shape and constitute the discourses, practices and institutions that to outside observers so often appear as a unitary organization? This methodological move has two interrelated consequences. First, it means that we have to confront the narratives that the Chinese state and party produce about themselves and their role in society. This we have to do without benchmarking them against what we think is true and proper socialism, or, conversely, true and proper liberal democracy. Here we are less concerned with the content of ideology than with the performative tasks that ideological work fulfils among the ruling elite of the party-state. Second, we have to get a grip on the *state's mode of reproduction* and the changes therein. As we have seen above, the neo-socialist Chinese state's mode of reproduction revolves crucially around the role of the CCP, which continues to suffuse the entire state apparatus, providing it with leadership, purpose and strategy, coordination, and its ultimate *raison d'etre*. Indeed, to the party itself the state simply is its main, but by no means sole, instrument of governance in Chinese society. Despite much official rhetoric about the separation of party and state, both structural and practical arrangements of governance continue to be informed by Leninist principles that assign to the party the status of prime and unchallengeable driver of governmental processes. Quite intentionally, exactly where the party stops and government begins remains anybody's guess.

CADRE MANAGEMENT AND CADRE TRAINING

In this book I tackle the issue of the neo-socialist state as society by interrogating the efforts to standardize, modernize and sanitize the practice and ethos of administration. The party has a range of tools at its disposal to maintain its grip over the state, but the key component of continued Leninist supervision is its control over the careers of the cadres that populate the government, public services, state-owned enterprises, the judiciary, the arms of representative government (people's congresses and political consultative conferences) and indeed the party apparatus itself. The party's management of cadres (*dang guan ganbu*) gives the party the ultimate decision-making power across the institutions of formal governance. To the party itself, this principle is the final guarantee that the party will continue to be unchallengeable as what used to be called the 'vanguard of the proletariat' and is now known as the 'ruling party'. If we can better understand the changes and continuities in how the CCP manages its own personnel, we will have gone a long way in understanding many other questions about the Chinese state in the reform process as well. Of course, efforts to strengthen the party's grip over its own cadres are hardly new in China. Many political campaigns of the Maoist era were partly or chiefly devoted to bringing local cadres to heel, fighting bourgeois corruption and bureaucratization, and reinvigorating their revolutionary spirit. Yet neo-socialist administrative changes are fundamentally different. The solution for the ills of China's administration is sought not in rekindling the revolution, but, quite the contrary, in strengthening and rationalizing bureaucratic structures, procedures and attitudes.

This observation might, at first glance, be counterintuitive, used as we are to thinking of socialist societies as giant bureaucracies, and market reforms as the means to counter the ills of this total bureaucratization of social life. Yet as we learn more about the past of state socialism, it becomes increasingly clear that its bureaucratic structures often had little to do with bureaucracies as described by Max Weber: rational, rule-bound, impartial, professional and impersonal. We do not have to go as far as Eddy U who, in his recent book, coined the word 'counter-bureaucracy' to highlight the reign of ideology, the arbitrary exercise of power and the priority given to political over professional qualifications in socialist party-states, to accept his argument that socialist societies went under because they *lacked* sufficiently bureaucratic organization (U 2007). Against this background, it is no longer that surprising that neo-socialism entails much more than the creation of markets. Neo-socialism is, in fact, predicated on the creation of a strong, effective and modern bureaucracy from the ruins of 'really existing socialism', while at the same time maintaining the party's Leninist control. This book scrutinizes the interlocking patterns of neo-socialist marketization, bureaucratization and party building. Specifically, it is about a vital aspect of neo-socialism – the reform of the cadre system (the training, appointment, evaluation, promotion and dismissal of government and party officials and locally elected or appointed leaders), and, more specifically, the education, training and qualification that is intended to raise the 'quality' of such cadres (Kipnis 2006).

However, both socialist and neo-socialist administration are about much more than bureaucratic effectiveness. In an influential article originally written in 1978, Kenneth Jowitt elaborated on the Weberian concept of charismatic leadership to explain the ethos of Leninist ruling parties. According to Jowitt, Leninist parties are unique organizations in that they have transferred the charismatic mystique of rule from the person of the leader to the party as an organization (Jowitt 1992). Here I would like to add the perhaps obvious observation that the charismatic mystique of the party is predicated not merely on its organization but also on the existence of an ideology that defines the ultimate goals that the party can refer to in its claims to infallibility: abolition of class exploitation, national salvation or nowadays simply 'development' and full membership for China of the modern world order. Although the ideological content and goals are variable and change over time (provided they refer to the canon of Marxist classics), having an ideology is indispensable: without it Leninist charismatic rule would degrade into mere authoritarianism.

It is my contention here that this 'organizational charisma' of communist parties is anything but faceless. Leading cadres are the embodiment of the party's charisma, a delegated charisma that they possess and display by being steeped in the party's power cult and the cult of eliteness. The party's power cult entails much more than the party's own anodyne discourse on 'quality': education, civilization, moderation, public spirit and selflessness. Being a party cadre is also about very specific 'techniques of the self': the cultivation and quite literally the incorporation of the accoutrements and mystique that make the party-state's delegated power real, tangible and imminent. These include manners of speaking, writing, listening and even walking, smoking, drinking, eating, singing and whoring that are part of cadre life, the network of relationships with people that matter within the party-state, and quite simply the fact that one is privy to the main manifestations and metonyms of the exercise of power within the party: policies, documents, opinions, speeches, exhortations and gossip that signify that cadre power is always delegated power emanating from a mysterious 'Centre' and whose exact source is always a cause of inference, suggestion and conjecture. The confidential nature and the varying degrees of access between cadres to policies and other documents create meticulous distinctions of knowledge and power that cover the rule of the party as a whole and that of individual cadres in a cloak of secrecy, adding greatly to its mystique and efficacy.

With a focus on the power cult and the cult of eliteness cadre training becomes of especial, even pivotal interest. Like all other forms of education, we can expect that the impact of cadre training lies only partially in its formal curriculum and objectives. Cadre training also socializes into the broader formal role expectations of a cadre and the informal cultural skills and expectations of the CCP's specific power cult. This study will show that cadre training is a strategic site where the party not only imparts the knowledge and skills needed of cadres. Cadre training also turns cadres into a ruling elite, whose whole composure expresses the mystique of the CCP's power. Cadre training may appear to be a dull Maoist backwater best left to the ideological hacks that instil sterile ideological messages on those who are paid to pretend to believe anyway. However, in reality, cadre training is a rapidly moving and actively debated policy area that puts some of the fundamental issues and choices that confront the party in especially sharp relief. An understanding of the policies and practices of cadre training yields a direct insight into how the CCP views and acts upon itself. These insights help us understand the future that the party charts out for itself as China's 'ruling party'. Cadre training and management are a truly national enterprise in which the central authorities are not only the driving force, but also take on an increasing number of tasks. At the other, regional end, cadre training is a crucially important prong in the Chinese state's long-term civilizing project to bring modern, unifying government to even the most remote corners of the nation. Cadre training involves not only the extraordinary system of thousands of party schools, but also a plethora of other training centres, cadre academies, regular schools and universities and ad hoc training programmes. Cadre training has developed important inter-regional and international dimensions, with countless programmes negotiated by local or national schools or authorities that enable cadres to spend periods of a few weeks to a few months in schools in other, more 'advanced' areas, or indeed abroad. By specifying how the many rules and regulations and the practice of cadre management, education and training shape real career opportunities and strategies in the Chinese administration, this ethnographic study presents an understanding of the Chinese Communist Party's rule not only as a set of institutional arrangements, but also as everyday communities and forms of administrative practice.

THE PROJECT

Research took place during a three-year period between March 2004 and April 2007. During this period, I undertook five research trips to China. In March and April 2004 I stayed for a period of four weeks at the Yunnan Provincial Party School near Kunming city in Yunnan province, southwest China. During this period, I mainly conducted interviews with students, administrators and teachers at the school, and I also was allowed to attend a few classes. In November and December 2004, I returned to Yunnan for a further stint of interviews at the Provincial Party School and two very useful trips to visit prefectural and county party schools in eastern and southern Yunnan. In September 2005, I paid my final visit to the Yunnan Provincial Party School to make arrangements for a questionnaire survey of all students that would attend training courses at school in the autumn semester of 2005. In December 2006 and again in April 2007 I visited Beijing for interviews with administrators and teachers at the Central Party School, the National Academy of Administration, the Beijing Municipal Party School, Tsinghua University, Peking University and Renmin University. I also made a short trip in November 2007 to the Universities Service Centre for China Studies at the Chinese University of Hong Kong to collect publications and other printed materials on party schools and cadre training at the Centre's library. In addition, I used my involvement in training programmes for Chinese cadres at the University of Oxford to gather information about such international programmes, talking to the Oxford organizers, attending some classes and associated ceremonial dinners, and talking with students and Chinese organizers. In Oxford, as the head of the Institute for Chinese Studies, I also received several delegations from the Central Party School in Beijing, which in at least one case I was able to follow up later on with interviews in Beijing.

Ethnographic work on Communist Party cadres and cadre training presents its own unique challenges, in addition to the already formidable ones associated with ethnography in less politically charged environments. These challenges have shaped the kind of fieldwork that was possible and imposed obvious limitations on both the research and the data that I was able to collect. It is important to discuss how I arranged the fieldwork and cooperation with my collaborators in China and how these evolved over a period of more than three years. A free and frank discussion of these matters will help us be aware of the strengths and constraints of my fieldwork, so that we can be clear from the outset what my data can and cannot tell us.

From the onset, I knew that research on cadre training and management would require ethnographic work at several different sites, not only to account for regional differences that no doubt would exist, but more importantly because of the great differences between levels of administration. At the Centre, I expected, cadre training would likely be much better funded. Cadres at the Centre would also be much more senior, knowledgeable and, not unimportant from a party school's point of view, demanding. The strategy that I settled on was to try gain access to a school at the provincial level, which I expected to combine characteristics of both national and local institutions. From there, I would try to establish connections up and down the hierarchy to help me broaden the picture gained from my initial work at the provincial level. In other words, I prepared myself for a project that would be multi-sited and would need several years to gather its own momentum and evolve.

The choice of Yunnan as my primary fieldwork site was less a matter of design than of opportunity. Yunnan is located in China's extreme southwest on the border with Myanmar, Laos and Vietnam. The capital Kunming is a large modern city which attracts many foreign and Chinese residents for its pleasant climate and life style, and the province as a whole is a premier tourist destination, mainly because of its stunning landscape and the exotic appeal of its many ethnic minority people. However, from the administration's point of view, Yunnan is simply a remote, mountainous and poor province. Yunnan is a frontier area where at many places the party-state's grip is less than fully secure, dominant Han-Chinese culture has to compete with many other cultures, and the economy is still predominantly rural and undeveloped. Yunnan should therefore not be taken as in any way 'typical' or representative of China as a whole. However, as a vantage point on the administration, its poverty, remoteness and ethnic plurality provides a very instructive contrast with the Centre (mainly but not exclusively located in Beijing). In Yunnan, central policies and institutional arrangements can be expected to be challenged, compromised, trimmed down or adapted much more than in most other parts of the country.

One of my academic contacts from earlier fieldwork in eastern Yunnan had moved on in life. He had become an important provincial cadre and volunteered to help me get in touch with a few teachers at the provincial party school that he had became friendly with during his own training stint there following his elevation to leading cadre status. He arranged a

Photo 1.1 Professor Duan Eryu and the author in front of the entrance of the Yunnan Provincial Party School (2004)

meeting between Professor Duan Eryu and me. In less than half an hour, Duan agreed to all the things I asked for: residence at the school, interviews with students, teachers and administrators, class attendance. Duan did not expect that the project would be vetoed by the school's leadership. There is now, he told me, a great deal of openness and international cooperation in cadre training, and the project might in fact be seen as an opportunity to improve the perception and image of party schools.

For all three years of the project, my collaboration with Duan Eryu and his student Li Yongkang, who served as my research assistant, ran extremely smoothly, with Duan not only trying more than his best to help me with my many requests, but also becoming my key informant on many aspects of cadre training and management in Yunnan. It transpired that Duan Eryu, as 'head of education' (*jiaoyuzhang*) was a key figure at the Provincial Party School, and moreover had an extensive network of contacts in party schools and the administration across the whole of Yunnan. At the Provincial Party School, I spent most of my time on formal interviews (sometimes as many as four or five a day), and I was also allowed to sit in on several classes and even one discussion session. I was free to mix with students and staff in the dining hall, during class breaks, or playing ping pong or tennis. Duan would also regularly take me out for liquor-soaked dinners, giving me the opportunity to talk more informally with some of his many colleagues, former students or friends in the government or party. While still falling short of full immersion in school life (for instance by being a member of one of the small groups around which much of the instruction and leisure activities of the students revolved), this fieldwork gave me enough of an insider's perspective to approach (or at least simulate) an ethnography of important aspects of the life of China's local political elite.

In return for Duan Eryu's cooperation, I had to agree that Duan would take political responsibility for my research by checking (*baguan*) all interview notes taken by Li Yongkang and the questionnaire survey that we jointly designed. However, rather than a serious restriction, as I had originally feared, this turned out to be a major asset. When my informants were told that Duan took political responsibility, they often said that in that case they could speak freely without worrying too much about transgressing the boundaries of what could be said to a foreign researcher. At many interviews I also took my own notes, and I never discovered any censorship in the (much more detailed and superior) Chinese transcripts that Li Yongkang produced. All that Duan would do was, in a few cases, add an explanation or correction of what he considered incorrect or incomplete statements by informants without, however, tampering with the original.

Duan Eryu also had no problems arranging my visits to local party schools elsewhere in Yunnan that were some of the most useful periods of my fieldwork. However, as a provincial cadre he unfortunately had no power to make any arrangements for me to do fieldwork in Beijing. A friend of his at the National Academy of Administration was keen to help me, but after very considerable effort and time the School's Administration in the end turned down my request to do research there. As I fully expected that the Central Party School would give me even shorter shrift, I embarked on an approach more akin to what Tom Gold has called 'guerrilla interviewing' (Gold 1989). Unashamedly using each and every connection that I could think of, I arranged interviews, informal chats, seminar meetings or whatever other format suited the informant with teachers, administrators and cadres at the Central Party School and other institutions involved in cadre training in the capital. Although by no means as systematic and complete as my work in Yunnan, these interviews have nevertheless been invaluable in putting my work in what is a backward and remote province in a national and comparative context.

An additional but very important source of information has been the Internet. Originally, I searched the Internet simply for online versions of public documents, such as laws, regulations and newspaper articles, but suggestions from my informants in Beijing gradually made me realize that I would be able to find much more. The Chinese party-state has invested very heavily in electronic government. Websites of central and local government agencies contain many surprises, especially when insiders tell you where to look. Moreover, party schools use the Internet as an instrument to disseminate information about teaching and research to students, teachers and other schools in the party school system. The websites of the Central Party School and other party schools helped me fill in the blanks and check the accuracy of information gathered in the field, and find comparable information on party schools elsewhere in China.

In sum, my research for this project was much less constrained by the secrecy that one might expect to surround the inner workings of the CCP. The Central Party School remained out of bounds for direct fieldwork, but this is not that unreasonable given the fact that quite often highly confidential policy research, lectures and seminars take place there that are intended for very highly placed officials. Yet this was less of a problem than it might seem. After all, my project was not so much about the content of training as the organization, delivery and reception of training and teaching, and much of this could be gleaned from my detailed fieldwork in Yunnan supplemented by the interviews in Beijing.

This project is about administrative practices aimed at realizing a new vision of the Chinese party-state. My focus on training and education documents neo-socialist governance as an ongoing effort to build new institutions, mould the agents of the state and realize a particular vision of China's modernity. My research has sensitized me to the perspective of the people who rule China, which I believe is crucially important to our understanding of contemporary China yet ruefully under-researched. Who would want to write about the faceless bureaucrats that rule China with all the exciting developments that take place in Chinese society? Yet the point that this book wants to make is that this elite and their organizations, guiding ideology and power cult are important and, as the CCP reasserts itself, arguably become more important with each passing day. I believe that, on the whole, the Chinese people have benefited immensely from the political stability, prosperity and above all the hope that tomorrow will be a better day that neo-socialism is bringing. However, the acknowledgement of the CCP's success should not be misread as an attempt to whitewash the many injustices that also are part of its autocratic rule and ruthless market-driven development logic. In previous research in China I have had ample exposure and understanding of the iron fist that still hides in the velvet glove of neo-socialism (Pieke 1996). While I certainly have become a lot more sympathetic to the achievements of the CCP than I was before the project, I have no illusions about what the CCP is capable of doing, if it felt so compelled by what it perceives as separatism, political dissidence or a foreign threat.

CHAPTER 2

Cadres, cadre training and party schools

SOCIALIST GOVERNANCE

The Communist Party's dominance in China amounts to much more than simply holding on to power. In Soviet and Chinese communist political theory, the Communist Party is intimately linked to, but remains separate from, the government. The party does not govern, but leads, directs, controls and inspires all institutions of governance: state, army, judiciary, mass organizations, 'functional' work units, state enterprises. The party even guides, mainly through its United Front Department (*Tongzhan Bu*), the formal institutions of representative government, such as the people's congresses and the people's consultative conferences. In addition to having its own separate organizational setup, the party has created cells of party members in institutions everywhere, ensuring the party's role as the leading force that holds society together. With only slight exaggeration we can indeed say that the party is 'the organized expression of the will of the dominant class in society, the proletariat' (Schurmann 1968: 109). This role is predicated on socialist ideology as a mode of governance. Without such an ideology, the party would quickly decay into an electoral machine or a patronage network for the competition and sharing of power: effective perhaps at just that, but no longer a party capable of exercising leadership across society.

In the reform era the party has diminished its control over many parts of society, but has by no means wholly given it up. The party's continued control over the people who rule the country is the essential feature of China's uniquely socialist mode of governance: despite much talk of separation of party and state, the state continues to be the party's chief instrument of rule.[1] The grip of the party on its personnel is evident in how ideology and policies are transmitted and put into practice, how appointments to

---

[1] It is therefore quite pointless, as Shiping Zheng does in his book *Party vs. State in Post-1949 China*, to maintain that the party has been a major obstacle to state building in China (Zheng 1997).

leading positions are made, and, perhaps most unambiguously, how training programmes prepare cadres for the exercise of leadership on behalf of the party. All of these reveal that the party remains firmly in control of Chinese society. Socialism as a revolutionary ideology may be dead, but (neo)-socialism as a form of rule and a transformative vision of modernity is alive and well.[2]

The emphasis in the reform period on bureaucratic-organizational efforts to rebuild the cadre system should not be mistaken for a fundamental change of colour. The Communist Party remains to this day an organization firmly anchored not only in Leninist organizational principles, but also in the Maoist tradition of campaign-style politics. In this tradition, campaigns can be mounted for just about any policy objective, but what concerns us here in particular are the so-called rectification campaigns that take the party-state itself as their object. During the reform period, the party has returned to this tradition as it was developed in the Yan'an period of the late thirties and early forties and further refined during the first decade of communist rule after 1949. Such campaigns are not all-out efforts to achieve a fundamental social and political transformation like those attempted during the late Maoist period, such as the Great Leap Forward or the Cultural Revolution, but amount to a targeted deployment of the party organization to achieve a general ideological transformation or renewal that is limited to party and state cadres. Such campaigns are deliberate attempts intended to reinvigorate party discipline (*dangji*) and the party spirit (*dangxing*) of cadres in order to restore rather than undermine the normal rhythm of socialist administration.

During the reform period, at least three such campaigns have been launched: the 'spiritual pollution' (*jingshen wuran*) campaign in 1983, the 'three emphases' (*san jiang*) campaign in 1999 and most recently the 'educational activities' (*jiaoyu huodong*) campaign in 2005.[3] Each of these campaigns explicitly state that the party's socialist rule is threatened by the rising tide of capitalism in China that has tempted cadres to stray from the socialist path. The prescribed medicine for this creeping illness is invariably a large dose of diligent regular group study of Marxism, backed up by demotions, dismissals or sentencing of the worst culprits. In each of these

---

[2] In this book, I do not, therefore use the term socialism to point at a way of organizing the economy (i.e. the 'planned economy'), as was quite common in the past.
[3] See Fewsmith 2005. I exclude the period immediately after the 1989 crackdown, which saw a much more extreme reaction (including a party purge) in the face of a perceived acute threat to party rule. This period was more reminiscent of the line struggle campaigns and purges of the Maoist period than of the orchestrated rectification campaigns.

campaigns, the party leadership apparently felt that the problem was large enough to justify a general campaign, but also ensured that the campaign coincided with, or was followed by, other, less disruptive measures. These are normally grouped together under the heading of administrative system reform. Rectification campaigns – and for that matter other types of campaigns as well – and administrative reform are therefore not separate or perhaps even conflicting instruments. Both are tools of the trade of socialist rule as it has evolved in China that support and are used in conjunction with each other.

CADRES

In the West, the term 'cadre' (*ganbu*) is often not well understood. Even in China there is sometimes considerable confusion. In socialist and communist parties, the term cadre tends to refer to members who are in a position of leadership and authority: they are the professional staff that is the backbone of the party apparatus. When after 1927 the Chinese Communist Party was forced to retreat to rural revolutionary base areas and rely on the mass mobilization of peasants, the term cadre began to denote a much broader range of local party leaders in addition to high-level professional leaders. As Mao Zedong put it back in 1938: 'The Chinese Communist Party is a party at the head of a great revolutionary struggle in a nation of several hundred millions of people and cannot fulfil its historic task without a large number of leading cadres who combine ability with character.'[4]

In post-1949 China, cadres became a meritocratic power elite, the opposite of the 'people' (*renmin*) or the 'masses' (*qunzhong*) who they lead. Cadres are also contrasted to the ordinary members of the party, who may have a strong ideological commitment, but are not fully involved in day-to-day management and leadership. When such cadres are on the state's payroll, they are often referred to as 'state cadres' (*guojia ganbu*). As a heritage of the Maoist revolutionary struggle referred to above, the word 'cadre' in addition has the much looser connotation of just anybody in a position of officially sanctioned authority – regardless of whether or not this person is a party member or in the state's employment – in a village, neighbourhood or work unit (Schurmann 1968: 162). Such cadres are often referred to as 'basic cadres' (*jiceng ganbu*) or 'local cadres' (*difang ganbu*; Barnett 1967: 39–40). Furthermore, under the planned economy

[4] Mao Zedong, 'The Role of the Chinese Communist Party in the National War', *Selected Works of Mao Tse-tung*, volume II, p. 251.

no distinction was made between enterprises, service organizations, the party and the administrative apparatus; leaders and managers in all these organizations were uniformly referred to as cadres.

Despite the attempt to introduce a civil service system over the past twenty-five years, to professionalize the administration, and to separate government, party, enterprises and service organizations, the slippage between these different meanings still often makes it difficult to ascertain what it is that people in China are talking about when they use the word 'cadre'. Although in this study the main focus is on higher-level political leading cadres (i.e. close to the original meaning in communist and socialist parties), in practice it is impossible fully to tease them apart from all sorts of other cadres in China: the phrase 'cadre training' (*ganbu peixun*) is used equally for the ideological education of provincial governors as for computer training courses for staff in a township office.

Cadres in China and other socialist societies should not be thought of simply as either bureaucrats or, alternatively, as a gloss for cognate concepts such as 'leader', 'politician', 'official' or 'manager'. The concept of cadre includes all of these, but is moreover directly linked with the unique nature and role of the Communist Party discussed earlier. Consequently, the concept reveals all the contradictions inherent in the party itself in terms of its organizational nature, position vs. the state and society, and stated objectives. Cadres ought to be, in Maoist terms, both 'red' and 'expert': they have to be as fully committed to socialist ideology and practice (their 'party spirit') as to possess the professional skills and knowledge needed for their job. Cadres are impersonal bureaucratic instruments of rule, ideological exemplars, and autonomous combat leaders of men and women all at the same time. Cadres both connect and separate the party-state and society. The recruitment and deployment of cadres is one of the most important ways in which the party-state integrates itself with society and guides and directs the project of socialist transformation. This is one of the main sources of ambiguity in the cadre system. The party's self-assigned transformative mission and leading role make it conceptually difficult to separate out the party from the government and society; ultimately, the party cannot step aside and can only lead and change by remaining involved. Despite more than fifteen years of separation of party and government (*dang-zheng fenkai*), administrative rationalization, democratization and the development of a socialist legal system, the party continues to manage and control the cadres and organs of government, the judiciary, the legislative and even the other officially recognized democratic parties and other parts of the 'United Front'. The cadre system, as the party's main instrument, also continues to impinge equally on all these branches of the party's domain of governance. Appointments to all institutions of governance continue to be managed as part of one comprehensive system, and individual cadres move freely from posts in government to party positions and appointments in legislative and united front branches.

Cadres are not a uniform category. The most important distinction is that between leading cadres (*lingdao ganbu*) and all other, regular cadres (*yiban ganbu*) or non-leading cadres (*feilingdao ganbu*).[5] This distinction is to a large extent separate from rank (see below): many administrators or professionals may have a high rank, but nevertheless do not hold leading positions. The distinction between leading and regular cadres cannot be easily mapped onto the categories of western administrative systems. Most importantly, as in some other political systems where bureaucratic and political elites are fused, in China leading cadres occupy the strategic positions that would be held by elected politicians and political appointees in a democratic political system. Appointments to these leading positions and the careers of the cadres who occupy them are controlled by the party's organization department (*Zuzhi Bu*);[6] by contrast, the careers of high-level non-leading cadres are managed by the government's personnel ministry or bureau.[7] Crucially, leading cadre positions are controlled by the organization department at one level above the positions and cadres that it controls; by contrast, the government's personnel bureau controls positions and cadres at the same level (Burns 1989; 1994; Huang 1996; Burns 1999; Pieke 2004; Fu Libai 2004: 258; Manion 1985). Lower-level non-leading cadres are usually managed by the personnel department of their work unit, and their career is normally confined to that unit.

All national cadres have a specific grade (*jibie*), of which there are currently 15 with 1 being the highest and 15 the lowest. Grade determines the salary they earn, although the salaries that come with each grade vary regionally and by the level (rank) of both the job that the cadre in question has and the organization a cadre works for.[8] All national cadres and cadre

---

[5] *Temporary Regulations on National Public Servants* (*Guojia gongwuyuan zanxing tiaoli*), State Council document no. 15, 14 August 1993, article 9. Reprinted in Fu Libai 2004: 263.

[6] On the organization department, see Huai 1995a.

[7] In 2008, the Ministry of Personnel was merged with the Ministry of Labour and Social Security to form the new Ministry of Human Resources and Social Security.

[8] However, official wages account only for a minor portion of the differences in actual income earned in the bureaucracy. Apart from institutional or individual corruption and abuse of power, there are also many legal sources of income that account for major income differences. For some fascinating details on this point, see Zhonggong Fujian shengwei zuzhibu ketizu (Research group of the organization department of the Fujian Chinese Communist Party committee) 2003: 73–80.

posts also have a specific level/rank (*zhiwu*, literally 'post') that mirrors the ranks given to all party and state institutions in Chinese society. A cadre's rank determines the level of positions he or she can occupy: for instance, a deputy office level (*fuchuji*) cadre can only be the deputy head of a county or an office (*chu*) level organization or department. Likewise, cadres have to have a specific grade in order to occupy a post of a particular rank. For instance, the head of a ministry has to be a grade 3 or 4 cadre; the head of a county has to be between grade 7 and 10.[9]

As far as leading cadres go, ranks start at the level of 'section' (*keji*), equivalent to either a township or a bureau in a county government. The next levels are the 'office' (*chuji*, county or bureau in a prefecture), 'department' (*tingji* or *siji*, prefecture or bureau in a province), and 'ministry' (*buji*, province or ministry at the central level), and finally the central (*zhongyang*) level. In 1998, there were a total of forty million cadres in the whole of China, of whom only 466,000 were cadres of county or office level or higher, 39,000 of prefecture or department level or higher, and only 2,600 of provincial or ministerial level (Brødsgaard 2003: 212). All levels of leading and non-leading cadres, including the central one, are divided in a deputy (*fu*) and a full (*zheng*) level. Non-leading cadre positions mirror those of leading cadre posts, but bear different names. The highest rank of non-leading cadre posts is that of 'inspector' (*xunshiyuan*), equivalent to the *ting* or *si* rank of leading cadre posts. This is followed by 'investigator' (*diaoyanyuan*), equivalent to the *chu* level for leading cadres, and 'chief section member' (*zhuren keyuan*), equivalent to the *ke* level. Similar to the leading cadre ranks, these three non-leading cadre ranks are subdivided in a deputy and a full level. Below the *ke* level, which is the lowest leading cadre rank, are two further ranks of non-leading cadres, namely 'section member' (*keyuan*) and 'office worker' (*banshiyuan*). The nomenclature of the ranks given here is that laid down in official regulations. In actual bureaucratic practice, other names are often used, especially that of 'bureau level' (*juji*), which usually refers to a post, cadre or organization at either the *chu* or the *ting/si* level.[10]

Both rank and grade are nationally unified. This has the vitally important effect that cadres and institutions across the country immediately can and do determine the hierarchical relationship between any two individuals or organizations. This universal framework for the assessment of rank

---

[9] *Temporary Regulations on National Public Servants* (*Guojia gongwuyuan zanxing tiaoli*), State Council document no. 15, 14 August 1993, article 10. For a table mapping cadre ranks onto cadre grades, see Fu Libai 2004: 182.
[10] *Temporary Regulations on National Public Servants* 1993, article 10.

provides a ready reference point for social relationships across the country: it determines for any person or organization in China whether or not they have to comply with (or least listen to) any other given individual or organization. As a result, practising rank reproduces the Chinese bureaucracy as a community of belonging and practice in much the same way as generational rank (*beifen*) structures social relations and practice in local Chinese kinship groups (Eyferth 2001).

ADMINISTRATIVE REFORM AND CADRE MANAGEMENT

Centralized control over leading appointments is an integral aspect of the party's methodology of socialist governance: cadres are as much a trusted instrument of transformative rule as the party's primary object of transformation. From the earliest days of the CCP, recruitment, training, deployment and rectification of its own corps of cadres has been a centrepiece of the party's Leninist strategy (Barnett 1967: 38–63; Harding 1981: 72–78; Oksenberg 1968). The reform period has been no exception. The post-1978 reforms started as a near-desperate attempt to salvage socialism from the wreckage caused by the Cultural Revolution and its aftermath. One of the main prongs of the reform strategy was to strengthen the party's leading role in society. One of the most essential components of this was the transformation of the cadre management system, a view that was expressed very clearly by Deng Xiaoping himself in his famous speech 'On the Reform of the System of Party and State Leadership', delivered in 1980 (Deng 1984a; Manion 1985; Zheng 1997: 193).

In 1978, the party was saddled with a cadre system that was staffed by poorly qualified personnel. Many cadres at that time had been recruited as activists in the late forties and fifties. They usually had little formal education or professional skills. In addition to them, the Cultural Revolution had witnessed the appointment and rapid promotion of large numbers of cadres whose main qualification for the job was their ability to 'make revolution'. In 1984, as soon as the even more urgent task of economic reform was firmly on track, the party embarked on a programme of cadre system reform. Its main aspects were mandatory retirement ages and minimum education qualifications for specific levels of appointment.[11] By 1987, these

---

[11] Regarding the latter, appointment to a section (*ke*) level post now requires at least senior high school (*gaozhong*) or middle vocational (*zhongzhuan*) education; a department (*ting* or *si*) level job requires at least higher vocational (*dazhuan*) education; a ministry (*bu*) level job requires at least university undergraduate education (Fu Libai 2004: 105). On a 'rational age composition' of the cadre corps, see Brødsgaard 2003: 224.

two requirements had been successfully (albeit somewhat superficially) imposed across the cadre system (Lee 1991: part III; Manion 1993; White 1998, chapter 4.1) laying the foundations for generational change and the professionalization of the cadre corps.

As a bold new step in the reform process, in 1987 Prime Minister Zhao Ziyang announced the creation of a civil service system. Although this in itself was a collective decision of the leadership at the time, it included the radical proposal that the party should also relinquish its control over leading appointments in government (Chan 2001: 405–411; Lee 1991: 374– 384). If implemented, the proposal would have left the party with much reduced power to steer the evolution of Chinese politics and society, cutting right at the heart of socialism as understood by a majority of party leaders. Unsurprisingly, this aspect of the proposals met with great hostility.

Zhao's fall after the 1989 movement provided the opportunity to eliminate this aspect of civil service system reform (Huai 1995b). After 1989, the deepening of the reforms in general had to wait until Deng Xiaoping's celebrated southern tour in 1992, and administrative reform was no exception. Only in 1993, therefore, was a civil service system (*gongwuyuan zhidu*) officially established with the promulgation of the *Temporary Regulations on National Public Servants* (Guojia gongwuyuan zanxing tiaoli). Since then, the terms 'civil service' and 'civil servants' are routinely used, but they speak to a much broader and less threatening agenda of administrative reform than Zhao's original version. The CCP's control over the cadre system remained as solid as it was.[12]

Like in so many other aspects of policy making in China, reforms announced and regulations promulgated should not be read as established fact, but as aspirations that are usually still quite contentious within the leadership. The *Temporary Regulations* are no exception, which is why it took until 2005 for the promulgation of the full *Civil Servants Law* to replace the *Temporary Regulations*.[13] One glaring hole in the 1993 regulations that may have been caused by resistance within the leadership was

---

[12] Burns 2004. According to Brødsgaard, in the nineties the status and grip of the CCP's organization department nevertheless suffered from the emphasis on the role of the Ministry of Personnel in the building of a civil service system. Since 1998, the organization department bounced back again and with it the inviolability of the principle of the party's leadership over cadre management (Brødsgaard 2003: 218–220).

[13] The full text of the law, which became effective on 1 January 2006, is available on politics.people.com.cn/GB/1026/3354665.html. For an English translation of the law, see fdi.gov.cn/pub/FDI_EN/Laws/GeneralLawsandRegulations/BasicLaws/P020060620318525786351.pdf. The new law is different mainly in that it incorporates new developments since the promulgation of the regulations in 1993, such as the public examination, selection and election of officials that we will discuss later in this chapter.

that they only applied to personnel in administrative departments. The regulations did not apply to employees in functional organizations, mass organizations, the judiciary and procuratorial organizations, the organs of the People's Congresses and People's Consultative Conferences, the Communist Party and the patriotic democratic parties, despite the fact that these organizations act as organs of the CCP's system of governance rather than being independent institutions.[14] Until this was changed in 2004 (and confirmed in the 2005 *Civil Servants Law*), the regulations were out of synch with China's administrative reality and therefore did not have nearly as much bite as they otherwise could have had. Likewise, the position of leading cadres remains decidedly ambiguous. Leading cadres are on the state's payroll and in this regard are considered civil servants, but their appointment and dismissal remain firmly under the control the CCP, a fact that is confirmed in article 4 of the 2005 *Civil Servants Law*.[15]

Civil service reform is a part of the broader agenda of administrative reform that serves to enhance the legitimacy of the Communist Party's rule, while at the same time reducing direct government interference in the management of society and the economy. In 1999–2000, the government under Premier Zhu Rongji aimed at a far-reaching restructuring of the government system and a drastic reduction of the number of government departments. In 2003, a further fine-tuning of government reform was completed. These two restructuring efforts were important steps in moving away from old style government still fundamentally predicated on a Stalinist planning ethos, to a government that limits itself to providing the institutional framework to facilitate and supervise the orderly conduct of social and economic life (Yang 2004: chapter 2).

However, discarding the party-state's totalitarian ambitions should not be read as the establishment of a genuine 'rule of law' and a retreat from the Leninist principle that the party is the leading force in society. The party's continued dominance of social and political life was enshrined as integral to the reforms in 1979 as the third of Deng Xiaoping's 'four cardinal principles' (Deng 1984b).[16] Throughout the reform period, the

[14] See 'China intends to include in the scope of public servants personnel of party and state organs and mass organizations' (Zhongguo nijiang dang-zheng jiguan qunzhong tuanti renyuan naru gongwuyuan fanwei), Renminwang 25 December 2004, online at www.people.com.cn/GB/shizheng/1026/3079363.html (checked on 24 May 2006); 'Chinese leader stresses importance of Law on Civil Servants', 22 September 2005, nz.china-embassy.org/eng/xw/t213283.htm (checked on 30 August 2007).
[15] Fu Libai 2004: 8.
[16] The four cardinal principles are keeping to the socialist road, upholding the dictatorship of the proletariat, upholding the leadership of the Communist Party and upholding Marxism–Leninism and Mao Zedong Thought.

importance of party leadership and party building have frequently been reasserted, most recently in the 2004 *Decision of the Chinese Communist Party centre on the strengthening of the building of the party's ruling capacity building*.[17] The party continues to reflect on its relevance to and hold over China's rapidly changing society, and repeatedly takes initiatives in this regard. For instance, in the nineties and beyond, the party has stepped up efforts to extend its membership to include the new entrepreneurial elites of reform-era China and to establish party branches in private and even foreign enterprises (Dickson 2003). The party also emphasizes the importance of inner-party democracy to stay in tune with the times, which became a major theme at the 17th Party Congress in October 2007.

The adherence to Leninism is very clearly visible in the management of leading cadres. As Deng himself said in 1980 in *On the reform of the system of party and state leadership*, '[t]he purpose of reforming the system of Party and state leadership is precisely to maintain and further strengthen Party leadership and discipline, and not to weaken or relax them' (Deng 1984a: 324).[18] Already from the early eighties onward, party policies and documents offer guidelines that aim to finesse – but not resolve – the conflict between the desire for greater transparency, democracy and non-political meritocracy in cadre management on the one hand, and the need to uphold the ultimately conflicting principle of party control (Lee 1991: chapter 15; White 1998: chapter 4.1; Bo 2004). This tension also continues to inform that aspect of cadre management reform that is the topic of this book, namely the evolution of cadre training.

PARTY SCHOOLS AND CADRE TRAINING BEFORE 1978

Formal study and training is where ideology and organization in Leninist parties meet, and is at the very core of the CCP's tradition of revolutionary governance. Cadre training therefore serves as a fascinating window on the continuities and changes in CCP governmental practice.[19] In the only

---

[17] 'Decision of the Chinese Communist Party centre on the strengthening of the party's ruling capacity building' (Zhonggong zhongyang quanyu jiaqiang dang de zhizheng nengli jianshe de jueding). Beijing: Renmin Chubanshe, 2004.
[18] This point is made time and again by all top leaders throughout the reform period, see for instance the collection of Jiang Zemin's speeches in *On Party Building* (Jiang Zemin 2001).
[19] Despite the central role that cadre training plays in the CCP's form of governance, there are only two books on the development of Chinese communist cadre training before 1949, one in Chinese (Wang Zhongqing 1992) and the other in English (Price 1976). In addition, for the Yan'an period (1936–1947) there are a few more studies specifically on party schools and cadre training, mainly because the Central Party School was one of the main sites of the pivotal Rectification Campaign

English language book on cadre training before 1949, Janet Price documents how, on 1 January 1921, less than a year after its founding, members of the fledging Chinese Communist Party already established a workers' school in Beijing as part of their effort to awaken and recruit among China's urban proletariat. Nevertheless, in the early years the training of party leaders generally did not take place in formal institutions. There was, however, one exception. In August 1921, Mao Zedong and other members of the New People's Study Society in Changsha, Hunan, founded the Self Education College that, according to Price, prefigured later communist training programmes (Price 1976: 11–27).

In the course of the twenties, schools and training programmes played a prominent part in the CCP's efforts to recruit and groom a cadre of leaders, activists and ordinary members, particularly after the May Thirtieth Movement of 1926 had given the nationalist and communist movements a shot in the arm (Price 1976: chapter 3). In addition, Chinese communist leaders gained first-hand experience in the Soviet Union not only with communist theory and Stalinist practice, but also with formal cadre training (Price 1976: 30–38, 89–103). The first official mention of 'party schools at the highest level' dates from the special central conference in February 1926, when a decision was passed to establish two such schools in Beijing and Guangzhou, although this decision evidently was not carried out.[20] Nevertheless, it was only in the early 1930s, when the party was fully thrown back on its own organizational and mobilizational resources, that a network of party schools was set up, including, in 1933, the Ruijin Marxist Communist School (*Makesi Gongchan Zhuyi Xuexiao*), the first real precursor of the future Central Party School (Price 1976: 105–134).

in 1942–1943 (Apter and Saich 1994: 228–242; Dangxiao jiaoyu shi yanjiu zu (Research group on the history of party school education) 2002). There is equally little work on cadre training after 1949. There is only one early book chapter on cadre training that briefly mentions party schools and training programmes but mainly deals with small study groups at the workplace (Lewis 1963). For the contemporary period, there are Emilie Tran's article on the Shanghai Party School (Tran 2003), and Wibowo and Fook's article (Wibowo and Fook 2006) and a brief discussion in David Shambaugh's recent book (Shambaugh 2008: 143–151) on the Central Party School. In addition, I know of two very interesting but as yet unpublished papers, one on the Central Party School (Anonymous 2008) and the other more broadly on cadre training (Lee 2007). Official histories of many local party schools were published in the late eighties and nineties, while many others are available on these schools' Internet sites. Official histories focus heavily on the reform era, but usually also contain some information on the period before 1977. The Central Party School itself has until now refrained from publishing its own history, a decision no doubt inspired by the school's involvement in the factional struggles among the CCP's top leadership.

[20] 'Kaiban zuigao dangxiao wenti' (The question of opening party schools at the highest level), decision at the Special Central Conference, Beijing, February 1926; see www.people.com.cn/GB/paper83/3819/462404.html (checked on 18 February 2008).

After the Great March (1934–1936), the Marxist Communist School was re-established as the Central Party School at the CCP's new headquarters in Yan'an in central Shaanxi province. The relative isolation and stability of Yan'an enabled the party massively to expand its membership, organizational resources and military capacity. Education and training played a central role in this enterprise, producing the vast numbers of political and military cadres that the CCP's revolutionary war needed. This effort involved a range of institutions. As is the case until this very day, the Central Party School almost exclusively focussed on high-level cadres groomed for top leadership position. Better known, however, was the Military and Political University of Resistance against Japan (*Kang-Ri Junzheng Daxue*, or Kangda for short), whose role was to groom the leaders of the communist armed forces and to train non-communist intellectuals and local peasant cadres who wished to join the anti-Japanese resistance. At Yan'an, Mao Zedong also fully established his political and ideological dominance of the party, culminating in the famous Rectification Campaign of 1942–1943. Both Kangda and the Central Party School were centrally involved. In 1942, Mao delivered his famous *Report on the work style of party rectification* at the ceremony at the Central Party School's start of term; in the same year, he also took on the post of the Central Party School's principal to ensure the proper handling of rectification at this key site (Price 1976: chapter 8; Apter and Saich 1994: chapter 7).

With its defeat of the Nationalist troops between 1947 and 1949, the CCP was confronted with the daunting task of government and revolutionary transformation across the length and breadth of mainland China, posing tremendous challenges to the party's capacity of recruitment and training of activists, party cadres and government officials. The establishment of cadre training programmes was a vital component of the transformation of Chinese society and government, and is itself a testimony to the enormity of the organizational task that the CCP undertook following its conquest of China. In most localities, cadre training classes were initially organized by the party's propaganda or organization department.[21] Only several years later were party schools set up as a standard 'work department' of local CCP committees. As the Chinese administrative system and planned economy developed, party schools continued to be established when new counties, prefectures, provinces, state enterprises and government

---

[21] This sequence of events is found in most of the local party school gazetteers that I have perused for this study; see also Barnett 1967: 168–169.

departments were created, a process that continues to the present day.

In 1947, with the move of the CCP's central command away from Yan'an, the Central Party School temporarily ceased operations. In 1948, the school was reopened as the Marx–Lenin Academy (*Makesi-Liening Xueyuan*) with Liu Shaoqi as principal. The Academy was renamed the Central High-Level Party School (*Zhongyang Gaoji Dangxiao*) in 1955, and continued to operate under this name until the school's closure at the start of the Cultural Revolution in 1966. With the school's reopening after the Cultural Revolution in 1977, the name was changed back to the original Central Party School (*Zhongyang Dangxiao*) of the Yan'an period. Given the dearth of sources and published research, little information is available on the teaching and research at the Marx–Lenin and Central High-Level Party School. However, the 1985 'Resolution on outstanding issues regarding degrees conferred on students at the Central Party School', published in the first yearbook of the Central Party School, does give some idea.

During the period between the establishment of the Marx–Lenin Academy in 1948 and the closure of the school in 1966, six types of classes were taught. The first type were classes of the school's 'second department' (*er bu*) that were intended for party cadres with five or more years of work experience, who had been party members for at least three years, had held leadership positions at the county level or higher, had a middle level education and had the ability to independently research problems. Between 1948 and 1952, nine such classes were enrolled with a total of 670 students. The course lasted three or four years, and the last students graduated in 1955. The course was heavy loaded with Marxist, Leninist and Maoist theory and the history of revolutionary socialism, but also contained elements of general Chinese and world history, geography and logic, and instruction in language and writing. The second type of class was intended to train teachers for the rapidly expanding system of party schools across the country. In total 835 students were enrolled between 1953 and 1956 on a course that lasted two years. The third type of class was the theory class, which was a four-year course that enrolled a total of 515 students between 1959 and 1961 who were admitted by means of an entrance examination and inspection of their qualifications. Because of involvement in 'political movements', the class of 1959 took six years to graduate, the 1960 cohort five years and the final cohort of 1961 took four years. The other classes taught at the Central High-Level Party School were a 'natural dialectics class' and a 'logics class' which together took 98 students in 1958 and 1959; a 'news class', a two-year course with a total of 152 students in three cohorts between 1954 and 1956 for editors of newspapers and news agencies; and a three-year 'theory class' that enrolled 28 students in 1960.[22]

Unfortunately, the document only specifies the long-term courses that entitled students to a formal degree; no information exists on the undoubtedly much larger number of students on short-term courses. Nevertheless, a picture emerges of teaching provision laid on in a rather ad hoc fashion to provide for specific needs or groups of students, a picture which one suspects may also have been typical of the school's short-term training courses. Moreover, what little continuity may have existed in terms of content and methods was interrupted by the severe campaigns that became an endemic feature of Chinese politics after 1956–1957, and very little teaching and learning seems to have taken place at the Central High-Level Party School in the early sixties even before the full closure of the school in 1966.

RE-ESTABLISHING CADRE TRAINING AFTER THE DEATH OF MAO ZEDONG

Like most other parts of the government and party administration, party schools at all levels suffered badly during the Cultural Revolution. Some schools had been closed or abandoned altogether, while others, particularly in rural areas, had been turned into so-called May seventh cadre schools (*wu-qi ganxiao*). The latter sought to instil revolutionary values by participation in production that differed little from forced labour.[23] Cadres sent down to May seventh cadre schools also included teachers and staff of other party schools.[24] Despite the many upheavals and the closure of party schools during this period, what were called Mao Zedong Thought study classes and other cadre training classes continued to be organized in

---

[22] 'Resolution on outstanding issues regarding degrees conferred on students at the Central Party School (passed by the Central Party School Committee on 31 May 1985)', *Zhonggong Zhongyang Dangxiao nianjian 1985* (Yearbook of the Central Party School 1985), Beijing: Zhonggong Zhongyang Dangxiao Chubanshe, 1986: 70–75.

[23] For two accounts of life at May seventh cadre schools translated in English, see Chen (1973) (which toes the party line of the time and is extremely positive) and Yang (1982) (which exposes the hardships that cadres at these schools went through; for other translations see Yang 1983/1984; Yang 1986). The conversion of party schools to May seventh cadre schools is documented in some of the published histories of local party schools, for instance the one for Qianyang county in Hunan province (*Zhonggong Qianyang xianwei dangxiao zhi 1959 nian -1985 nian* (Gazetteer of the Qianyang county party school 1959–1985), n.a., n.d.: 1–2).

[24] Zhonggong Yunnan Shengwei Dangxiao jianshi bianxiezu (Editorial group of the brief history of the Yunnan Chinese Communist Party Committee Party School) 2000: 77.

many localities, which at least in some cases seem to have amounted to some form of continuation of the local party school.[25]

In 1977, the Central Party School opened its doors again. In an unknown number of cases, local party schools had resumed operations sometimes several years earlier than that, for instance by formally merging with the local May seventh cadre school.[26] After assessment of the first term of training at the Central Party School, in October 1977 the party centre issued a decision to reopen or re-establish party schools at all levels and in all areas, or more than a year before the Third Plenum of the Eleventh Central Committee that later became enshrined as the official start of the reforms.[27] The *Decision* met with rapid success: at the end of 1980, more than 5,800 party schools and cadre academies had either been reopened or newly established.[28] Yet so soon after the fall of the 'Gang of Four' the time was not ripe to simultaneously discontinue the May seventh cadre schools, and the *Decision* is careful to specify that each type of institution 'for a long time' would have its own role to play, and until the central decision to close the May seventh cadre schools in 1979, party schools and May seventh cadre schools indeed existed side-by-side, and often even on the same premises.[29]

In the 1977 *Decision* there is an almost exclusive emphasis on ideological orthodoxy without any mention of other skills or types of knowledge that cadres ought to possess.

Party schools, according to the historically given work methods of our party, allow cadres after a certain period on the job to focus their mind for a period of time on reading a bit from the works of Marx, Lenin and Chairman Mao, or to read important party documents, in order to engage in study to rectify their [political] line and thought. Its main objective is to raise the cadre's level of Marxism and Mao Zedong Thought... Reading the original works and self-study must continue to

---

[25] Zhonggong Yunnan Shengwei Dangxiao jianshi bianxiezu (Editorial group of the brief history of the Yunnan Chinese Communist Party Committee Party School) 2000: 79; Zhonggong Baoji shiwei dangxiao xiaozhi bianxiezu (Editorial group of the Baoji city party school gazetteer) 1989: 8.

[26] Meizhou City Party School (in remote southern Jiangxi province) reportedly opened again on 1 January 1974, training a total of 3,174 cadres between 1974 and the official end of the Cultural Revolution in October 1976. See 'Zhonggong Meizhou shiwei dangxiao yange' (The course of change and development of the Meizhou City Party School), dated 25 September 2005, www.mzps.gov.cn/ReadNews.asp?NewsID=531 (checked 18 February 2008).

[27] 'Zhonggong Zhongyang guanyu banhao geji dangxiao de jueding' (Decision of the Chinese Communist Party centre on the correct handling of party schools at all levels), 5 October 1977.

[28] 'Song Renqiong tongzhi zai quanguo ganbu jiaoyu gongzuo dianhua huiyi shang de jianghua' (Speech of comrade Song Renqiong during the national tele-conference on cadre education work), 1 February 1981, *Zugong tongxun* 1981: 31.

[29] *Zhonggong Qianyang xianwei dangxiao zhi 1959 nian -1985 nian* (Gazetteer of the Qianyang County Party School 1959–1985): 2.

be the main study methods, and there should not be lectures expounding on everything... [Teachers at party schools] should not steer students to side issues and engage in unnecessary debate on unimportant words and phrases, nor lead students to engage in pedantic textual research. [They] should raise questions and stimulate debate in order to deepen students' understanding of the essence of the spirit of the original works, and they should stimulate students' independent reflection.[30]

This focus on the self-study of original Marxist classics was not only caused by the need to tread very carefully so closely after the death of Mao and the fall of the Gang, the scarcity of teachers with more than just the most basic knowledge, or the tradition of teaching at party schools before 1966 that also put a very heavy emphasis on the understanding and correct interpretation of ideology. In the immediate aftermath of the Cultural Revolution, emphasizing self-study and the critical faculties of individuals was hugely significant. Mao's mistakes meant that even among leading cadres, the first priority was to re-establish their commitment to the party-state and its mission. Healing the wounds of the Cultural Revolution meant more than rebuilding the institutions of party rule: its organizational charisma, the very source of its authority, had to be re-created. This required that the party's bedrock supporters had to go through the experience of conversion to communism all over again, and the leadership knew no better method than a fresh immersion in the iconic source of truth, the original Marxist classics. In 1977, party schools were thus key instruments to help assert reformist control over the orthodox Marxist–Leninist–Maoist canon and to undo the legacy of the Cultural Revolution with its uncritical acceptance of whatever Chairman Mao said or wrote, its fetish of manual work and physical suffering and its deep suspicion of learning, intellectuals and the capacity for independent thought.

At the end of 1978, the 'Four Modernizations' had become the party's new programme of action, posing demands on the party-state's governmental capacity that had never been faced before. In this context cadre training attained a whole new significance and, as a result, underwent a process of fundamental changes that, in many respects, is currently still underway. In 1980 Deng Xiaoping himself said that China's 'cadre corps should become more revolutionary, younger, more knowledgeable and more specialized'.[31]

[30] Zhonggong Zhongyang guanyu banhao geji dangxiao de jueding: 3–6.
[31] The earliest occurrence of Deng Xiaoping's call appears in his famous speech 'On the reform of the system of party and state leadership' on 18 August 1980 (Deng 1984a). This slogan has now been incorporated in article 33 in the CCP's party constitution itself. Online at news.xinhuanet.com/ziliao/2002–11/18/content_633225_7.htm (checked 28 August 2007).

In a 1981 speech during a tele-conference on cadre education, the CCP's organization work supremo Song Renqiong elaborated on central documents issued in 1980 that were intended to carry out Deng's wish.[32] He emphasized that cadre education and training should not be limited to ideological study, but should prepare cadres with the management skills and specialist knowledge needed to face the new challenges of the Four Modernizations. Cadre training should be flexible, catering to the specific needs of all cadres in particular localities or departments. Cadre training should also be inclusive and be ruled by comprehensive plans that were to be drawn up and managed by a group of leaders in each locality, lead by the organization department and including the propaganda department and the relevant economic and educational departments. Participation in training should become a recurring requirement of all cadres, even the most important and busiest leading cadres, and should be linked with decisions on appointments and promotions. Very much in the spirit of the reforms, the CCP was prepared to consider novel approaches as well. A document published in 1980 discussed the rising need for specialist training that cannot have easily been catered for in existing party and cadre schools. To help large numbers of cadres acquire the knowledge and skills that they require, the document recommended following the example of the Ministry of Agriculture and its subordinate bureaus across China that enlisted the services of regular higher educational institutions in delivering customized training courses to their cadres, an approach that would attain mainstream status as 'high-end training' (*gaoduan peixun*, see chapter 5) only twenty years later.[33]

The new policies provided the framework for a comprehensive system of cadre training, which, as we will see throughout this book, would be fleshed out and further developed, hesitantly at first, and much more fully in the nineties and the first decade of the twenty-first century. The long lead time of these reforms was most likely mainly caused by financial constraints. My interviews with older teachers at the Yunnan Provincial Party School indicate that in the eighties party schools were poorly funded, and the quality of their facilities and consequently teaching was rather low. However, despite issues of funding and quality, in the course of the eighties cadre training had already become much more systematic and

---

[32] 'Song Renqiong tongzhi zai quanguo ganbu jiaoyu gongzuo dianhua huiyi shang de jianghua' (Speech of comrade Song Renqiong during the national tele-conference on cadre education work), 1 February 1981, *Zugong tongxun* 1981: 31–49.

[33] 'Ba ganbu zhuanye peixun gongzuo zhuajin zhuahao' (Grasp firmly and well cadre specialist training), *Zugong tongxun* 1980: 168–175.

comprehensive than it had been in the fifties or sixties. Party schools at different administrative levels were required to train and retrain all leading cadres of a specific rank in their area. Schools also had to organize training classes for outstanding new leading party cadre recruits (*youxiu qingnian ganbu peixunban*), thus preparing the way for a generational shift in the cadre corps. Party schools also played a vitally important role in the teaching and examination of degree courses after the introduction of the requirement of minimal educational qualifications for specific positions mentioned earlier in this chapter.[34]

In 1986 the Centre also called for the organization of ideological and professional mandatory training specifically for administrative non-leading cadres in specialized schools of administration (first called *xingzheng guanli ganbu xueyuan*, later *xingzheng xueyuan*). Although some headway was made with this in the latter part of the eighties, only a few provinces actually established such schools before 1989, Shanghai being one of them.[35] In Yunnan, the Provincial Academy of Administration started operations only in 1991. As in most other parts of China, the new academy of administration was added on to the existing party school, a very common practice in the Chinese bureaucracy called 'two signs, one group' (*liang kuai paizi, yi tao banzi*), to accommodate the frequent changes in the names and number of administrative departments and offices (Zhonggong Yunnan Shengwei Dangxiao jianshi bianxiezu 2000: 177–178). Internally, at the Yunnan school no separate organizational setups exist for the Academy of Administration and the party school,[36] although it is known of specific classes or administrative responsibilities whether they are of the party school or the Academy of Administration.

The standing of cadre training and party schools again changed greatly from 1989 onward. The 'turmoil' (later reclassified as 'disturbance') of that year and its violent repression served as an important wake-up call to the Chinese leadership. After the crackdown, the party leadership was quick to formulate a strategy to avoid a repetition of such events in the future. While reaffirming the general economic policy of market reform and opening up to the world, it was also acknowledged that socialism needed to be put on a solid footing through administrative reform, party building and political education. Harking back to Deng's own speech in 1980 on *The reform of*

---

[34] See Zhonggong Yunnan Shengwei Dangxiao jianshi bianxiezu (Editorial group of the brief history of the Yunnan Chinese Communist Party Committee Party School) 2000: 116–123 and Tran 2003.
[35] Fieldnotes 22 April 2004; Tran 2003. According to Emilie Tran, the Central Organization Department had already issued a decision to this effect in 1983.
[36] For instance interview 9, 5 April 2004.

the system of party and state leadership (Deng 1984a), administrative reform, including the modernization and professionalization of the cadre system, was reaffirmed as a cornerstone of the reform project. New, however, was the much greater prominence as part of this accorded to ideological training and party schools.[37] In September 1990, the party centre issued the *Circular regarding the strengthening of the work of party schools*.[38] The *Circular* urged party schools 'to become the smelting furnace in which the strengthening of cadres' party spirit is forged'. This phrase, in which the word 'smelting furnace' (*ronglu*) is a direct reference to Mao Zedong's views on the relationship between the party and its members,[39] would become a stock formula in all official documents on cadre training. The *Circular* specified that party schools should systematize and standardize their education to ensure a regular pattern of rigorous and high-quality training and retraining for all leading party cadres. Moreover, party schools were given a much higher profile in research and propaganda than in the past to help the party tackle the new challenges created by reform and opening up in a way that continue to be consistent with socialism. In other words, party schools were to be the party's principal ideological and policy think tanks, and were encouraged to seek greater autonomy in carrying out their work. As part of this, the image of party schools would also have to be changed. Party schools should no longer be seen as the mouldy remnants of a tainted past, secretive and inward looking. Party schools were to become part of the sanitized and modernized exterior of party rule, a symbol and promise of the party's new confidence that continued market reform would deliver not a grubby capitalist, but a bright socialist future.

[37] Only a few days after the crackdown in June 1989, in his address to martial law troops, Deng had already stressed the role of political education: 'I once told foreigners that our worst omission of the past ten years was in education. What I meant was political education, and this does not apply to schools and young students alone, but to the masses as a whole' (Deng 1990: 380). Soon, the new General Party Secretary Jiang Zemin would start elaborating on these words of Deng; see for instance Jiang Zemin, 'Wei ba dang jianshe cheng gengjia jianqiang de gongren jieji xianfengdui' (The struggle to build the party into an even stronger vanguard of the working classes)', in Jiang Zemin 2001: 1–20; Jiang Zemin, 'Guanyu jiaqiang dangxiao jianshe de ji ge wenti' (On several questions regarding the strengthening of the building of party schools)', summarized in Zhonggong Yunnan Shengwei Dangxiao jianshi bianxiezu (Editorial group of the brief history of the Yunnan Chinese Communist Party Committee Party School) 2000: 170–172.

[38] Guanyu jiaqiang dangxiao gongzuo tongzhi (Circular regarding the work of the strengthening of party schools), summarized in Zhonggong Yunnan Shengwei Dangxiao jianshi bianxiezu (Editorial group of the brief history of the Yunnan Chinese Communist Party Committee Party School) 2000: 170–172.

[39] In 1935, Mao had said that 'We should make the party a smelting furnace of Communism and take numerous new members who wish to struggle for what the Communist Party advocates and temper them into Bolshevik fighters with the highest class consciousness' (Mao Zedong 1970–1974, volume v, p. 38). For a further discussion of this quote, see Wylie 1980: 44.

However, in 1990 all of this was still a promise. The role of the party schools in reaching out to society and indeed the world gradually rose with the increasing prominence of Hu Jintao at the Centre from 1992 onwards. Hu had a particularly strong and enduring commitment to cadre training and the modernization of the cadre system through his tenure as President of the Central Party School from 1993 until 2002. In 1995, the party Centre promulgated the *Temporary Regulations on the Work of the Party Schools of the Chinese Communist Party*.[40] These regulations mainly restate the policy of the 1990 *Circular* and pre-1989 practice, but, by more clearly explicating and standardizing them as formal regulations, put them on a more solid footing. The regulations provide a clear template for the nature, function, educational principles, basic tasks, leadership system, order of classes, educational and degree system, educational and research work, organizational, ideological and political work for the party, staff building, and logistical and financial guarantees of party schools. The regulations reaffirm that the formal head of a party school ought to be the secretary or deputy secretary of the party committee at the same administrative level, and that party schools should be run by their own committee for school affairs (*xiaowu weiyuanhui*) rather than directly by the party committee, as used to be the case before 1983, although the members of that committee are still appointed by the party committee. The regulations also stipulate that all running expenses of a school should be met by a budgetary allocation of the finance department of the government at the school's administrative level, while the costs of infrastructural construction would have to be borne by the government's planning department at that level. These regulations thereby affirm that party schools were considered elements of the party's inner core of institutions and activities, directed by the party committee and bankrolled by the government. Party schools were thus treated as fully administrative departments and not, for instance like ordinary schools and hospitals, as 'functional units' (*shiye danwei*). As the reforms progressed in the nineties and 2000s, the functional units were more and more cut loose from direct government planning and funding and more exposed to the forces of the market economy, along the same lines but with a few years delay as state-owned enterprises.

The nineties also saw serious progress with academies of administration for the training of non-leading government cadres. In 1993, the National

---

[40] *Zhongguo Gongchan Dang dangxiao gongzuo zanxing tiaoli* (Trial regulations on the work on Chinese Communist Party schools) as summarized in Zhonggong Yunnan Shengwei Dangxiao jianshi bianxiezu (Editorial group of the brief history of the Yunnan Chinese Communist Party Committee Party School) 2000: 190–193.

Academy of Administration (*Guojia xingzheng xueyuan*) was established in Beijing. Unlike the provincial academies of administration that in some cases had already started operations in the late eighties and early nineties, the National Academy is located at a different site and is completely independent from the Central Party School.[41] The establishment of a fully fledged system of academies of administration from the Centre all the way down to the county level is an aspect of the creation of a civil service system. With the desire to staff the state bureaucracy with qualified and professional personnel came the fear of their possible lack of ideological commitment to the party and socialism. At the same time, the party also realized that such personnel required regular training to acquire, improve and update their professional skills, knowledge and qualifications.[42] In subsequent chapters we will see that many government and even party departments in fact fill the need for specialist training through a gradual proliferation of in-house and outsourced training courses. However, the academies of administration continue to fulfil an important need to control and monitor high-level staff and staff promotions through their unique combination of ideological training, monitoring and assessment, and non-political education. Indeed, academies of administration can perhaps best be described as party schools for non-leading cadres. As far as the party is concerned, party schools and academies of administration are simply different aspects of the same task. The head or deputy head of the government at a particular academy's administrative level is the formal head of the academy, just as the party secretary or deputy party secretary is the head of the party school. The annual targets of an academy are part of the overall cadre training plan (*ganbu peixun guihua*) set by the party leadership committee or group for education (*ganbu jiaoyu weiyuanhui* or *ganbu jiaoyu peixun xiaozu*). This plan also sets the targets for the party school and the so-called academy of socialism (*Shehui zhuyi xueyuan*) that trains leading cadres who are members of the eight democratic parties.[43]

To sum up, in the eighties and nineties the regulatory framework was put in place for the standardization and systemization of cadre training. The nineties also saw the establishment or strengthening of the institutions

---

[41] Some localities also operate separate party schools and academies of administration. One example is Kunming municipality, where 'personal factors' were cited as the reason for keeping the two establishments separate.

[42] Guojia gongwuyuan peixun zanxing guiding (Trial rules on the training of national civil servants). Ministry of Personnel document no. 52, 1996. Online at www.zytzb.cn/zytzbwz/jiaoyupeixun/fagui/80200306121035.htm (checked on 15 May 2006).

[43] Field notes 18 November 2004. I will return to the cadre educational and training plans and academies of socialism below.

that were supposed to deliver this training. However, cadre training only became a truly important priority after the turn of the century in the run-up to the transition of power to the 'fourth generation' of leaders around Hu Jintao, when the party started in earnest to put its money where its mouth was.

CADRE TRAINING IN THE TWENTY-FIRST CENTURY

In the year 2000, the party centre issued the *Decision on the strengthening and improvement of party school work in the twenty-first century*,[44] followed in 2001 by the *2001–2005 national plan for cadre training*.[45] The *Decision* starts out by making very clear that leading cadre training is vitally important, because the changes forged by market reform and opening to the west have also had important implications for the cadre system. Many young and well-qualified cadres have joined the ranks, but they are often insufficiently steeped in Marxist theory, party history and tradition, the party's internal life and work with the masses, and they lack the ability to find their way through complicated situations and resolve complex contradictions. However, the real meat of the *Decision* is arguably that the salaries of staff in party schools have to be brought in line with those in regular universities. Investments should be made to upgrade the facilities for students and staff, and to meet the financial needs of modernizing teaching and research, including the use of information technology to enable distance learning throughout the party schools system. Through their finance and planning departments, governments at all levels are required to make adequate funds available to make these improvements possible.

The *Decision* is a relatively short and almost improvised document that may have been written in some haste, perhaps connected to the Party's reflections on its future role in the new century as an emergent super-power under a new leadership that also spawned the new theory of the 'Three Represents' announced in the same year. As these reflections took place in large part in the Central Party School itself, it is not altogether unsurprising that prioritizing party schools and cadre training was given a prominent place. In 2001, with the 'Three Represents' firmly in place

[44] 'Ershiyi shiji jiaqiang he gaijin dangxiao gongzuo de jueding' (Decision on the strengthening and improvement of party school work in the twenty-first century), 5 June 2000, online at aixin.njmu.edu.cn/jcdj/xxcl/200603/5948.html (checked 14 June 2006).
[45] '2001 nian – 2005 nian quanguo ganbu peixun guihua' (2001–2005 national plan for cadre training), in Zhonggong Zhongyang Zuzhi Bu ganbu jiaoyu ju (Cadre education bureau of the Central Organization Department of the Chinese Communist Party) 2001: 1–14, online at www.china.org.cn/chinese/zhuanti/177926.htm (checked 14 June 2006).

as the new orthodoxy, the spirit and many of the concrete initiatives of the *Decision* were incorporated in the more comprehensive and more carefully wrought *2001–2005 national plan for cadre training*. Unlike the 2000 *Decision*, the plan not only includes training for party and state leading cadres, but also lower-level civil servants in party and state organizations, state enterprise managers, cadres in the juridical and legal system, grassroots cadres below the county level, minority cadres, cadres who are not members of the Communist Party, female cadres and cadres working in the remote western parts of the country. The plan reaffirms the central role of party schools in cadre training, but also sanctions much more explicitly than earlier documents the role that other institutions may play in delivering training programmes for cadres, including 'other schools and centres for cadre training' and other 'higher education schools'. The *Plan* also actively encourages exchanges and cooperation between party schools within China, and with institutions abroad.[46] As I found in the course of my fieldwork, this endorsement of the diversification of cadre training has had important implications, but the *Plan* itself is still rather short on detail in this regard. Yet, policy making on this issue continued and, as we shall see, by 2006 the diversification of cadre training had become a major element in the Centre's strategy to push change further.

The *Plan* is quite extensive in its exhortations of efforts to raise the quality of teaching and research staff, infrastructure, teaching materials and assessment of cadre training. As with the 2000 *Decision*, all of these entail very considerable needs for extra funding, supervision and leadership, and it is the final sections that deal with these issues that are perhaps the most important. The *Plan* stipulates not only that adequate funding should be made available by each level of government, but also that funds should be used more effectively. The *Plan* also explicitly states that cadre training should not be done for profit. Classes should not arbitrarily be organized, fees charged, or certificates issued simply to make money. The party meant what it was saying. In 2002 the Centre reportedly allocated one billion yuan in additional capital funds to the Central Party School and the National Academy of Administration, mostly for new infrastructure.[47] However, the *Plan* remains silent on where local governments should find the funds to pay for these improvements. As I learned during my fieldwork, this would have very major consequences for the shape of local administration in the years to come.

[46] *2001–2005 national plan for cadre Training*, pp. 10–11.　　[47] Field notes 22 April 2004.

NEW INSTITUTIONAL ARRANGEMENTS FOR CADRE TRAINING

The *2001–2005 national plan for cadre training* set the framework for cadre training in Yunnan when I did my fieldwork there in 2004 and 2005. However, the plan was merely the first step in a policy area that was, and continues to be, very much in flux. After the installation of the new leadership around Hu Jintao had been successfully completed at the Sixteenth Party Congress in 2002, a series of new initiatives have seen the light of day as part of a further drive to strengthen the party and its leading role.[48] Several of the developments that I witnessed at or below the provincial level in Yunnan and which I will discuss in detail in the chapters ahead were clearly influenced by these national developments. Conversely, some of the chronic problems in cadre training that persisted at the local level were the reason for further initiatives, particularly the most recent round of changes in the run-up to the new, Eleventh Five-Year Plan in 2005 and 2006. Before turning to the fieldwork, I will therefore briefly dwell on these new policy initiatives between 2002 and 2006.

In the new era, the CCP leadership tends to react to priority issues and problems largely by strengthening central institutions, spending more money at the central level and centralizing control over policy making and implementation. There is, in general, a great belief in social engineering that applies modern scientific methods to developmental issues (*kexue fazhanguan*): the party puts even greater faith in the healing power of science than in the past. This explicitly also includes the humanities and the social sciences that were recently singled out for special attention in this regard.[49] Centralization and modernization mean that the party will have to break the mould of the traditional governmental structures that

---

[48] The key document here is the *Decision of the Chinese Communist Party centre on the strengthening of the party's ruling capacity building* (Zhonggong Zhongyang Guanyu jiaqiang dang zhizheng nengli jianshe de jueding) passed at the Fourth Plenum of the Central Committee of the Sixteenth Party Congress on 19 September 2004, online at www.people.com.cn/GB/40531/40746/2994977.html (checked 2 March 2008).

[49] See the *Opinion of the Party Centre on taking a further step in the promotion and development of the humanities and social sciences* (Zhonggong Zhongyang guanyu jin yi bu fanrong fazhan zhexue shehui kexue de yijian), Central document no. 3, March 2004, online at www.sicau.edu.cn/web/xcb/llxx2/3.htm (checked 17 September 2006). See also 'The Centre issues "Opinion on taking a further step in the promotion and development of the humanities and social sciences" ' (Zhongyang fachu 'guanyu jin yi bu fanrong fazhan zhexue shehui kexue de yijian'), *Xinhuanet News* 20 March 2004, online at news.xinhuanet.com/newscenter/2004-03/20/content_1375777.htm (checked 8 September 2007). Margaret Sleeboom has shown how independent social science research and party leadership have gradually been welded together since the 1989 crackdown at China's main social science research institution and former hotbed of heterodox thinking, the Chinese Academy of Social Sciences (Sleeboom 2007: parts IV and V).

are not only highly compartmentalized and ossified, but also devolve a great deal of autonomy to local levels of government. This new ethos impels the leadership to take bold steps quickly and tackle problems that previously seemed intractable. However, such solutions can often seem more apparent than real. As local government still by and large remains the same, the centre's many initiatives are therefore often not or only imperfectly transmitted downwards. Even if they reach the lowest levels, local administrations of counties and towns, especially in poorer areas, often simply do not have the budget to comply with central demands for action.[50] As we shall see in chapter 5, this approach also deepens the developmental and political rift between the developed coastal areas that have the money and political access to accommodate the Centre's wishes, and the central and interior parts of China that, on the whole, do not.

The belief in the malleability of society is also played out clearly in cadre training: strengthening the ideological and administrative 'quality' of cadres is reduced to a governmental problem than requires the right application of technocratic solutions. The common thread that runs through the initiatives and exhortations of recent years is a clear impatience, if not frustration, with the conventional methods and institutions of cadre training and the intransigence of local government. Cadre training had already been given much more prominence and priority in the nineties, yet much of what had been done then had in fact amounted to just more of the same. Cadre training was better funded, much more professional, broader in scope, emphasized both ideology and skills training, and catered for a much larger constituency of leading and ordinary cadres than ever before, but the basic philosophy behind it had not changed from the early days when the party still was a revolutionary organization. In short, the cat might have become a lot fatter, but not necessarily caught more mice.

Training in the new era has to balance more the requirements of 'quality' and 'ability'. A proper understanding of ideological orthodoxy ensures that cadres continue to submit to Leninist party discipline, including resisting the temptations of official graft. However, training should also equip cadres with the ability to deal flexibly with complex issues, apply their knowledge creatively and independently, and accept that continuous learning is a

---

[50] The paradox created by central fiscal health and local budgetary squeeze is discussed in Christine Wong's recent work (Wong 2008). While local governments in richer areas can still find ample sources of income, those in poorer areas have directly been hit by the recent central abolition of local levies and fees. Their only recourse is often the diversion of centrally earmarked transfers (thus increasing even more their lack of compliance to central wishes) and the appropriation and sale of land, which is arguably the most contested and politically explosive issue in local state–society relations in recent years (Liu, Wang, Tao and Murphy 2008; Zhou Feizhou 2008).

normal part of their work. The professional training that cadre training has to supply is no longer limited to specific skills (English, computer use) and specialist knowledge, but calls for a completely different style of work. In other words, the party wants to have its cake and eat it. Cadres continue to be bound by the ideology and practice prescribed by Leninist party discipline, but should also become modern, competent managers of increasingly complex organizations.

The initiative in the developments after 2002 is clearly in the hands of the Centre (including the Central Party School) and a very few model regional party schools, such as the ones in Shanghai and Shenzhen, that are closely associated with the Centre. Interestingly, these initiatives have established specialized institutional arrangements for revolutionary 'theory' and administrative 'practice', which are traditionally united in conventional cadre training in party schools. In 2003, the Centre, reportedly at the insistence of the then Head of the Central Party School Zeng Qinghong (Shambaugh 2008: 148), decided to establish and fully fund three completely new, high-profile cadre academies (*ganbu xueyuan*, translated as 'executive leadership academies'). The schools opened in 2005. They are located in Pudong, Shanghai, the place where the party was founded, but more importantly also the pinnacle of China's modernity and international opening up, and the sacrosanct revolutionary sites of Jinggangshan (Mao's first revolutionary base area and the 'cradle' of the party) and Yan'an (the revolutionary base area from where Mao launched the party's revolutionary conquest of China). Together, these three sites offer a carefully constructed, material representation of the party's auto-narrative on its own birth, growth and maturation.[51] Both in the very choice of their location and in their objectives these academies offer a curious blend of orthodox modernization, reinvented revolutionary tradition and international exchange. In 2006, a fourth school of management and economics was opened in Dalian city, the party's own model of the symbiosis between strong government and the market economy. Training at this fourth academy is especially aimed at high-level cadres in state enterprises and financial institutions.[52]

---

[51] 'Congratulatory letter from Hu Jintao on the completion and formal start of study at the three cadre schools' (Hu Jintao wei san suo ganbu xueyuan jiancheng bing zhengshi kaixue fa hexin), 21 March 2005, online at www.jxgdw.com/news/gnxw/2005-03-21/3000036162.html (checked 19 September 2006); 'A look at the innovation of cadre training from the perspective of the three cadre academies' (Cong san suo ganbu xueyuan kan ganbu jiaoyu peixun de chuangxin), online at www.jxgdw.com/news/gnxw/2005-03-21/3000036162.html (checked 19 September 2006).

[52] Interview 93, 27 April 2007. The Dalian Academy of Economics and Management (*Dalian Jing-Li Xueyuan*) was officially opened on 12 January 2006, online at politics.people.com.cn/GB/14562/4026576.html (checked 18 June 2008).

Apparently, the Centre believes that whirlwind trips to these ultra-modern new academies can be used to enforce centralist loyalties and traditional revolutionary virtues: Maoist revolutionary theory and Leninist centralism reduced to package tourism.

Training at the academies is supposed to complement conventional cadre training by educating cadres in the party's revolutionary tradition and exercising party spirit. One of the key tasks of the academies is to offer 'experiental education' (*tiyanshi jiaoyu*), experience which includes both the party's revolutionary roots and its modernist future. Administratively, the four academies fall directly under the Central Organization Department. The department coordinates with the Central Party School and the National Academy of Administration to ensure that trainees at these two schools will also receive a stint of ten days or so at one of the academies to charge their revolutionary batteries.[53] Training at the four new academies is also available to lower cadres whose training is the responsibility of organization departments at the provincial or even lower level. No doubt one of the attractions for lower-level organization departments – apart from the need to conform to central wishes – is that the costs of training at the new academies is supposed to be paid fully out of the Centre's coffers.[54]

FURTHER REFORMS OF CADRE TRAINING

Apart from the creation of the new cadre academies, the conventional programmes of cadre education and training themselves were also directly targeted for reform. In October 2003, the Central Organization Department, the Central Propaganda Department and the Central Party School jointly issued the *Relevant opinions on further deepening the reform of cadre education in the Central Party School*.[55] After party building was put at the

---

[53] See 'Training classes at the three cadre academies innovate the model of training for party and state leading cadres' (San suo ganbu xueyuan peixunban chuangxin dangzheng lingdao ganbu peixun moshi), 4 August 2005, online at politics.people.com.cn/GB/8198/60906/61581/4269456.html (checked 18 June 2008). Also interviews 94 and 95, 28 April 2007.

[54] Field notes 17 December 2006.

[55] Central Organization Department, Central Propaganda Department and Central Party School, *Relevant opinions on further deepening the reform of cadre education in the Central Party School* (Guanyu jin yi bu shenhua Zhongyang Dangxiao ganbu jiaoyu gaige de ruogan yijian), 2003. This document is not publicly available, but much of its content is cited in other sources, some of which have been referenced in the following sections. Additionally, a summary of the content of this document is posted on the website of the party school of the Guangxi Autonomous Region see 'Important news about the immediate future: the Central Organization Department, the Central Propaganda Department and the Central Party School jointly issue a document demanding the upholding and perfection of the new arrangement of education Take one step further in deepening the reform of the

Further reforms of cadre training 53

centre of the political agenda at the Fourth Plenum of the Central Committee in 2004, the suggestions for reform contained in this document were quickly disseminated to provincial party schools across the nation.[56] The Centre itself focussed its budgetary and capital construction spending on the new cadre academies, the Central Party School, the National Academy of Administration, and, interestingly, on web-based distance learning for rural party members. In 2005, the Ministry of Finance raised its own (non-capital construction) spending for cadre training at the central level by 10.2 per cent.[57] At both the central, provincial and even lower levels, a period of experimentation, implementation and reflection followed,[58] culminating

---

education at the Central Party School' (Jinqi yaowen: Zhongzubu Zhongxuanbu Zhongyang Dangxiao lianhe xiafa wenjian yaoqiu jianchi he wanshan jiaoxue xin buju Jin yi bu shenhua Zhongyang Dangxiao jiaoxue gaige), online at www.gxdx.gov.cn/readarticle.asp?newsid=371 (checked 18 June 2008).

[56] See for instance Shi Taifeng, 'Earnestly carry out the spirit of the Fourth Plenum of the Sixteenth Central Committee: further deepen the reform of the party school education – speech given at the discussion meeting on the reform of education in the national system of party schools' (Renzhen guanche luoshi dang de shiliu jie si zhongquanhui jingsheng, jin yi bu shenhua dangxiao jiaoxue gaige – zai quanguo dangxiao xitong jiaoxue gaige yantaohui shang de jianghua), 11 October 2004, online at www.ltdx.com/Article/Print.asp?ArticleID=397 (checked on 18 September 2006). 'Party schools from four cities discuss deepening educational reform' (Si zhixia shi dangxiao yantao shenhua jiaoxue gaige). Online at www.ccps.gov.cn/xinwen.jsp?daohang_name=%E6%90%9C%E7% B4%A2%E7%BB%93%E6%9E%9C&daohang_uri= search.jsp&content_uri=/root/jqyw/111336-1568890 (checked on 18 September 2006).

[57] National Development and Reform Commission, *Actively encourage large scale cadre training work* (Jiji zhichi da guimo ganbu peixun gongzuo); Ministry of Finance, *Secure the funds for cadre education and training* (Zhuahao ganbu jiaoyu peixun jingfei de baozhang luoshi). Reports at the Tenth National Joint Conference on Cadre Education (*Dishi ci quanguo ganbu jiaoyu lianxi huiyi*), 2005.

[58] To understand what the demand for innovation and change meant for local party schools and academies of administration, a report from one locality, Jiangjin city in Chongqing municipality, gives a refreshingly candid insight. In Jiangjin city, raising the 'quality' of cadres seems to have brought a fusion of the Renaissance man, Confucian gentleman, CCP cadre and MBA graduate, leaving the impression of a confused, but no doubt rather interesting, cadre training pedagogy. The Jiangjin report summarizes the work in 2004 and 2005 under three delightfully simple headings, namely 'who teaches' (*shei lai jiao*), 'what to teach' (*jiao shenme*) and 'how to teach' (*zenme jiao*). The first mainly involves attracting external well-known teachers to give one-off lectures and, conversely, sending local Jiangjin teachers to schools in the developed coastal parts of China for retraining or further degree work. The second entails that in the design of the curriculum a special emphasis is placed on theory, applicability, innovation, practical issues, education, diversity, student participation, orientation on the future and strategy. For senior cadres this includes adding to the curriculum classes that test cadres' 'psychological quality' and adaptability. Other classes are supposed to raise their civilization, decency or vigilance. Yet others have as their subject reporting on the state of the municipality and strategic issues in the development of Jiangjin. For younger cadres, classes are organized on art appreciation, military training and shooting, music appreciation, calligraphy and debating. Finally, the third heading of 'how to teach' starts with a crackdown on cadres who take leave from training whenever they please. A range of new teaching methodologies is then listed, including case analysis, discussion, lectures, debate, simulation, exercises and exchange. More attention is also given to field trips and the use of audio-visual equipment in the classroom. This report, 'Jiangjin party school

in the Tenth National Joint Conference on Cadre Education (*Dishi ci quanguo ganbu jiaoyu lianxi huiyi*) in 2005. Following the conference, in March 2006 a new central document was promulgated, the *Trial regulations on cadre education and training work* that broke important new ground in the field of cadre training.[59]

The *Trial Regulations* express the Centre's disquiet over the lack of fundamental change and formalize a development that was already well underway: the emergence of a market for many aspects of cadre training. Even the monopoly of political training of party schools, academies of administration and the new central cadre academies is no longer unchallenged: for the first time it is also permitted that such training be given by other institutions (article 13). Furthermore, it is recognized that the requirements of individual cadres may be very different, and that cadre training should cater flexibly and effectively for these individual training needs in ways that party schools and schools of administration are illequipped to do. The *Trial Regulations* however won't (yet) go as far as saying that conventional party schools no longer are up to the job. Rather than acknowledging the direct conflict between these two elements of cadre training they are simply mentioned alongside each other, and cadre training will henceforth have to have many different faces.[60] The key element in the *Trial regulations* to make this happen is that individual cadres and their work units are given much greater autonomy and choice in selecting the kind of training and the specific providers of that training. Cadres have a general obligation to undergo twelve days of full-time training a year, and can opt for a variety of study methods, providers and content. This includes a specific encouragement of self-study and study while on the job, participation in study tours or coursework elsewhere in China or abroad, and web-based distance learning. Cadre training should moreover use a

---

deepens educational reform and raises the quality of training' (Jiangjin shiwei dangxiao shenhua jiaoxue gaige tigao peixun zhiliang), is part of a set of such local reports and reports from central organizations at the 2005 Tenth National Joint Conference on Cadre Education that were given to me in 2006. Several of these reports were still available on the website of the Jiangsu Province organization department in the summer of 2007, but not including this particular one. The fact that it was the Jiangsu organization department that made these documents publicly available is unlikely to be a coincidence. The provincial party secretary at the time, Li Yuanchao, was preparing himself for an appointment at the Centre, and at the Seventeenth Party Congress in October 2007 was indeed given a key central post, interestingly enough that of head of the Central Organization Department.

[59] *Trial regulations on cadre education and training work* (Ganbu jiaoyu peixun gongzuo tiaoli (shixing)), online at politics.people.com.cn/GB/1026/4250946.html (checked on 15 September 2006).

[60] *Regulations (trial)*, articles 16 and 27.

variety of methods, including lectures, seminars, case analysis, simulation, research and direct experience.[61]

CONCLUSION

Cadre education and training is a reform programme that continues to develop in a manner that is beginning to be more similar to other reforms, for instance those of state enterprises and public services. In 2008, just before the completion of this book, it was rumoured in Beijing that county-level party schools might be abandoned altogether, a development that would be entirely in line with the trend in policy making since 2000. The endorsement of 'orderly competition' gives market forces an important role right at the deepest core of Leninist governance: the party's grip over its own cadres. Clearly, this is not uncontentious, which explains why the Centre at the same time spends increasingly large sums on the very institutions (party schools, cadre academies, schools of administration) whose monopoly is being challenged. We can only guess at the political machinations in Zhongnanhai (China's Kremlin) that lie behind the complexities in this area, but in a way they matter less than what actually happens with cadre training in the field. The daily realities of cadre training are not simply determined by the policy pronouncements at the top. As in many other areas of reform, local initiatives are in many ways ahead of the Centre. In fact, local realities often function as an important driver of further reform policies, and it is to these realities that we must turn in the next chapters.

[61] *Regulations (trial)*, articles 23 to 26.

CHAPTER 3

Cadre training and education in the twenty-first century

THE INSTITUTIONS OF CADRE TRAINING

Cadre training involves a great many party and state institutions. Although overall responsibility at each level of administration rests with the general party committee, this responsibility is delegated to a separate committee directly under the party committee called the cadre education and training committee (*ganbu jiaoyu peixun weiyuanhui*, or *ganjiaowei* for short). This committee is responsible for drafting the annual cadre educational and training plan, and is the main forum for political decision making on cadre education and training. All other party and government departments, the party school, the academy of administration and the academy of socialism essentially have executive, rather than decision-making, responsibility for parts of the plan. It is therefore very telling that this committee is a party, rather than a government committee: it is in coordinating committees such as this that the party's Leninist leading role over state and society finds concrete expression.

The formal chair of the cadre education committee is the full party secretary. The deputy chair – and the person normally running the committee – is the deputy party secretary in charge of ideological work, who also doubles up as the full head of the party school. Other members include the party secretary of the party's discipline inspection committee, the standing deputy head of the party school, the head of the party's propaganda and organization departments, the head of the government's personnel bureau and also the party secretary of the working committee for directly administered departments (*zhishu jiguan gongzuo weiyuanhui* or *gongwei*, see below). However, the head of government and the chair of the people's political consultative conference are *not* on the committee, thus denying both government and representative organizations parity with the CCP in this crucial policy field. Instead, lower-level leaders have been charged to represent their interests. The head of the government personnel bureau, who is a member of the committee, deals with academy of administration affairs, while the interests of the democratic parties, non-party cadres and minority cadres are represented by the party's united front department, whose head is invited to attend meetings of the committee if relevant business is to be discussed.[1] Moreover, at the national level also represented on the committee is the commission for commerce and trade as the latter coordinates international exchanges and cooperation in the field of cadre training.

Like so many functional departments in the Chinese bureaucracy, academies of administration and party schools are therefore only directly responsible to the government or party committee at their own administrative level. Schools at different levels form a so-called 'system' (*xitong*), but higher-level schools cannot direct – let alone command – the work of lower-level schools. However, active working relations are encouraged and expected, and higher-level schools can be an important resource for lower-level ones. Moreover, higher-level schools give guidance and direction to lower levels through the issuance of documents and regular meetings of administrative staff. Party schools even have a separate section in the school's office for liaison with lower and higher levels (*lianluo ke*), including handling the large volume of official documents that travels up and down the chain.[2] Another section (the confidential correspondence section, *jiyao tongxun ke*) deals with the direct command relationship with the local government and party administration.[3]

Chief operational responsibility for the implementation of the annual cadre education and training plan is in the hands of the party's organization department, and more specifically its office of the cadre education committee (*ganjiaowei bangongshi*), also known as the cadre education department (*ganjiao bumen*). The office's job is not actually to organize training and teaching, but rather to ensure that the relevant functional departments carry out their part of the plan. These principally are the personnel bureau and the academy of administration for non-leading civil

---

[1] There is actually a certain amount of discrepancy between different accounts of the composition of the cadre education committee, and it seems likely that arrangements at the Centre and at different localities are not necessarily exactly the same. Here I have pieced together the features that seem to apply in most cases. Sources include a meeting with the leadership of the Qilin district party school, 18 November 2004; *2001–2005 national plan for cadre training*, pp. 13–14; interview with Duan Eryu, field notes 12 April 2004; interview with Teng, head of the educational affairs office of the Qujing Prefecture Party School, 18 April 2004; field notes 18 April 2004; interview with Rao Peihui, 29 November 2004.

[2] Likewise, the Central Party School has an office for local party schools (*difang dangxiao bangongshi*) which is part of the school's general office (Sun Xiangdong, personal communication, 6 May 2008).

[3] Interview 42, 25 November 2004.

servants, the party's united front department and the 'academy of socialism' (see below) for non-CCP leading cadres and the party school for the party's leading cadres. The office also supervises the training and reports back to the cadre training committee on training and education delivered. The head of the office of the cadre education committee in one prefecture described his office's job as follows:

There are three people in the office, [who] are responsible for the management of cadre education, like whether or not a particular department's training plan is suitable or not, or whether or not it has carried out the training according to the plan. In general, such plans have to be submitted to the cadre education committee. In general, training can only be organized after it has been reported to our office, and important training can only be carried out after it has been reported to the cadre education committee and approved by the leaders on it . . . We monitor the execution of the plan, for instance that the students have actually come and that their number does not exceed the target set, and also the quality of instruction given by teachers, whether the content that is supposed to be taught is finished and we evaluate the effectiveness of the training. We [do this by] listening to conversations between students, sitting in on classes, looking at the quality of class teaching, whether or not the students are interested. After completion of the training, the [organizing department] also has to write a report for our office. QUESTION: What do you do when you think a teacher is no good? ANSWER: Ask another teacher to teach this class next time. QUESTION: Who decides that? ANSWER: The [department in charge of the training class]. It is their class, our responsibility is to monitor and discover any problems. We can only make suggestions to the department; we cannot directly get in touch with the party school [to ask for another teacher].[4]

In addition, the office keeps track of the training received by all cadres in its jurisdiction, including the information that cadres submit in their mandatory report after their participation in a training session. The office uses this information later to identify which cadres are due for periodic retraining. The office also keeps itself informed on those cadres that are likely targets for promotion, giving such cadres preferential access to training opportunities. The information for this is gathered through the annual cadre evaluations that involve work reports from the individual concerned, and opinions from their colleagues and some of their subordinates.[5] However, much of the work of selecting cadres for particular training sessions is actually devolved simply by issuing quotas to the organization department at the level where the cadres actually work, rather than where they will receive their training.

---

[4] Interview 71, 29 November 2004. [5] On the cadre evaluation system, see Edin 2000; 2003a.

The institutions of cadre training 59

In delivering cadre training, at each level of the administration (central, provincial, prefectural, county and even township) the vertically integrated 'systems' (*xitong*) of party schools and schools of administration continue to be the main institutions. Apart from these schools at each administrative level, many other party schools exist in government departments and state-owned enterprises. In 1995, there were already considerably more than 2,000 party schools in the whole of China.[6] In addition, many other institutions are involved in cadre training. In the course of my fieldwork I discovered a seemingly never-ending range of party schools and other institutions and arrangements for cadre training and education, and further research would undoubtedly unearth yet more.

First of all, the Central Party School's Branch School for Central (Party) Organs (*Zhongyang Zhishu Jiguan Fenxiao*) and the Branch School for Central Government Organs (*Zhongyang Guojia Jiguan Fenxiao*) provide political training to leading cadres in the central administration in Beijing who are of insufficient rank to go to the Central Party School itself.[7] Both branch schools were established in 1980 with the explicit purpose of restoring ideological unity and order in the central administration. The branch schools seem to be not so much a school as a coordinating organ whose main task is to organize centralized ideological study classes in the party schools of individual central departments, committees, bureaus and offices. Students taking these classes are cadres of *ju* or *chu* rank in the department. The branch schools operate under the joint direction of one of the two Central Work Committees for Directly Administered Departments and the individual central administrative departments. The curricula are set by the Central Party School, which also provides many of the teachers. Despite their name, the Central Party's branch schools are not directly subordinate to the Central Party School, but have a looser business or guidance relationship with it, similar, in fact, to the relationship between

---

[6] A compendium of party schools in China was published in 1996. It contains short descriptions of the Central Party School, twenty-eight of the twenty-nine province-level schools (with Hebei province listing two and the Beijing municipal school being the only one missing), 1,991 prefectural and county schools, and a further 345 schools of state enterprises or departments of provincial-level governments. There are descriptions of only two ministerial party schools and only one description of a party branch school (namely the one in Beijing) at any level. Although impressive, the compendium clearly does not contain all party schools in China at the time: many government departments, state enterprises and local governments are missing. In addition, the compendium also makes no mention of any of the schools of administration or the academies of socialism that are important elements in China's cadre training infrastructure (Liu Yucheng 1996).

[7] The Central Party School has four branch schools. In addition to the two mentioned here, there are the Branch School for the Commission of State Assets (*Guoziwei Fenxiao*) and the Military Branch Department (*Budui Fenbu*). For more information on each of these branch schools, see the links provided at www.ccps.gov.cn/fxgz.php?col=13 (checked on 18 June 2008).

all party schools of different rank throughout the whole party school system.[8] This arrangement is repeated at lower levels of the bureaucracy. Provincial party branch schools (*dangzhi xuexiao*) train the on average 4,000 or so leading cadres in a provincial administration who are of insufficient rank to go to the provincial party school. These schools are independent institutions, but, like the party schools at lower levels of the administration, tend to have close working relations with the full party school at their level, and quite often hire teachers from that school to teach particular sessions or classes.[9]

At lower levels of the administration a similar situation pertains, although the number of lower-level leading cadres is of course much less and separate party branch schools apparently do not exist. Training for lower-ranked leading cadres in the localities is the responsibility of the work committee for directly administered departments, which is a department of the general party committee much like the organization department, the propaganda department and the discipline inspection committee.[10] Unlike the cadre education committee that, as we mentioned above, is just a periodic gathering of selected leaders, the committee for central administrative departments has its own staff and offices. The work committee is responsible for party work among lower-level leading cadres in the central administrative departments within its jurisdiction. This includes not only education and training, but also other aspects of normal party work, such as the oversight over party branches in the administrative departments, propaganda, party discipline and discipline inspection. The committee also carries out the annual evaluations of leading cadres, and its opinions and recommendations weigh heavily in decisions on promotions, demotions, transfers, bonuses and fines made by the organization department.[11]

---

[8] Interviews 94 and 95, 28 April 2007; 'Central Party School's Branch School for National Organs' (Zhongyang Guojia Jiguan Fenxiao), 18 April 2007, online at www.ccps.gov.cn/fxgz.php?col= 520&file=2414&onlyOne=1 (checked on 28 June 2008).

[9] Interview 1, 12 December 2004.

[10] At the central level there are actually two such committees, one for the central organs of the party, and another for the central organs of the government. See 'Circular from the Chinese Communist Party Centre endorsing "Opinion of the Central Organization Department, Party Committee for Directly Administered Central Organs and Party Committee for Central Government Organs on strengthening and improving party work of central organs of party and government"' (Zhonggong Zhongyang pizhuan 'Zhongyang Zuzhibu, Zhongyang Zhishu Jiguan Dangwei, Zhongyang Guojia Jiguan Dangwei guanyu jiaqiang he gaijin zhongyang dang-zheng jiguan dang de gongzuo de yijian' de tongzhi), 13 February 1988, online at cpc.people.com.cn/GB/64162/71380/71387/71589/4855226.html (checked on 18 June 2008).

[11] On the role of the committee for directly administrated departments in cadre training, Interview 71, 29 November 2004. For one of the few publicly available documents on this committee, see 'Proposal for the functional deployment, internal setup and personnel of working committee for

It may help to illustrate this issue by talking about a more concrete instance. In the case of a prefecture, the heads of the administrative departments of the prefecture (education, personnel, health, etc.) have *chu* level rank. The management of these leading cadres, together with the heads of counties under the prefecture, is the responsibility of the prefectural organization department, and they normally receive their training at the prefectural school. However, heads of sections within these departments normally have *ke* level rank. This is too low to be managed directly by the prefectural organization department, which is why a separate work committee for centrally administered departments was created. The work committee has the same rank as a county party committee, and in many ways the prefectural work committee is in fact the functional equivalent of a county party committee. However, the important difference is that county *ke* cadres are part of the county administration. Their management is the responsibility of the county organization department and their training is part of that county's cadre education and training plan. *Ke* level cadres in the prefectural administration, on the other hand, are only managed by the work committee, but remain the responsibility of the prefectural administration; likewise, their training is part of the prefectural cadre education and training plan.

Second, large government departments, state-owned enterprises and large service organizations have their own party schools that train those party cadres in the organization whose rank is too low to go to the party school or academy of administration within the jurisdiction of the state or party administration that controls the enterprise.[12] In total, no less than 56 such schools exist in Yunnan province alone. Such party schools also organize training classes for activists who are groomed for party membership.[13] The head of one very large state enterprise in Yunnan explained this in

---

directly administered departments of the Chinese Communist Party of Yangquan municipality' (Zhonggong Yangquan shi zhi jiguan gongzuo weiyuanhui zhineng peizhi, neibu sheji he renyuan bianzhi fang'an), no date, online at www.yq.cn/sw/jggw.htm (checked on 28 June 2008).

[12] Like everything else that has to do with the state, state-owned enterprises are owned and controlled by the government of a particular area and of a particular level. A state enterprise somewhere in Yunnan may, for instance, be a provincial-level enterprise and thus be responsible to the provincial government of Yunnan. This enterprise will have no relationship with the township, county or prefectural governments in whose area it is actually located: rank overrides geography.

[13] Training classes for activists or recent members of the CCP are organized, if they are large enough, by party committees in all Chinese organizations, including private enterprises and foreign-invested enterprises. However, in most organizations the party committees or branches are too small to run their own classes (let alone have their own party schools), and send their activists to general classes offered by either the party committee in their locality, or else their supervisory organization, such as the development and reform committee, the commerce and trade committee or their supervisory board. Interview 1, 12 December 2004.

more detail to me. His enterprise with 40,000 employees has the rank of a prefecture or provincial bureau (*diqu/ting*), and last year the central government handed it over to Yunnan province. The company's main party school has a rank one lower than the enterprise itself, i.e. county or prefectural office (*xian/chu*). Under the company's main school there are a further five party schools of township or county section (*xiang/ke*) rank. These schools serve as much more than just party schools and have in fact diversified into all kinds of more specialist professional training and education. Proper party training now is only a small part of their remit.[14]

Third, almost all departments of the party and the government have their own training centres (*ganbu peixun zhongxin*) or cadre schools (*ganbu xuexiao*) that are responsible for the professional, non-political training of cadres of various levels in their organization. Courses usually last no longer than a week to ten days and have a very specific focus relevant to the work of a particular group of cadres. Of course, only departments above a certain size can afford to run such a centre. At lower levels, departments therefore have to turn to another training provider to run the courses that they need, and this quite often is the local party school or academy of administration.[15] However, departments are entirely autonomous in their choice of provider.

Fourth, many government cadres are actually not members of the Chinese Communist Party at all, but are either members of the eight so-called 'democratic parties' (*minzhu dangpai*) or have no party membership (*feidang ganbu* or *dangwai ganbu*).[16] Greater participation in government by non-CCP members is actively promoted and engineered by the CCP that thus uses its time-honoured united front strategy for the purposes of strengthening its role as China's 'ruling party' by broadening the base of its government among the newly emerging social strata in Chinese society, particularly intellectuals and other highly educated employees, private entrepreneurs and independent professionals. Cadres who are non-party members or members of democratic parties are an integral part of the CCP-dominated cadre system. Non-party cadres not only include professional civil servants in non-leading positions, but also leading cadres. The latter tend to be concentrated in organizations that link government with

---

[14] Field notes 4 December 2004.   [15] Field notes 29 October 2004.
[16] In 2004, Yunnan province had about 18,000 state cadres who were members of one of the eight democratic parties, 1,090 of whom were leading cadres of county/office rank or higher; Interview 48, 26 November 2004.

non-communist forces in society (people's political consultative conferences, industry and trade associations, minorities work committees), and government departments whose work is largely non-political and requires a great deal of expertise (finance, management, trade, education, health). Increasingly, non-party members are also appointed to positions of deputy or full head of government, both because of a conscious effort of the CCP to increase the proportion of non-CCP leading cadres, and the impact of the introduction of procedures for competitive appointment or election (see chapter 6).

The careers of non-CCP cadres are shaped by essentially the same factors as those of party members. In the case of leading cadres this inevitably entails that the CCP is directly involved in their careers. Although the party's united front department is responsible for non-party cadre management, the organization department closely watches over and participates in this aspect of its sister department's work.[17] The accounts given by two cadres who happened to be on a non-CCP cadre training course when I visited the Honghe Prefecture Party School illustrate this point very well.

QUESTION: You are not a party member. Why haven't you applied for membership?
ANSWER: Once upon a time I thought about joining the party, but then later thought that it didn't really matter whether or not you join the party as long as you do your work well. In the beginning I also didn't really seek promotion. Later, the [CCP's] organization [department] got involved and they decided that I should develop my career as a non-party member.[18]

I am a member of the Guomindang Revolutionary Committee, which is one of the eight democratic parties. The party's political signature is very distinctive because it is the left wing that split off from Sun Yat-sen's Guomindang. I have relatives in Taiwan. After the relationships between China and Taiwan got better, the organization [department] mobilized me in 1985 to join the Guomindang Revolutionary Party: the elder generation of my family had been Guomindang members during the War of Resistance against Japan... I participate in this training as the chair of the Honghe Committee of the Guomindang Revolutionary Committee (...) The united front department required me to participate, I was able to relieve myself of my duties at work, and so I came.[19]

---

[17] In fact, the organization department is also involved in other aspects of united front work. For instance, the appointment of delegates at the political consultative conference, which is the public face of the CCP's united front work, is done by the CCP party committee after inspection of the delegates' credentials by a working party whose members are taken from the CCP united front department, the political consultative conference itself and the CCP organization department; Interview 78, 1 December 2004.
[18] Interview 74, Honghe Prefecture Party School, 30 November 2004.
[19] Interview 75, 30 November 2004.

As already briefly mentioned in the previous chapter, the ideological and theoretical training needs of leading cadres who are not CCP members are catered for at separate establishments that are known, without any irony intended, as 'academies of socialism' (*shehuizhuyi xueyuan*). Academies of socialism exist separately at the national and the provincial level, but, in Yunnan at least, at lower levels they have been combined with the party school/academy of administration, thus creating an institution that simultaneously fulfils three functions and boasts three separate signs at its main gate.[20] Academies of socialism are an old component of the People's Republic of China's administrative setup. The Yunnan Provincial Academy of Socialism was established in 1956, but after the Cultural Revolution it was not until 1992 that it started operations again.[21] At all levels, the work of the academies of socialism is directed not by the democratic parties themselves, but by the Communist Party and the government: although the head of the academy of socialism is the chair of the people's political consultative conference, the deputy head is the head of the CCP's united front department. Moreover, many of the teachers are members of the Communist Party. CCP staff at the Yunnan Provincial Academy of Socialism have their own party branch that plays an important role in supervising and guiding the work of the school, and the secretary of the CCP branch also holds an appointment in the province's united front department.[22] Academies of socialism are a fully integrated part of the cadre training infrastructure. Academies of socialism, party schools and schools of administration in a particular area closely coordinate their activities and routinely contract each other's staff to teach specific courses or sessions. Many of the teachers and leaders at the Yunnan Provincial Academy of Socialism had, in fact, either been recruited from the provincial party school or else had received their masters degree from the provincial party school or Central Party School. Furthermore, like lower-level party schools in Yunnan, the provincial academy of socialism also serves as a teaching site for the provincial party school's correspondence courses. Academies of socialism mainly provide short-term training to non-CCP leading cadres and enterprise managers and to cadres working in the people's political

---

[20] Interview 54, 16 November 2004.
[21] This was significantly later than the national school and the schools in other provinces that were re-established in the eighties. According to my informants at the school in Yunnan, the main reason for this tardiness was the difficulty in finding suitable premises (and quite likely even more important funding) for the school; Interview 48, 26 November 2004.
[22] Interview 48, 26 November 2004.

consultative conference and the CCP's united front department. In fact, academies of socialism function in large measure as the cadre training arm of the CCP's united front department, and are also tasked with training that is part of other aspects of the department's work, including private entrepreneurs, the industry and trade association, business associations, and the Taiwan and overseas Chinese associations.[23]

Part of the reason for the complexity of the general field of cadre training and education that I have briefly outlined above is historical. Traditionally, departments of government, functional units and state enterprises had a large degree of autonomy, and the presence of party schools was part of the inclusiveness of institutional life in most Chinese work units. Another explanation is sheer numbers. The party attaches great importance to cadre training and education, and the number and variety of courses and students that have to be taught is simply astounding. A final explanation of the institutional complexity of cadre training is the administration's preoccupation with hierarchical rank and administrative jurisdiction: any particular school only caters for cadres of a particular rank and from a particular area. In cadre training, as in the administration in general, hierarchical rank is mapped onto levels of local government and spatial units. Geography, bureaucratic level and rank are conflated and one often serves as a shorthand reference to the others. In view of this great variety, I have focussed my own research on cadre training at party schools and schools of administration, where the ideological and strategic connection between the party and its bureaucratic agents is forged most explicitly and directly. However, I will return to the issue of variety when discussing the promotion of competition in an emerging market for cadre training, which is clearly the direction that policy making in the last six years has gone.

THE CENTRAL PARTY SCHOOL

The Central Party School in Beijing is not only the pinnacle of the cadre training system in China, but in many respects is akin to regular research universities. Although numerically much smaller, in terms of quality its academic staff of 600 is on an equal footing with academics in top-flight universities in China. Among the staff, 168 are full professors and 159 associate professors; more importantly, as many as 70 of the staff have the right to supervise PhD students, arguably the most important indicator of

[23] Interview 48, 26 November 2004.

academic prestige in China.[24] Staff at the Central Party School only teach graduate students: between 1981 and 2007, 1,126 master's and 266 PhD students graduated from the school. In 2006, the school was building a new student dormitory to accommodate more graduate students. Competition for entry as a degree student at the school's graduate academy is even fiercer than at the top universities. This makes the school one of the elite graduate centres in the country: after graduation many find employment in regular universities, specialist research or teaching institutions, or in the administration.

Nevertheless, like lower-level party schools, non-degree cadre training remains the most important teaching duty at the Central Party School. On 1 October 2007, the school proudly announced that since 1978 it had trained more than 50,000 middle and high ranking officials. In the academic year 2007–2008, the school hosted about 1,300 training students per semester.[25] The school's main training courses are periodic retraining (*lunxun*) classes for prefectural/*ting* (or *ju*) and provincial/*bu* level cadres. Most students have a rank at the deputy (*fu*) level and their training is an important component of their preparation and selection for promotion to and appointment at the full (*zheng*) level. Shorter courses for full (*zheng*) rank cadres are offered to fulfil the five-yearly retraining requirement of such cadres. Training courses at the central school last longer than at lower-level schools. A typical course for deputy prefectural rank cadres lasts half a year (with four and a half months of actual training). A retraining course for full prefectural rank cadres typically lasts three months. In January and February, the school runs a special one-month retraining course for full heads of provinces and ministries, reportedly set up at the specific order of Hu Jintao. Deputy heads of provinces and ministries have to take a three- to six-month course. Since 2001 the school also has been tasked with running courses of just ten days or two weeks for selected county party secretaries who are being prepared for promotion to a higher rank and office. In

---

[24] 'The Central Party School' (Zhongyang Dangxiao), online at baike.baidu.com/view/125711.htm, no date (checked on 28 June 2008). Wibowo and Fook also give the number of 600 teaching staff, adding that 400 are professors or lecturers with doctoral degrees (Wibowo and Fook 2006: 149).

[25] 'Central Party School trained an aggregate of over 50,000 middle and high officials since 1978' (1978 yilai Zhongyang Dangxiao leiji peixun 5 wan yu ming zhong-gaoji guanyuan), 1 October 2007, online at news.xinhuanet.com/politics/2007-10/01/content_6820277.htm (checked on 23 June 2008). *Baidu baike*, China's online encyclopaedia, gives the somewhat higher figure of 1,600; see 'The Central Party School' (Zhongyang Dangxiao) baike.baidu.com/view/125711.htm, no date (checked on 23 June 2008). In 2001, a visiting Chinese journalist reported 1,300 students per semester at the school; see Wang Yueping, 'Inside the Central Party School' (Zoujin Zhongyang Dangxiao), *Shidai chao* 2001(13), online at www.people.com.cn/GB/paper83/3819/462405.html (checked on 23 June 2008).

The Central Party School

addition, the school runs training courses (*peixun*) for younger (typically forty-five to fifty years of age) cadres slated for promotion, usually to the deputy provincial level. Such courses include the relatively well-known special courses for minority cadres from Tibet and Xinjiang. Courses for younger cadres normally last half a year or a full year. In the case of the courses for Tibetan or Xinjiang cadres, the courses may even be two years long, and are an important component of the CCP's rule and civilizing mission in these two most remote and potentially secessionist territories. The two-year course is aimed at students who have not previously studied at university, and an undergraduate degree is given at the end of the course.[26]

Even more than at lower-level schools, training at the Central Party School revolves around current issues rather than a set curriculum. Although even these high cadres cannot escape the prescribed dose of set ideological training, this involves interpretation and application rather than the simple regurgitation of orthodoxy more frequently taught at lower-level schools. In 2002, the Central Party School published two volumes of lectures selected from the more than 1,000 lectures given at the school since the Fifteenth Party Congress in 1997. One volume deals with 'major issues in the contemporary world', the other with 'basic issues in Marxism' (Yu Yunyao and Yang Chungui 2002a; 2002b). Lectures under the latter rubric include not only predictable titles like 'Discussion of basic issues in Marxism–Leninism', but also 'Establish socialist democratic politics with Chinese characteristics and China's reform of the political system' and 'Economic globalization and the CCP facing the twenty-first century'.[27]

Despite the many classes, training at the school continues to emphasize self-study, reflection and reading of the original Marxist classics. Students on courses for younger cadres, for instance, upon entering the school gate are given a set of Marxist texts and other basic readings, including *Capital* and the *Anti-Dühring*, which they are expected to finish within

---

[26] Interviews 94 and 95, 28 April 2007; Zhou Tianyong, 'The place and function of the Central Party School in political life in the party and government' (Zhongyang Dangxiao zai dang he guojia zhengzhi shenghuo de diwei he zuoyong), *Guangming Guancha* 27 February 2007, online at guancha.gmw.cn/show.aspx?id=3645 (checked on 11 September 2007).

[27] In recent years, an increasing number of lectures at the Central Party School are broadcast by satellite or streamed over the Internet for use across the whole national system of party schools and other training institutes. The Central Party School's network centre for long-distance education (*yuancheng jiaoxue wangluo zhongxin*) regularly posts lists of these broadcasts on its own website (www.ccps.gov.cn/ycjx.php). Although only titles of lectures are given, these nevertheless are a useful source for tracking the current interests of the Chinese leadership. I will return to the use of the Internet in cadre training in chapter 5.

three months.[28] As we saw in chapter 2, self-study and the classics were the centrepiece of training when the Central Party School officially reopened in 1977. The highlight of training at the school is the weekly report session on a current topic with a senior figure in the party, government or army. These sessions are not only attended by students, but also by many members of the school's teaching staff.[29] A feature of particularly these sessions and other non-ideological components on the courses is the extreme frankness of the discussions that allows unusual or unorthodox viewpoints to be aired, a far cry from the Leninist and Maoist origins of cadre training with its emphasis on the imposition of uniformity and orthodoxy. Teachers and (former) students uniformly comment extremely positively on the wide-ranging and candid nature of the training that allows students to understand issues from many different angles that are often far beyond their normal core competency. These sessions are not only an invaluable experience for the students at the school, but are also an important opportunity for central leaders to test new ideas and policies. The candour at these sessions therefore allows for feedback and criticism from a sympathetic and highly qualified audience that makes for ultimately better policy.[30] The concentration of talent and expertise among training students at the Central Party School is also tapped into by means of special discussion classes and research classes. In these classes students and staff jointly investigate a particular problem or topic and often also undertake original research, conducting surveys, site visits or other forms of fieldwork. Because this research is conducted by high-level cadres themselves, results or recommendations can frequently be fed into ideological innovation or policy making at the central level.[31]

---

[28] 'Deciphering the Central Party School: already 1/3 of students from younger and middle aged cadre courses have been promoted to provincial-ministerial rank' (Jiemi Zhongyang Dangxiao: Zhongqingban xueyuan yi 1/3 jisheng sheng-buji), *Nanfang zhoubao* 8 November 2007, online at news.qq.com/a/20071108/001619.htm (checked on 23 June 2008).

[29] In 2003, a selection of thirty-three such reports from 2002 was published as Zhonggong Zhongyang Dangxiao baogaoxuan bianjibu 2003. Together with the two-volume selection of lectures at the Central Party School (Yu Yunyao and Yang Chungui 2002a; 2002b), this volume provides a valuable glance at central policy making and the content of cadre training at the school. This rare moment of openness has, at least to my knowledge, not been repeated since. Selected lectures are also regularly published in the journal *Zhonggong Zhongyang Dangxiao baogao xuan* (Selected lectures at the Central Party School), but this is a *neibu* (for internal circulation only) publication.

[30] Interviews 94 and 95, 28 April 2007; Interview 89, 20 December 2006; Interview Wu Zhongmin 96, 29 April 2007; fieldnotes 29 April 2007; Saich 2001: 91–92; Wibowo and Fook 2006: 149; Zhou Tianyong, 'The place and function of the Central Party School in political life in the party and government' (Zhongyang Dangxiao zai dang he guojia zheng zhi shenghuo de di wei he zuoyong), *Guangming Guangcha* 27 Febuary 2007, online at guancha.gmw.cn/show.aspx?id=3645, checked 11 September 2007.

[31] Wang Yueping, 'Inside the Central Party School', 2001.

TRAINING FOR CENTRAL LEADERS

Training of the highest cadres at the central level, the members of the Politburo, consists of periodic 'collective study' (*jiti xuexi*), essentially half-day seminars that are arranged upon request. Unlike cadre training at the Central Party School, these collective study sessions are not the responsibility of the Central Organization Department, but are organized by an office of the CCP's Politburo itself and take place in Zhongnanhai. Although these sessions predate the Hu Jintao–Wen Jiabao leadership, they have become much more prominent and regular since their ascent in 2002. A testimony to this is the fact that a list of topics and speakers since 2002 is publicly accessible, and in early 2007 extensive excerpts of the first forty-two sessions were published 'for internal use only' (*neibu shiyong*). Each session consists of a speech by Hu Jintao himself, followed by lectures by two prominent specialists, usually from the Central Party School, the Chinese Academy of Social Sciences, the Military Academy, Renmin University, or other research institutions, party schools, or universities. In addition, two groups of specialists are asked to prepare a class on the topic. After each teaching a trial class, one of these groups is selected to teach the class, while the materials of the other group are distributed.[32] In total, forty-four such sessions were held between the Sixteenth Party Congress in 2002 and the Seventeenth Party Congress in 2007.[33]

In addition, since 1999 a seven-day annual 'special discussion class for principal central cadres of provincial-ministerial rank' (*sheng-buji zhuyao lingdao ganbu zhuanti yantaoban*) is held during the winter vacation around Chinese New Year. These classes are about a topic of special interest at the time, such as finance (the first one in 1999), the WTO, the construction of the new countryside, the harmonious society and study of Jiang Zemin's selected works. The classes usually include speeches by the CCP general party secretary and other senior leaders followed by extensive discussions. Despite the fact that these classes are held at the Central Party School, the classes are organized by the Party Centre itself when the school is not in

---

[32] The internal publication is Gaoji lingdao juece xinxi ziliao bianxie zu (Editing group of the policy making information materials for high-level leaders) 2007. Details on the conduct of the collective study sessions were taken from the preface to this collection.

[33] 'A view of establishing a learning political party from the 44 collective study sessions of the CCP Politburo' (Cong Zhonggong Zhongyang Zhengzhiju 44 ci jiti xuexi kan jianshe xuexixing zhengdang), 10 October 2007, online at news.xinhuanet.com/newscenter/2007-10/10/content_6857255.htm (checked on 24 June 2008).

session and teaching staff and students are not invited.[34] Similar sessions, often called 'reading classes' (*dushu ban*), are also found at lower levels of the administration for the highest leaders at that level, particularly those who hold a full rather than just a deputy rank and thus have a much heavier workload and direct executive responsibility. Interestingly, the Yunnan Provincial Academy of Socialism also ran reading classes for non-CCP high-level provincial leaders, such as some provincial vice-governors and the deputy heads of the Provincial People's Congress and the Provincial People's Political Consultative Conference.[35] Although I do not have independent information on this point, it seems reasonable to surmise that similar arrangements also exist at the central level.

MAIN COURSES AND OTHER NON-DEGREE TRAINING COURSES
AT PARTY SCHOOLS

At each level, party schools and schools of administration deal with a range of short-term residential training courses, long-term residential degree courses and non-residential degree courses. In this section and the next I will first discuss non-degree training courses; I will turn to degree courses in the next section.

To party schools and schools of administration, the main training courses (*zhuti ban*) are their most important task, and they expect that they will gradually be made to concentrate more fully on these again as other tasks will either become less onerous, or will be taken over by other, specialized training institutions that the recent policy changes are encouraging. Short-term main training courses are the linear descendants of cadre training as it took place in party schools from the very beginning. Their main objective continues to be instilling knowledge of and conformity to the current ideological orthodoxy and administrative practice. Main courses are residential, last from one week to a few months (or more at the Central Party School) and are a requirement for cadres, both leading and non-leading. At all party schools, a distinction is made between specialized professional training courses that are organized for a specific purpose (such as a new law or skills training in electronic government), short refresher

[34] Interviews 94 and 95, 28 April 2007; field notes 6 November 2006. Some of the speeches and associated documentation are publicly available on the Internet, see for instance Hu Jintao's speech on 19 February 2005 'Speech at the special topic discussion class for central principal leading cadres on raising the capacity of building a socialist harmonious society' (Zai sheng-buji zhuyao lingdao ganbu tigao goujian shehuizhuyi hexie shehui nengli zhuanti yantaoban de jianghua), online at news.xinhuanet.com/newscenter/2005-06/26/content_3138887.htm (checked on 23 June 2008).
[35] Interview 48, 26 November 2004.

retraining courses and general main courses. In addition, schools will, for a fee, take on the organization and teaching of other short-term training courses for government departments or even enterprises that are not part of the school's own teaching plan. Examples of such courses 'outside the plan' (*jihuawai*) are induction courses for applicants for party membership at a particular department, or training courses for managers of a state enterprise. Usually, party schools secure contracts for these courses because of their relatively good facilities and, in some cases, also because they can provide specialist training in current policy and political developments in China and the west, further testifying to the broadly perceived usefulness of such subjects in China. However, one of my informants at the Yunnan Provincial Party School rather disarmingly admitted that the school was not very good at providing entertainment, an important aspect of such semi-commercial courses, although they were often praised for their expertise in promoting 'team spirit'.[36]

Two different types of general main courses exist with each type in turn having separate classes for leading cadres (taught through the party school) and non-leading civil servants (taught under the heading of the academy of administration). The first type of courses are called 'novice training' (*churen peixun*), 'reserve cadre training classes' (*houbei ganbu peixun ban*) or 'young and middle-aged cadre classes' (*zhongqing ban*), when the students are younger cadres who just have been recruited into the civil service, or else 'training for office' (*renzhi peixun*) for more experienced cadres who are slated for a promotion. Especially for new recruits, novice training at the party school is part of a longer period of training and preparation that also usually involves temporary, non-executive appointments (*guazhi*) as deputy head in an enterprise, government department or (at the lowest level) a village. Participation in such a course is a requirement for an appointment to take effect, although in the case of the promotions of more experienced cadres such training is in practice usually given after rather than before their appointment. In the case of novice training, the content of these courses also includes the basic skills needed in leadership positions, such as the handling of documents or oral presentation, in addition to the party's policies and direction, laws and regulations and other basic knowledge about the Chinese administration.[37]

The other type of course is called 'refresher training' (*lunxun*), which cadres are obliged to undergo every five years. Usually, a party school

[36] Interview 36, 24 November 2004. On party member induction courses, see Interview 65, 17 November 2004.
[37] Interview 43, 25 November 2004; Interview 55, 16 November 2004.

has different departments that deal with these two types of training: the training department (*peixun bu*) for novice training and the advanced study department (*jinxiu bu*) for refresher training. Early on in my first stint of fieldwork, Duan Eryu, the head of education and my main collaborator at the Yunnan Provincial Party School, explained the difference as follows:

> The first group often has just been recruited and has no experience in administration, but has a lot of theoretical knowledge from their time as undergraduate, masters, or even PhD students. They need to be taught knowledge about administration that they didn't get in university. The second group is different. They have substantial experience and need to know how to apply their knowledge to the handling of concrete issues. The main content of their training is the analysis and discussion of case studies with the objective to reach a consensus between teacher and students in the class. For instance, this morning I taught a class on administrative management. The main topic was how to move from an administration based on power to one based on service and the understanding of obligation. This is an important theme for the central government, as many leading cadres still operate on the basis that theirs is the final word (*wo shuo le suan*), whereas they have to work on the basis of the law and regulations, that is, they have to deal with issues on the basis of what the law says.[38]

Schools also offer special main course training classes for certain categories of cadres, such as female cadres, youth league cadres, minority cadres, and (in areas without a separate academy of socialism) democratic party members, non-party cadres and private entrepreneurs. Categorial training classes are usually organized on behalf of a specific administrative department. In the case of non-party leading cadres, for instance, the CCP's United Front Department and the people's political consultative conference are the leading departments, while for minority cadre training the government's minorities committee (*shaoshu minzu weiyuanhui*, or *minwei* for short) takes the lead, but in close cooperation with the CCP's united front department. Categorial training is part of the CCP's long-term effort to broaden the social base of the administration. In order to boost the participation of minorities in the administration, minority cadres in minority areas, for instance, may also receive other forms of preferential treatment in their training, such as preferential access to study and inspection trips in advanced areas in the east of China or to general training courses.[39]

The length and intensity of main courses depends greatly on the bureaucratic rank and political importance of the cadres involved and the administrative level of the school. At prefectural party schools, for instance, refresher training for office (*chu*) cadres usually lasts about a month, while

[38] Field notes 2 April 2004. [39] Interview 71, 29 November 2004.

at the provincial school it may last up to two months, with the extra time mainly spent on more thorough theoretical (ideological) training. Novice training for cadres of deputy department (*ju* or *ting*) level or higher at the Central Party School lasts from six months up to a full year, while such training of lower-level cadres at prefectural or provincial schools lasts at most three months. Training classes for private entrepreneurs or members of the democratic parties at prefectural or provincial academies of socialism may be as short as ten days. At county schools, refresher training for deputy section (*fuke*) cadres or village cadres might simply be a meeting instead of formal training (*hui dai xun*), attending a few lectures for a day or so, participation in short inspection trips, or, if the county can afford it, training at a party school in a more 'advanced' part of China such as Shanghai. If formal training is organized, it usually lasts only for about a week or so. Novice training for new civil servants or cadres at county schools takes a bit longer, but will not exceed half a month. County schools are also responsible for providing the teachers for training sessions for cadres at township or town party schools. Township party schools themselves only take care of the practical organization of these sessions.[40] In Yiliang county in central Yunnan, a week's training for village and party committee members is provided by the county party school, which includes question-and-answer sessions with cadres of the county's organization department. In addition, each year separate ten-day training sessions are held for both the secretaries of village party committees and the chairs of villagers' committees. These sessions are very much top-down efforts to turn these elected officers into responsible cadres. Topics include the basic skills needed for members of such committees and briefings to bring their work in line with the general policies at the Centre and the economic development plan of the county. Certain sessions are taught by higher-level cadres or teachers. For instance, when a central document on rural work has been issued, personnel of the provincial policy research office would be invited to speak on the province's take on the new policy.[41]

At the Yunnan Provincial Party School, two main objectives of cadre training were mentioned to me time and again. First of all, training should instil a better understanding of Marxist theory in general and the CCP's own theory, ideological line, orientation and policies. When discussing the content of training courses, party school teachers and students normally distinguish between such 'theory' (*lilun*) and 'practical' (*shiji*) subjects. Theoretical study instils a 'correct' understanding of ideological orthodoxy

---

[40] Interview 69, 27 November 2004.   [41] Interview 69, 27 November 2004.

with a special focus on the most recent policy changes at the Centre. This is indeed exactly the point of these subjects: students expect from their teachers expansions on the most recent developments at the Centre, both in terms of general policies and ideology and policies and trends in their own field of work. As a rule, the higher the rank and the more political the post of the cadres involved is, the more attention is paid to theory in the curriculum. Although it would be tempting to read an implicit criticism of the uselessness of 'theory' in its distinction from 'practice', this was not the case for leading cadres whose very career depends on their ability to bend with the changing ideological wind from Beijing.

The distinction between theory and practice is a core aspect of Marxism, but so is their ultimate unity. Teaching of theory therefore has to cater to the second main objective of training: uniting this theory with the practice of administrative and leadership work. This is obviously easier said than done. As a general rule, training courses at all levels and areas lack the rigidly set curriculum of degree education. Lower-level party schools look very carefully at the most recent annual teaching programme and teaching materials of the Central Party School in Beijing, but combine this with teaching materials of their provincial school and elements that are specific to their own area and the target group of students of a particular class. Uniting theory and practice happens more specifically by adding other elements to the course. In addition to the relatively standard lectures by the school's staff and external specialists, local leaders are often invited to expand on the significance of recent policy changes. Students also spend considerable time analysing cases in class discussions, on visits or inspection tours locally or in more advanced areas, or even on their own research. 'Practical' aspects of a course also include more properly academic subjects that are not necessarily more locally informed, but are simply considered useful in day-to-day administration, including computer skills, English or standard Chinese, accountancy, public management, economic management and law. Organizers of training courses quite often try to inform themselves of the wishes of the students and their institutions. In designing courses they take into account the feedback of previous cohorts, meetings with the students' departments during inspection tours, meetings with departments directly involved in cadre training such as the organization department, the propaganda department and the personnel bureau, surveys and lastly also meetings with students at the commencement of the course. Catering for the students' specific needs is also in line with the thrust of recent policies on cadre training that were discussed in the previous chapter. One informant at the Yunnan Provincial Party School in fact used the term '*à la carte* education' (*caidanshi jiaoyu*) to describe what the school aspired to deliver, a term that features regularly in central policy documents on cadre training.[42]

CORRESPONDENCE DEGREE COURSES

By referring to the short-term residential training courses as 'main courses', these are distinguished from 'degree courses' (*xueli ban*). There are two quite different types of degree courses. At provincial party schools and the Central Party School in Beijing, a relatively small number of students are taught full-time (*tuochan*, meaning that the student (temporary) has left his or her job) or part-time (*zaizhi*, i.e. while in employment). Although residential degree teaching continues to blossom at the Central Party School, the number of full-time students at provincial schools is much lower now than in the nineties. At even lower levels, residential degree courses had already been phased out in the late eighties or early nineties. Instead, lower-level schools took on the teaching for separate correspondence courses set by higher-level schools that teach the vast majority of degree students within the party school system.[43] Both on-site and correspondence degree courses at party schools originated in the early eighties, when the massive drive to raise the educational standards of China's cadre corps suddenly required millions of cadres to obtain the minimum degree deemed necessary for the level of job they were in. Correspondence courses prepare for a range of degrees, from middle vocational school (*zhongzhuan*) all the way up to master's degrees. Degrees can be taken in many subjects, but the most popular ones are economic management, law and public management. Students are recruited by open examinations, and prospective students as a rule have extensively prepped through self-study, or in tutorial classes organized by the school or through the Internet.

Correspondence courses are colloquially often called sidelines (*fuye*),[44] a term used in agriculture to distinguish grain production (main crops, *zhuye*) from other crops such as vegetables, and a reference to Maoist agricultural policy that emphasized grain production over sidelines. In the sixties and seventies, sideline production was politically suspect: very profitable perhaps, but also a capitalist distraction from grain, the mainstay of socialist production. Degree correspondence courses are very similar to that: they may raise most of the income for the school, be good for the

---

[42] Interview 36, 24 November 2004.
[43] Interview 54, 16 November 2004.   [44] Field notes 17 November 2004.

vast majority of students, and occupy much of the time of the staff, yet are not considered core business. Correspondence degree courses are taught to prepare students for degree examinations. As one of my informants put it: 'non-residential degree education teaches for degrees, cadre training is education for the quality of cadres.'[45] A fairly typical example of the difference in cadres' attitude to non-degree training and degree education is that of the following forty-year old county cadre, who I interviewed while on a short-term course at the Honghe Prefecture Party School:

This [training course] is study arranged by the organization department of the higher level. It helps in raising one's own quality, and acquiring some further knowledge is also my own aspiration. After the organization department has made the arrangement, you must participate in study. When I am busy working at the county I have no time to study, I do not have the opportunity to participate in theoretical study. This is what the organization department is concerned about, and I myself also want to participate (...) I have studied for degree courses ever since I graduated from middle vocational school. In 2000 I got my higher vocational degree, and in 2002 I started on the undergraduate correspondence course of the Provincial Party School in economic management. I am almost finished with that now. QUESTION: Do you study for this degree because it was a requirement from your superiors, or because you want it yourself? ANSWER: Studying is the individual's own wish. QUESTION: What do you expect from your undergraduate diploma? ANSWER: Competition in society is very strong. The main reason is not to be out-competed, and I also do not want to fall behind.[46]

The term correspondence course actually does not adequately describe the pedagogy or institutional setup. Students continue in their normal daytime job. During most of the time they do indeed study on their own and are guided through assignments by postal or email correspondence with their teachers. However, there is also a requirement to spend a fixed number of days per year in class, and employers (as a rule, a state organization) are obliged to give the students adequate time off to do so. Unlike main courses, the curriculum of correspondence courses is entirely set by the degree-awarding school, leaving little room for the initiative of the local teachers and schools that deliver the teaching.[47] Degree courses impart

---

[45] Field notes 18 November 2004.
[46] Interview 74, 30 November 2004.
[47] For instance, the Qujing Provincial Party School in 2004 taught about five thousand students on correspondence courses. About half of these studied for an undergraduate degree, the other half for a vocational (*zhuanke*) degree. According to the regulations of the degree-giving school (i.e. either the Provincial or the Central Party School), each group of students had to be taught in-class for twenty days per semester. During these twenty days, the class got examination preparation instruction for three different subjects. About one-third of classes received their in-class teaching at the prefectural school itself, the other two-thirds were taught at lower-level county party schools in the prefecture. County schools were rather autonomous in providing the teaching for vocational

knowledge and skills. This includes a certain amount of ideology and Marxist orthodoxy, but on the whole this is very different from the ideological training on main courses that aims to convey the most recent ideological and legal developments and to link this with administrative practice.

As the sole purpose of instruction, examinations are taken incredibly seriously. In order to avoid any leak of the content of the examinations, the teachers who set the examination are held in full detention (*fengbi*) from when they get together to set the papers right up until the end of the examinations. The papers themselves are put under lock and key. In this period the examiners are confined to a separate office building on campus and are not allowed to have any contact with the world outside: telephones are disconnected, mobile reception is screened off and even food is provided by cooks who silently hand their meal through a hole in the door. If the examiners have to have contact with the outside, several people stand around to listen in, including a person of the discipline inspection department of the party.[48] The downside of the exam-driven nature of the courses is, as teachers regularly complain, that students on degree courses tend to be very uncritical and uninterested in discussion, which is very different from students on the short-term main courses.

With the exception of the Central Party School, until recently party schools did not have the right to confer full academic degrees, called *xuewei* in Chinese. However, the central and provincial party schools since the eighties have nevertheless given out large numbers of degrees called *xueli*. These degrees are not recognized by the State Council's degree committee, but have been approved by the party school system, and are thus good enough to fulfil the requirements for positions in the state sector.[49] It is this right to confer *xueli* degrees that provides the regulatory basis for the thriving distance learning operation of the Yunnan and other party schools. The central and provincial party schools hold the profitable right to give out *xueli* degrees, but do not have (or probably would not want to have) the capacity to teach the tens of thousands of students that sign up for

---

classes. Undergraduate classes were more strictly in the hands of the prefectural school, dispatching its own teachers to teach the classes. County schools only provided classroom facilities, a class teacher and just a few trusted teachers that were hired by the prefectural school. The content of the degree programmes was entirely set by either the central or the provincial party school, while the prefectural school was responsible for organizing in-class teaching and administration. Interview 54, 16 November 2004.

[48] Field notes 11 April 2004.

[49] China has three independent educational hierarchies ('*systems*'): the state's supervised by the Ministry of Education, the party's and the army's. Interview 90, 21 December 2006. I will return to the increasing importance of *xuewei* education at party schools in chapter 5.

their courses every year, all across the country in the case of the central school and across Yunnan in the case of the provincial school. It is here that the full network of party schools kicks in. Party schools at the prefectural level and below do not have any independent right to confer degrees, but provide the bulk of the teaching, both by correspondence and in-class. Entrance and final examinations are set by the degree-giving school. The entire curriculum and teaching materials are likewise designed and provided by that school. However, in offering degree classes, local schools sometimes take into account the requirements of local government. In Qujing prefecture, for instance, the party school offered special degree classes for cadres of the local public security bureau to enable them to obtain the minimally required advanced vocational (*dazhuan*) degree.[50]

Lower-level schools have entered into agreements with specific degree-giving schools to teach the students according to the specifications of the degree-conferring school for a specific share in the income. At one prefectural school that I visited, in the case of degrees from the Central Party School, 40 per cent of fee income went to the central school, 20 per cent to the provincial party school and the remaining 40 per cent to the prefectural school. In the case of a degree from the provincial school, 40 per cent is for the provincial school and 60 per cent for the prefectural school.[51] Prefectural and county schools are responsible for supplying teachers of the required standards, classrooms, timetabling and everything else that is needed. In fact, a prefectural school may in turn farm out to their subordinate county-level schools much of the teaching for degree courses.[52]

Until 2007, the Central Party School was the leading school to offer *xueli* correspondence degrees. The Central Party School's Correspondence Academy was formally set up in 1984 after pioneering efforts at party schools in certain provinces (including Yunnan) in the years before. In 2006, the school had 3.7 million graduates and 600,000 students on courses. Correspondence degree education requires a great deal of coordination between the central school and lower-level schools to design the curricula and teaching plans and to produce the teaching materials. In this vertically integrated network the central school acts as the general academy (*zongyuan*), with under it branch academies (*fenyuan*), followed by study districts (*xuequ*) and teaching stations (*fudaozhan*), corresponding to the provincial, prefectural and county party schools. The network also includes branch academies, study districts and teaching stations in government institutions and in the

---

[50] Interview 64, 17 November 2004.
[51] Interview 65, 17 November 2004. [52] Field notes 17 November 2004.

army. Nationally, the school has fifty-five branch academies and over three thousand teaching stations.[53]

According to the head of the educational affairs office of the Central Party School's Correspondence Academy, distance learning plays a very important role. Students are taught in classes at their local schools and mostly at the weekend when they are free. Classes are taught in Beijing by lecturers and are broadcast by satellite to the branch academies in the network. Local schools and teachers are responsible for making sure that the students are actually in class, and in addition teach tutorial classes and answer questions. Questions can in principle also be asked from the teacher in Beijing directly, usually by email.[54]

Lower-level party schools as a rule teach degree courses for both the provincial and the central school. Students in one classroom may then for instance take the more expensive and prestigious Central Party School degree in, say, public administration, while students in the next classroom are taught on the basis of a different curriculum for the same degree given out by the provincial school. Degrees taught at county and prefectural party schools include a wide range of subjects far beyond the traditional remit of party schools (including finance, management, accountancy, IT, economics) that attract not only government cadres, but also students from many other backgrounds.[55]

Courses for *xueli* degrees have created a market in higher education in which party schools are operating very actively. Schools that have the right to give out degrees have used this to create a steady income stream. Schools without this right have capitalized on other resources: their teaching staff, buildings and, most importantly, proximity to students. The market has created a system that actually works remarkably well: it has brought degree education within the reach of millions of cadres across China, fulfils the party-state's ambition to raise the educational level of its staff and has created a substantial and reliable income stream for party schools across the country, keeping them afloat despite very restricted local budgets.

The massive scale and increasing marketization of degree course work also had another effect. As we have seen in chapter 2, since 2000 central policy emphasizes the importance of high-quality teaching staff as one of

---

[53] Interview 90, 21 December 2006. For a list of all branch academies and study districts in 2002, see Huang Shi'an, *Yearbook for 2002 of Correspondence Education of the Chinese Communist Party Central Party School* (Zhonggong Zhongyang Dangxiao hanshou jiaoyu 2002 nianjian), Beijing: Zhonggong zhongyang dangxiao chubanshe, 2003: 610–643.
[54] The school is reluctant to broadcast classes directly over the Internet to be watched at home rather than in class. Students only take the classes because they need the degree, and may be tempted to log on and then go off to do something else, or have a friend or their wife log on instead.
[55] Field notes 22 April 2004 and 4 December 2004.

the ways to raise the overall level of cadre education. Although this has had the effect of much stricter standards in the appointment, appraisal and promotion of academic staff in party schools, it has also created a very active, secondary market in teachers. This seems to be especially true for degree courses that put a very considerable strain on existing human resources and at the same time generate the cash that can pay for outside teachers.

Schools at all levels recruit well-known (or not so well-known) teachers for specialist sessions or subjects. Nationally, famous scholars fly about the country giving special lectures at provincial schools. Prefectural and especially county schools recruit teachers from higher-level party schools, or from regular schools or universities in the area. At the Qujing Prefectural School, for instance, 10 to 20 per cent of teachers for correspondence courses were recruited from local middle and vocational schools, especially for subjects such as English or computer use.[56] Sometimes, and especially in the case of special lectures on main courses rather than degree courses, this also happens as 'support' as part of the 'work guidance relationship' (*yewu zhidao guanxi*) that exists between party schools of different levels, and payment is quite modest and nominally voluntary (several teachers mentioned a sum of around one hundred yuan per session at the time of fieldwork). However, outside these relationships, the arrangement is entirely private. Payment in those cases can be considerably higher and on the basis of norms set by the home institution of the teacher. Such fees can be an important supplement to the wages of teaching staff.[57]

However, this financial lifeline for local party schools is in the process of being cut. Dissatisfaction with the variable quality of correspondence degree courses urged the Centre in 2006 to phase out this aspect of party school work. At the same time, the marketization and diversification of cadre training and degree work was put on a more solid regulatory footing. By 2007, the centre of gravity of cadre training was moving rapidly to well-funded central and provincial institutions and a range of other providers, including regular universities and schools. We will return to these very recent changes in degree work in chapter 5, but first take a closer look at life and work at party schools.

[56] Interview 54, 16 November 2004.   [57] Field notes 18 November 2004.

CHAPTER 4

Life and work at party schools

Like many other party schools, the Party School of the Yunnan Provincial Party Committee (*Yunnan shengwei dangxiao*) *cum* Yunnan Provincial Academy of Administration (*Yunnan sheng xingzheng xueyuan*) is located at the edge of the capital, in this case the city of Kunming. This location keeps the school in the immediate proximity of the province's administrative centre, but away from the noise, stress and pollution that are a normal part of city life in contemporary China. The party school is located in the small town of Haikou on the shore of Tianchi, a large mountain lake immediately to the southwest of the city. This location gives the residents of the school not only a stunning view of Kunming city on the other side of the lake, but also places the school in an area that until very recently was largely rural and at the foot of a range of forested hills. The proximity of the hills allows invigorating after-dinner hikes along carefully constructed footpaths leading through the forest and botanical gardens on the hillside to the top. The area is praised for its fresh, crisp air, which clears the mind and helps the students recover from the stress of their work and the onslaught of the unhealthy city environments that they normally inhabit.

Unfortunately, the realities of economic development, so dear to the party itself, have also caught up with the party school. Uncontrolled drainage of raw industrial waste have poisoned Tianchi with heavy metals for which no treatment exists, turning the lake into a dead body of water in which only certain algae and a particularly large species of mosquito seem to flourish. The relative seclusion of the school will also soon come to an end when the city of Kunming finally finishes construction of the elevated motorway around the shores of Tianchi, no doubt bringing not only the convenience of access, but also noise and exhaust fumes. Like many other party schools, extensive new build since 2002 has transformed the look and feel of the place. Students are housed in comfortable dormitories with all the trappings of luxury hotels, except, unfortunately, heating during the

Photo 4.1 Inside the Yunnan Provincial Party School (2004)

cold and damp winter months. Facilities include good buffet-style catering for all meals at very heavily subsidized prices. Staff no longer live on campus in the cramped blocks of flats that were built in the early eighties, but have moved into apartments in new residential areas across the city. On campus, the office buildings, library, lecture buildings, dining halls and sports facilities are all new, comfortable and spacious. During my two visits in 2004, the school's new indoor tennis and badminton hall was

Photo 4.2 Student dormitory at the Yunnan Provincial Party School (2004)

under construction. When I returned in 2005, the hall had just opened, its facilities rivalling those of luxury private rackets clubs in the UK.

The party school clearly is more than just a school. It is quite openly also a retreat, a place for reflection, rest and relaxation away from the pressures of the normal working day. Much like corporate training sessions in the west, training is not only an opportunity for intellectual and professional refreshment, but also an occasion for mental and physical recuperation. The school is both a place for work away from work, and a vacation away from home. Sports (mainly basketball, badminton, volleyball, table tennis and now also tennis) are actively encouraged: at least a token commitment to physical health is an important component of leadership in China. The school regularly organizes fixtures between teams of different classes or areas of origin. In the evening, students who haven't gone out for dinner with other students or friends in Kunming often end up singing karaoke in the bar in the main dormitory building, a near-universal lubricant of social relations among China's elite. However, it would be a mistake simply to dismiss the school's luxury as mere self-indulgence. Cadre training and

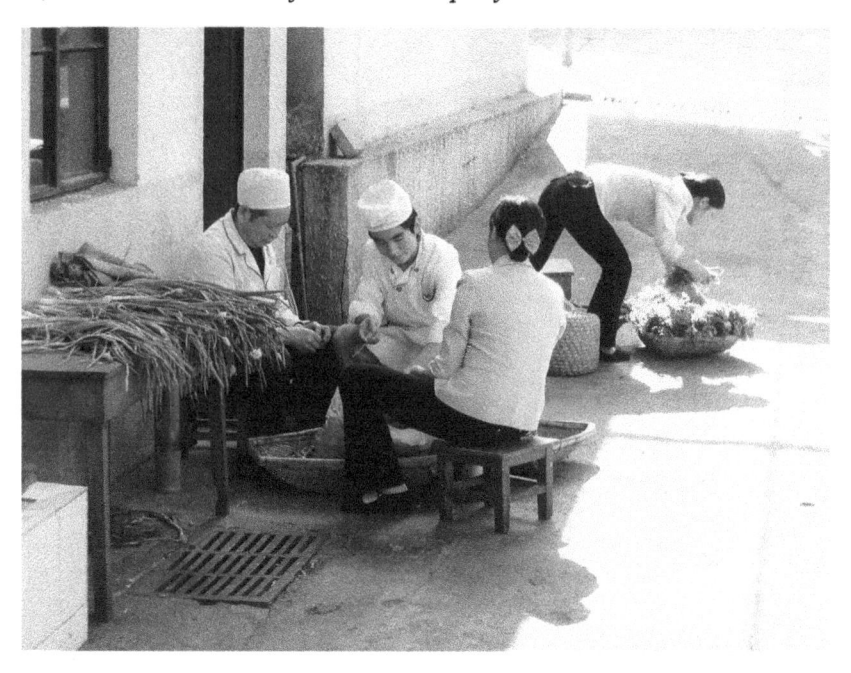

Photo 4.3 Getting ready for lunch at the Yunnan Provincial Party School (2004)

the raising of the 'quality' of the cadre corps of which this is part are integral to the party's vision of its own modernity. Spending on state-of-the art facilities – together with the fetish of modern teaching methods – is therefore also symbolically important. As the new cityscapes across China testify, modern, luxurious buildings are an iconic representation of China's new 'well-off' (*xiaokang*) society. By erecting such buildings for itself, the party signals that it is an intrinsic element of this new Chinese society. The cloak of Maoist 'arduous struggle and plain living' (*jianku pusu*) no longer befits the party's self-image: measured luxury serves as an index of the party's leading role in the modern world.

Despite the excellent facilities, two months of training away from home and work is a long time. Students are supposed to hand over their responsibilities to other people in their office (usually a deputy), but many find it impossible to remain completely detached from the goings-on at work. Mobile phones are an indispensable tool in the life and work of cadres anyway, and while at the school students spend even more time on the phone with people at work than they normally would. Even so, a crisis at work (or sometimes at home) means that students sometimes have to return at very short notice. Although they have to ask for written permission from their class teacher (*ban zhuren*) to leave, this always seems to be given; indeed, it is hard to imagine how such a request from a senior official could be refused.[1] Students, even those living in Kunming, are not allowed home visits on weekdays, but almost all students on short-term training courses return home for the weekend. School activities on Friday afternoon are not very well attended, as most students are busy packing up to be driven off in the black luxury cars that are a ubiquitous icon of official status and privilege all across China. During the weekend, the school is left largely to the small number of students on full-time degree courses who have no jobs and salaries while studying for their degree. They tend to return home only in vacation time, and sometimes their spouses and children visit them at the school for short periods. The school does not provide family accommodation and moving the entire family is usually not a realistic option anyway: in almost all households in urban China both spouses have full-time jobs.[2]

ADMINISTRATION

The Provincial Party School's organizational setup and administration is in part immediately recognizable to a researcher who spends most of his waking hours in a university environment in the west. The school has academic departments responsible for the delivery of teaching and research. A central administration manages and oversees the strategy and running of the school. Central departments also administer and direct teaching and research. The school has a correspondence course department, academic services departments (computer centre, library, publishing department),

---

[1] At the Central Party School, cadres arguably find it even more difficult to fully extract themselves from their responsibilities. However, the school wishes to maintain the ethos of strict detachment from the outside world, and cadres, no matter how important they are, are supposed to be just students during their stay. According to a Chinese journalist who visited the school in 2001, this is reinforced by the story of 'Huang Ju asking for permission to leave' that circulates among the students. Huang Ju, the party secretary of Shanghai at that time, had to attend a vital meeting back in Shanghai and received permission to leave the school on condition that he would be back at the school on the same evening. He indeed returned promptly that evening, even in time to watch the evening news together with his fellow students that showed him attending the conference in Shanghai earlier the same day; see Wang Yueping, 'Inside the Central Party School', 2001.

[2] I only know of one case of a student who had lived with his wife and child in a rented flat near the school for a year because she had managed to get a temporary placement in the area.

and non-academic support services, although several of the latter are quite unlike those in universities outside China. Academic staff are graded as full professor, associate professor and lecturer. Staff are obliged to teach and do research and their performance is regularly monitored by the school. Unlike at certain universities in the west, those who perform well are eventually promoted, while those who perform exceptionally badly at least in theory run the risk of dismissal. Finally, full-time students at the school study for recognizable degrees (BA and MA). They take courses, get credits, write papers, attend lectures, read books and articles, do research, meet their supervisor and write and defend their thesis much as in any other university.

However, this is where the similarities end. A party school is a department of the relevant party committee, and it shares important features with other party and government departments. The school is governed by a separate party committee that acts like a board of directors or management committee. Its non-academic support services not only include a finance department, a support centre and an administrative department, but also party committees and branches. Party branches include the staff party committee (*jiguan dangwei*), including a discipline inspection committee (*jiwei*), and temporary party branches for all students who are party members that are headed by a member of the teaching staff.[3]

Clearly, the party school is not intended to be a fully independent institution of academic learning, but is part of the apparatus of the party (as the party school), the state (as the academy of administration) and at lower levels even the organs of representative government (as the academy of socialism). As we saw in chapter 3, the local administration's cadre education committee decides on the annual cadre education and training plan at its level of administration. Responsibility for the execution of the plan rests with the cadre education and training office of the organization department. The office in turn delegates specific aspects of the plan to government departments (such as the personnel bureau) or educational establishments, chief among them the provincial party school. However, like other party schools, the Yunnan Provincial Party School does not take direct orders and has been given substantial autonomy in the execution of its tasks. To ensure autonomy, the school's annual teaching plan and the management of the school are the responsibility of the school's own party

---

[3] A separate party branch structure is found in all party schools; Interview 70, 28 November 2004.

committee.[4] In addition to the formal head of the party school and the formal head of the academy of administration, the ten other members of the committee include the five deputy heads of the school, two heads of education, the head of the school secretariat, the head of the general office and the head of the organization and personnel office.[5]

Final responsibility for the day-to-day running of the school rests with the standing deputy head of school. Like in other state and party organizations, the other deputy heads are responsible for more specific areas, such as education or research. Quite unconventional is the position of head of education of whom there are three in Yunnan: the main head of education and two deputies. Although the Central Party School also has a head of education, my informants in Yunnan told me that in most other schools this position no longer exists as its tasks overlap with those of the deputy heads of school above it and the heads of administrative departments below. The main head of education was also my collaborator and main contact in the school, and I had the opportunity to witness at least some of his daily work directly. In the Yunnan school at any rate, the head of education's tasks included both teaching and research, with a focus on the academy of administration rather than the party school side of things. Apart from his own teaching, examination and research, the head of education's role was a very broad one of coordination and trouble-shooting and liaising between the party committee, administrative departments and academic departments.[6]

The provincial organization department's cadre training office's normal point of contact within the school is the school's educational affairs office (*jiaowuchu*). Both offices have the same bureaucratic rank. By virtue of this horizontal bureaucratic link, the educational affairs office has first operational responsibility for most activities in the school and serves as the executive arm of the school's party committee. The key element in this is that educational affairs drafts the school's overall teaching plan, which is then finalized and approved by the school's party committee. After approval of the plan, the educational affairs office is tasked to ensure its implementation. Although the plan is determined by the school itself, planning and coordination meetings are held with provincial departments (mainly the organization department, the propaganda department and the

---

[4] According to the 1995 *Temporary Regulations on the Work of the Party Schools of the Chinese Communist Party* this role should be fulfilled by an educational affairs committee (*jiaowu weiyuanhui*) in the school, but in Yunnan at any rate such a committee is now either defunct or, more likely, was rolled immediately into the school's party committee.
[5] Interview 34, 19 April 2004.   [6] Interview 34, 19 April 2004.

personnel bureau) about the timing of courses and the kind and numbers of students the courses should cater for. After a timetable has been agreed upon, documents are sent to all provincial departments and prefectural administrations inviting them to select their quota of students for each course.

Within the school, the educational affairs office delegates responsibility for specific parts of the plan to other offices or departments of the school. Short-term training courses for leading cadres awaiting promotion or appointment are delegated to the training department (*peixun bu*), refresher courses for senior leading cadres are dealt with by the advanced study department (*jinxiu bu*), while academy of administration short-term training courses for non-leading cadres are the responsibility of the civil servants training department (*gongwuyuan peixun bu*).[7]

The school's educational affairs office also actively monitors and evaluates teaching and learning. Both the educational affairs office and the academic departments arrange for assessors to attend classes, afterwards giving feedback on their performance to the teachers. Students routinely have to fill out teacher evaluation forms. Educational affairs also organizes feedback meetings with students, and suggestions and criticisms are fed back to the teachers in the form of written reports. Teacher evaluation is directly connected to personnel management, and in this area educational affairs works closely together with the organization and personnel office (*zuzhi renshichu*)[8] of the school. The Organization and Personnel Office conducts mandatory annual evaluations of academic staff that rely mainly on the input of both the educational affairs office and the research office (*keyan chu*). Academic staff is evaluated excellent, good, adequate or inadequate. In terms of teaching, the chief criterion is whether the teacher has fulfilled her or his target of teaching commitments translated in 'study units'.[9] Annual evaluations are also fed into assessments for promotions to a higher rank: for instance, lecturers who want to be promoted to associate professor must each year have had roughly 250 teaching hours.[10]

---

[7] Interview 33, 18 April 2004.

[8] At lower administrative levels it is very common that tasks of separate departments at higher levels are combined in one office, usually with just a few staff. In this case, the work of the party's organization department and the state's personnel bureau have been merged into the school's Organization and Personnel Office.

[9] Teaching counts for a set proportion of a teacher's annual evaluation. Although I do not know the exact proportions in the provincial school, at the Qujing prefectural school teaching counts for 60 per cent of the total, with research and 'other duties' weighing in at 20 per cent each; Interview 65, 17 November 2004.

[10] Interview 22, 13 April 2004.

In terms of the evaluation of research, the Organization and Personnel Office at the Yunnan Provincial Party School similarly takes a quantitative approach, relying on a specialist panel and the research office to assess the research of staff. Moreover, research is deemed to support teaching, and so there is additional pressure on teachers to conduct research. The research of academic staff is mainly judged by their publications. The school's Research Office maintains electronic files on the publications and research projects of staff, and in 2004 the office was working on adding the full text of publications to this database. The required number and quality of publications are set in national guidelines for promotions, although these are applied 'flexibly'. Quality is assessed on the basis of the standing of the journal or publisher that has published the article or book.[11] An associate professor or lecturer without a single publication in a year will get a yellow card. A teacher who has been yellow carded in three consecutive years receives an evaluation of 'inadequate'. If such a situation arises, staff on fixed-term contracts will simply find that their contract is not renewed, while for others their salary and bonus are cut. However, full dismissals of tenured staff have not occurred.[12]

ACADEMIC DISCIPLINES AT PARTY SCHOOLS

Teaching and research are geared towards the specialized needs of a modernizing socialist party-state. This is reflected in the nature of the disciplines represented at the Yunnan Provincial Party School. Certain academic departments (*jiaoyan bu*) bear names that are directly equivalent to (and often borrowed from) western disciplines, namely philosophy, language and literature, economics, law. The names of other disciplines (economic management, public administration, and science and technology) represent a combination of selective borrowing and local elaboration. The final three disciplines present at the school are home-grown: party history, scientific socialism and party building.[13] Together with philosophy and political economy, the latter three subjects constituted the 'five old courses' (*lao wu men*) taught at party schools until the start of the cadre training modernization drive in 1993.[14]

Unsurprisingly, almost all disciplines have in common that they can be more or less readily applied in administration and management. Potentially

---

[11] Interview 27, 16 April 2004.   [12] Interview 22, 13 April 2004.
[13] This information is drawn from an organizational setup of the school provided in interview 1 on 1 April 2004.
[14] Wibowo and Fook 2006: 144.

relevant disciplines prominent in regular Chinese universities, for instance political science, sociology or ethnology, are conspicuously absent at the Yunnan school. The research in such disciplines tends to be focussed more on 'pure' than applied research, and I suspect, might also be too explorative, innovative and independently minded for the taste of most local party committees.[15] The school's lack of comprehensive coverage is also in part simply a matter of scale. The Yunnan Provincial Party School employs about 450 people, of whom only about 200 are teaching and research staff.[16] At the Central Party School, the situation is very different. Not only is disciplinary coverage much more comprehensive, including political science and sociology, but the school also has much greater ambitions. Since the early nineties, the Central Party School has gone through an extensive and expensive process of 'disciplinary construction' that has placed it in the top league of research-intensive universities in China. The Central Party School sees its research actively contributing to policy making and ideological innovation and its researchers are involved in scholarly exchange across China and abroad.[17]

When assessing the disciplines that are represented at party schools and the teaching and research that takes place within them, we also have to bear in mind that even the seemingly most familiar academic disciplines have their own, unique history in China. Academic disciplines, in China as elsewhere, are not only a way of looking at and understanding a specific aspect of reality (say the economy, politics or social structure); they are also centrally involved in the creation and maintenance of these aspects as separately knowable entities that can than be acted upon, managed and controlled by governing institutions (Rose and Miller 1992: 182). Disciplines are the product of non-academic political agendas, academic debates and turf wars. These conditions constitute the environment in which disciplines develop and the academic and non-academic purposes to which they are put in a range of environments, including universities,

---

[15] Not all party schools are identical in their disciplinary setup. The Central Party School, for instance, has a much broader coverage of disciplines, including a department of political science (Interview 89, 20 December 2006). The Beijing Municipality Party School's main department is that of public management, while the school also has departments of foreign languages and sociology. This reflects the much greater involvement of the school in the market for higher education and training, including tailor-made non-political training courses and courses for foreign students (Interview 93, 27 April 2007).

[16] Interview 22, 13 April 2004.

[17] See 'Central Party School 1996–2000 plan for disciplinary construction' (Zhonggong Zhongyang Dangxiao 1996–2000 xueke jianshe guihua), posted online on 19 April 2007 at www.ccps.gov.cn/dxjx.php?col=671&file=2423 (checked on 24 June 2008).

Academic disciplines at party schools 91

party schools, cadre schools, schools of administration, business schools and the like. For instance, a seemingly abstract discipline like philosophy is actually directly relevant to cadre training and policy making, because most of it is concerned with Marxism and its derivative ideologies all the way from Leninism to the 'Three Represents' and the harmonious society.[18] The central position of philosophy in party schools is expressed very clearly in the 2007–2010 development plan of the philosophy department of the Central Party School, which states that the main characteristic of contemporary Marxist philosophical research is that it leads research on the big real issues. Moreover, on the basis of their philosophical research, 'specialists in the department will continue to give advice on policy making to the government both through their reports and internal consultation'.[19]

An example of more recent disciplinary innovation at the intersection of the production, management and control of an aspect of reality is provided by the disciplines of public administration and public management. This example reveals how administrative and ideological change within the party is shaped by actors that 'amphibiously' (Ding 1994) inhabit the institutions of the party-state, while also trying to change them. In traditional, pre-Cultural Revolution cadre training, the closest thing to administrative science was the discipline of 'party building' (*dangjian*). This discipline continues to exist in party schools, and still no other academic discipline in China can explicitly take the Chinese Communist Party and its role in government and administration as its object of study. By contrast, administrative science (*xingzhengxue*) or administrative management (*xingzheng guanlixue*) started out as a subject within political science. It developed quickly from 1984 onwards, was officially recognized as a separate discipline in 1988 and in the nineties became a mainstream discipline not only in universities, but also in party schools and the new schools of administration.[20]

---

[18] As a nineteenth-century thinker working in an environment in which the modern social sciences were only in their earliest infancy, Marx first and foremost thought of himself as a philosopher. According to Wibowo and Fook, at the Central Party School philosophy lectures also cover western philosophy (Wibowo and Fook 2006: 152). Although it is hard to imagine that high-level leaders have a great deal of enthusiasm for the intricacies of, for instance, German phenomenology, occasionally foreigners in China find themselves embarrassed in encounters with leaders with a detailed knowledge of such matters.

[19] Philosophy Department of the Central Party School (Zhongyang Dangxiao Zhexue jiaoyanbu), 'Makesi zhuyi zhexue guojia zhongdian xueke jianshe yu fazhan guihua (2007–2010)' (Construction of national disciplinary centre point and development plan of Marxist philosophy (2007–2010)), 20 November 2007, online at zhexue.ccps.gov.cn/jxkngl/knlw/879.html (checked on 25 June 2008).

[20] Huang Da-qiang 1993 and interview 91, 26 April 2007.

Administrative science in China focuses on the institutions, the law and the formal arrangements of government; it is allowed to study neither the formal institutions of representative government and the CCP nor the compromises and deals, influence peddling and jockeying for power that constitute the messy side of politics. Furthermore, as a highly sanitized version of political science, administrative science approaches issues of governance as they appear to government officials, namely as limited to questions of the government's control over and management of society. Despite that, the growth of administrative science has been an important component of the administrative reforms: by at least pretending that party and government can be separated, a vision of a stable Chinese state is presented that is unencumbered by the factional competition, purges and campaigns that were (and to certain extent continue to be) the mainstay of party life.

However, in the latter half of the nineties, administrative science was increasingly criticized as an anodyne and limited enterprise ill-suited to China's changing administrative and social reality. Inspired by western scholarship on civil society and the public sphere and World Bank support for non-governmental organizations, scholars such as Liu Xirui at the National Academy of Administration argued that administration amounted to much more than the work of the government. With the growth of the market economy, a public sphere had emerged in which the government was just one of the many providers. Governance, moreover, was not chiefly a matter of control over the population. The preoccupation with control by rulers, Liu argued, was something that China's feudalism and state socialism had in common. Modern governance should aim at providing services for the population in ways that are democratically controlled by the people. As a result, China no longer needs mere administration and administrative science, but the practice and study of public administration (*gonggong xingzheng*) and public management (*gonggong guanli*).[21]

The introduction of public management as the future of Chinese governance illustrates a clever use of a foreign neoliberal discourse on 'public management' – which in itself is an application of the language of business administration to public administration – to depoliticize calls for the development of civil society and democratization, instead presenting them as intrinsic to the CCP's vision of a modern Chinese state and society. As Liu himself put it:

---

[21] Interview 91, 26 April 2007, and Liu Xirui 2002; 2004; for a recent textbook on Chinese public management, see Jun 2006.

Western new public management... has drawn on the experience of business administration and the market mechanism ... for the development of a movement for government reforms that emphasizes efficiency. However, [when] we [in China] talk about new public management, in addition to considerations of efficiency, we are even more concerned with questions of the public nature of management, such as democratic participation, democratic management, democratic supervision, democratic investigation and so on. This is something that we must pay attention to when establishing a system for public management in our country. (Liu Xirui 2002: 33)

Rather than antagonistic calls for democracy outside of the established administrative system, democracy is depoliticized by its inclusion in the larger neo-socialist project of technocratic administrative reform, a strategy reminiscent of the promotion of village committee elections in the eighties and nineties. The fusion of technocratic reform and democratization may strike westerners as odd or naive. It does, however, make sense in the Chinese context, where the professionalization of administration and the depoliticization of democracy are both aimed at limiting the direct and arbitrary power of the CCP and its individual leaders over society. This incidentally is also the reason why western interpretations of Chinese administrative reforms as simply leading to the growth of a technocratic regime are missing at least part of the point: in China, the promotion of technocratic rule serves enduring political agendas.

The creation of a succession of new academic disciplines since the early eighties thus follows a logic that is both highly political and explicitly aimed at depoliticizing governance in China. What is remarkable about this is that first administrative science and now public administration and public management have been so readily endorsed by the party-state. Since the turn of the century, almost all major universities and party schools in China have included public management or public administration as a core discipline. Naturally, in each university or school the way in which this has been achieved varies,[22] but the outcome has been that schools or departments of public management in public universities now rival party schools as key institutions in the delivery of cadre education and cadre training. These schools are one of the main providers of the plethora of tailored short-term training courses that we will discuss in the next chapter. Schools of public administration also offer full degree courses for the Master's of Public Administration (MPA) that deliberately and

---

[22] On Renmin University, Interview 86, 16 December 2006; on Beijing University Tian Kai, personal communication 3 December 2006; on Tsinghua University, Interviews 92 and 93, 27 April 2007.

directly compete with higher degrees taught at party schools. As early as 1999, the Degree Office of the State Council had already approved the establishment of twenty-four MPA programmes to start in 2001, including those at Peking University, Renmin University and Tsinghua University. In 2003, the State Council approved an MPA in China to be taught jointly at the National Academy of Administration and Peking University.[23] These initiatives were clearly designed to deliver the new kind of cadres that conventional party education and training had proven unable to produce, and took their cue explicitly from the educational programmes offered at foreign business schools and schools of administration. In an article on the new MPA programmes the Central Party School's own *Study Times* makes this very clear:

Building the capacity of civil servants requires the best effort in 'specialization,' which is a great task that... the original civil servants' training finds hard to complete. Therefore, organizing MPA education is an important way for civil servants in active service to study the theory of public administration systematically, and to cultivate their capacity for public management.[24]

By drawing on foreign experience and China's specific circumstances, the article states, the MPAs will produce a new type of high-level managers, administrators and policy makers that possess practical, useful and specialized skills. The MPA programmes are intended to break through the conventional barriers between existing disciplines: their training can therefore be practical, comprehensive and strategic. Their flexible structure will allow students and their work units the freedom to create a programme of training tailored most to their needs. Teaching on the MPA programmes will deploy a range of methods, including group discussion, simulation exercises, case analysis, site visits and social investigation.

---

[23] See Li Junpeng, 'China's MPA education: an innovation in the model for the education and training of cadres', (Zhongguo MPA jiaoyu: ganbu jiaoyu peixun moshi de chuangxin), *Xuexi shibao* 18 October 2004, p. 6, online at www.studytimes.com.cn/txt/2004-10/19/content_5682610.htm (checked on 18 September 2006). A brief introduction to China's MPA degrees can be found at 'Prospects and policies of China's MPA education' (Woguo MPA jiaoyu fazhan de qianjing yu zhengce), online at www.mpa.org.cn/displaynews1.asp?id=142 (checked on 18 June 2008). According to the head of Tsinghua University's School of Public Management, they were the first to offer MPA degree programmes in 2001; Interview 92, 27 April 2007.

[24] Li Junpeng, 'China's MPA education'.

RESEARCH

All recent policy documents about cadre training and party schools emphasize that research is an important aspect of the work of party schools. Yet surprisingly, contract research does not count directly in the annual evaluations of academic staff, although participation in important provincial or national projects is given some consideration. At the Yunnan Provincial Party School, academic staff only get a little financial incentive to gain projects, apart of course from the fact that they can keep the income from projects for themselves. The school gives 500 yuan for applications made to national or provincial departments, 1,000 yuan for a successful application at the provincial level and 3,000 yuan at the national level.[25]

The strong emphasis on clear quantitative quota in teaching and research has been borrowed from neoliberal management practices that are increasingly dominant in the western academic world, as part of the effort to upgrade party schools to serious academic institutions. This has had results that are immediately familiar to the western eye. As in many western universities, teaching staff at party schools have to publish in order not to perish, and this in turn has led to an outpouring of publications both as books and in a plethora of academic journals published by party schools and schools of administration. Nationally, research has become increasingly prominent among the tasks of party schools. In 1997, the State Council's degree committee published the formal list of academic disciplines and specializations that the committee recognized for the conferment of masters and doctoral degrees. It also issued criteria for recognition of such disciplines and degrees at individual institutions.[26] This made the lack of academic standing of party schools much more visible than in the past. Not only were long-standing disciplines at party schools like 'party building' and 'scientific socialism' completely lacking from the committee's list of recognized disciplines, but the committee's list and criteria also brought the problem of the non-recognition of party school *xueli* degrees into sharper relief.

Party schools have responded by a programme of 'disciplinary construction' (*xueke jianshe*) that aims at improving their academic credibility. Funds have been poured into upgrading the staff at party schools and

---

[25] Interview 27, 16 April 2004.
[26] 'List of disciplines and specializations that confer Master and doctoral degrees and train graduate students' (Shouyu boshi, shuoshi xuewei he peiyang yanjiusheng de xueke, zhuanye mulu), 2007, online at 202.117.24.24/html/CALIS/daohangku/xkml.pdf (checked on 11 September 2007).

incentivizing them to engage in research. Another aspect of the aggressive upgrading of party schools as research institutions has been the emphasis on the unique nature of their research. Recent policy documents and writings on research and disciplinary construction at party schools invariably begin with the observation that party schools continue to be the 'main channel' (*zhu qudao*) for cadre training and that research and teaching at party schools have to be fully integrated. Research projects are carried out because they help academic staff to gather materials, insights and practical experience on policy issues that are immediately relevant to their teaching. Conversely, the presence of leading cadres as students provides teachers with a unique advantage. Students have direct experience with the problems confronting administrators in China: teaching them therefore helps staff identify those issues that are most urgently in need of research. Staff also frequently point out that a network of (former) students is an invaluable resource: they provide access, assistance and ideas than money alone cannot buy. At the Central Party School cadre-students even join research project teams as full members.

However, the development of research at party schools is not simply left to the initiative of academic staff and their students, but is actively nurtured and guided. In March 2004, the CCP Centre issued an 'opinion' on the development of philosophy and the social sciences in China. The document puts a heavy emphasis on the socialist nature of teaching and research. Research should be based on the party's ideological orthodoxy, and moreover should also be actively engaged in the further development and growth of socialist theory. Teaching materials to be developed in all social sciences should have an adequate base in the party's ideological orthodoxy in order to train a new generation of socialist social scientists. The document also emphasized that philosophy and the social sciences should be vigorously promoted and that there are no forbidden zones where research cannot go. However, much more prominent in the document is the need for stronger party management of state and non-state institutions engaged in research in the humanities and the social sciences, an approach that obviously constrains the freedom of academic enquiry.[27]

---

[27] 'Opinion on taking further the efforts in the promotion and development of philosophy and the social sciences' (Guanyu jin yi bu fanrong fazhan zhexue shehui kexue de yijian), central document no. 3, 5 January 2004, online at www.360doc.com/showWeb/0/0/349896.aspx (checked on 11 September 2007). See also 'Centre issues "Opinion on taking further efforts in the promotion and development of philosophy and the social sciences"' (Zhongyang fachu "Guanyu jin yi bu fanrong fazhan zhexue shehui kexue de yijian"), Xinhua online 20 March 2004, online at news.xinhuanet.com/newscenter/2004-03/20/content_1375785.htm (checked on 11 September

The emphasis on the development of socialist theory and practice smacked clearly of the Central Party School's own research role. The Central Party School's standing head of school, Yu Yunyao, almost immediately endorsed the CCP Centre's opinion, pledging the school's full compliance to the opinion's emphasis on the role of social science research in developing socialist theory and policy making.[28] Subsequently in May 2004, the school's party committee issued its own *Regulations for the management of research projects at the Central Party School*. These *Regulations* stipulate that research projects should serve the strengthening of the ruling capacity of the CCP. Internal school projects should contribute to the unity of teaching and research, and should reflect the issues and problems that cadre-students at the school raise, in addition to catering to the needs of the commissioning and funding body. Project approval is based on the administrative rank of the commissioning organization, and their importance and conformity to the Centre's spirit and requirements.[29]

Between the start of 2004 and early September 2005, the Central Party School embarked on no less than 110 projects at ministerial, provincial or school level alone, involving all disciplines at the school, a major contribution, according to the school's *Study Times*, to the school's disciplinary construction and the further establishment of recognized degree points (*xuewei dian*)[30] across all specialisms. Moreover, the school has engaged lower party schools in setting up branch projects, further broadening the impact and scope of these projects. Financially, research projects are important as well. From 2004 until the end of September 2005, 125 projects

---

2007). The slogan 'the promotion and development of philosophy and the social sciences' had already been around for a number of years, but gained much more prominence with the 2004 Document no. 3. For a study on the party's involvement in social science research, see Sleeboom 2007.

[28] Yu Yunyao, 'Make new contributions to the promotion and development of the humanities and the social sciences' (Wei fanrong fazhan zhexue shehui kexue zuochu xin gongxian). Speech at the discussion meeting on the party Centre's Opinion on the promotion and development of the humanities and the social sciences, 25 March 2004, published online on the *Xuexi Shibao* website www.china.org.cn/chinese/zhuanti/xxsb/547875.htm (checked on 11 September 2007).

[29] 'Regulations for the management of research projects at the Central Party School' (Zhongyang Dangxiao keyan xiangmu guanli tiaoli), issued by the Central Party School party committee in May 2005. I have been unable to get access to these regulations. Information on the regulations used here has been taken from an article on the *Regulations* in the school's weekly newspaper *Study Times* (*Xuexi Shibao*); Zhang Boli, 'Research projects are the management pivot: promote the reform and development of research at the Central Party School' (Yi keti xiangmu wei guanli shuniu cu Dangxiao keyan gaige yu fazhan), *Xuexi Shibao* 27 October 2005, online at cpc.people.com.cn/GB/47817/3805957.html (checked on 11 September 2007).

[30] Degree points are disciplines and specializations whose (Masters) degrees have been recognized by the National Degree Committee. For a list of the Central Party School's degree points, see www.ccps.gov.cn/dxjx.php?col=671&file=2422, 19 April 2007 (checked on 1 July 2008).

were funded at a total of 7.75 million yuan, 6.43 million of which came from external sources.[31] According to an article written by Zhou Tianyong, a leading economist at the Central Party School, the most influential projects recently were on the 'four how to understand' (*si ge ruhe renshi*), which are four questions raised in 2000 by then Party Secretary Jiang Zemin himself, namely the history and progress of socialist development, the development and progress of capitalism, the ideological impact on people of China's socialist reform, and the influence brought by the international environment and conflict. Other influential projects were carried out on party building, the theory of labour value, building an all-round prosperous society, and the concept of scientific development. According to Zhou, other examples of theoretical research that made its impact felt in changes in the party's orthodoxy include research on Maoism, Deng Xiaoping Theory and the 'Three Represents', and especially the significance of Marxism. According to Zhou, since the Sixteenth Party Congress in 2002 research at the Central Party School has yielded the concepts of 'scientific development', 'harmonious society' and 'new socialist countryside' that have become the fundamental building blocks of the developmental socialism of the Hu Jintao and Wen Jiabao leadership. The school also conducts projects for ministries, prefectures and even enterprises, helping them to think through and formulate their strategy and plan for reform and development.[32]

However, we should not make the mistake of thinking that research at the Central Party School (or any other government, party or academic institution for that matter) always feeds into policy making; as Joseph Fewsmith cautions, there is a considerable difference between developing radical proposals and actually adopting them (Fewsmith 2003: 162). Research at the school can therefore cover a broad range of topics and political positions without this necessarily feeding into policy making. Recently, for instance, researchers at the Central Party School published a report under the title *Storming the Fortress: A Research Report on China's Political System Reform after the 17th Party Congress*. This report makes a whole range of recommendations for far-reaching reform, many of which have been around for years in one form or another. Some of these may ultimately become

---

[31] Zhang Boli, 'Research projects are the management pivot'.
[32] Zhou Tianyong, 'The place and function of the Central Party School in political life in the party and government' (Zhongyang Dangxiao zai dang he guojia zhengzhi shenghuo de diwei he zuoyong), *Guangming Guancha* 27 February 2007, online at guancha.gmw.cn/show.aspx?id=3645 (checked on 11 September 2007).

policy – albeit in a much diluted form – but many others very likely will not.[33] Nevertheless, research at the Central Party School – and by extension at lower-level schools as well – plays a unique role. The Party School is further removed from the immediacy of daily policy making than other well-known 'think tanks', such as the CCP's Central Policy Research Office (*Zhonggong Zhongyang Zhengce Yanjiushi*), the Development Research Centre of the State Council (*Guowuyuan Fazhan Yanjiu Zhongxin*), or research institutes at individual ministries and central departments and commissions. Project research at the Central Party School can take a more detached, comprehensive and long-term view. Yet its proximity to the party Centre and its daily involvement in the training of high leading cadres lends researchers at the school a closeness to the Centre's needs and political sensitivities that are not necessarily found at China's research universities or the Academy of Social Sciences.[34]

Although efforts at streamlining and managing research have reportedly been undertaken at certain provincial party schools as well,[35] I did not come across evidence for such efforts at the Yunnan Provincial Party School, although this might be explained by the fact that my field visits to the school took place in 2004 and 2005, too early perhaps for the Centre's *Opinion* to have an effect. Nevertheless, much of the research done by academic staff at the school in Yunnan is contract research or consultancy for government departments. The Yunnan Party School research office's main role is in fact that of intermediary between provincial or national government departments and the school's staff who are looking for funded research projects. In addition, the school also received prestigious funding for projects from the United Nations Development Programme (UNDP) and the Ford Foundation. Given its location in Yunnan, relatively many

---

[33] Richard McGregor, 'Party think-tank calls for checks on China's rulers', *Financial Times* 20 February 2008, p. 10; Chris Buckley, 'Elite China think-tank issues political reform blueprint', *Reuters*, 18 February 2008, online at www.reuters.com/article/worldNews/idUSPEK20590720080219 (checked on 17 March 2008).

[34] Zhou Tianyong, 'The place and function of the Central Party School in political life in the party and government'. On think tanks in contemporary China, see Fewsmith 2003.

[35] Lin Shushun, 'Analysis of disciplinary construction at a provincial party school' (Shengji dangxiao xueke jianshe tanxi), *Guangming Ribao* 1 April 2005, online at theory.people.com.cn/GB/40551/3286724.html (checked on 11 September 2007); Xiao Hai, 'Creation of a new work environment at the Shandong Party School is keeping up with the times – an interview with the Standing Deputy Head of the Shandong Provincial Party School An Shiyin' (Yu shi ju jin kaichuang Shandong Dangxiao gongzuo xin jumian – fang Shandong Shengwei Dangxiao Changwu Fuxiaozhang An Shiyin), *Xuexi Shibao* 6 June 2007, online at www.studytimes.com.cn/txt/2007-06/05/content_8345925.htm (checked on 11 September 2007).

external research projects are about culture, administration, cadre training and development in minority areas.³⁶

At the central level, the Central Party School's publications are each aimed at a different readership. Fully publicly available (*gongkai faxing*) are the *Study Times* (Xuexi shibao), aimed mainly at teachers and administrators in party schools and other parts of the CCP's propaganda system, and the Central Party School's main academic outlet, the *Journal of the Central Party School* (Zhongyang Dangxiao xuebao), and several other journals. The school also publishes several periodicals for internal circulation (*neibu faxing*), such as *Theoretical Trends* (Lilun dongtai). Most restricted is the school's *Internal Reference for Ideological Theory* (Sixiang lilun neican), which is directly circulated among selected central leaders. This tiered system of publication enables the school carefully to target its audience and to ensure that its most important outputs are read by the country's highest leaders.³⁷

The Yunnan Provincial School also publishes at least one restricted circulation newsletter for the province's leadership, but I have not been able to get more information about it during my fieldwork. In addition, the school publishes three main journals, all for public consumption. *Creation* (Chuangzao) is the journal of the party school and has been established longest, having started as *Theoretical Study* (Lilun xuexi) in the eighties under the personal patronage of Pu Zhaogui, the then provincial secretary and head of the party school. Its aim is 'to link theory and practice' and its readers are both scholars and cadres in the province. *Lilun xuexi* changed its name to *Chuangzao* in 1991, after the journal of the provincial party school before the Cultural Revolution. Its 'for internal circulation' only restriction was lifted at the same time. The *Journal of the Yunnan Academy of Administration* (Yunnan xingzheng xueyuan xuebao) is a more strictly scholarly journal, established in 1999 when central regulation allowed the establishment of such journals to raise the scholarly profile of schools of administration and give their staff an outlet for their work. The third journal started as the internally circulated journal of the school's Centre for Research on Deng Xiaoping Theory, established in 1996. In 2001, the journal was given the name *Journal of the Yunnan Provincial Party School* (Yunnan Shengwei Dangxiao xuebao) and became publicly circulated. All three journals have their own editors and editorial boards, although the

---

[36] Interview 27, 16 April 2004.
[37] Zhou Tianyong, 'The place and function of the Central Party School in political life in the party and government'.

editors of *Creation* and the *Journal of the Yunnan Academy of Administration* work in the same department and cooperate closely.[38]

The three journals are an important element of the school's claim to academic respectability and a way to link its theoretical and research-focussed work with the practical concerns of leading cadres in the province. In the case of the *Journal of the Yunnan Academy of Administration*, the school provides a modest operating budget of 100,000 yuan (excluding personnel costs) that is used to pay authors a fee (30 yuan per 1,000 words) and for printing. In addition, the institution of the author itself may give a bonus for publications.[39] The journal itself makes some money from subscriptions, but most of the 2,500 copies are distributed free of charge in exchanges with other party schools or schools of administration or as complementary copies sent to university libraries.[40]

As in the west, not all academic journals in China have the same standing. The more prestigious the journal, the better the publication is for the scholar involved. However, the academic quality of the journal does not enter directly in the annual research evaluations of staff, and in order to fulfil their annual quota staff can publish in any journal that wants to take the article. American-style management methods coupled with an emphasis on both the freedom and the obligation to engage in original research have spawned a burgeoning field of academic discourse that is largely specific to the world of party schools and schools of administration. This discursive field exists wholly outside and unbeknownst to academic discourse outside China. What is even more significant is that it also has only limited connections with academic discourse in regular universities and research institutes in China itself, with the exception of university researchers in fields such as public administration or party building. The journals that service the two academic systems of party schools and regular universities and research institutes remain separate from each other, although leading scholars in party schools increasingly engage other scholars in China and abroad. Moreover, editors of party school and academy of administration journals regularly attend meetings of editors of regular academic journals in the humanities and social sciences.[41] The separation between these two worlds is clearly demonstrated by the 'Index to the list of main periodicals in the Chinese humanities and social sciences' (*Zhongguo*

---

[38] Interview 37, 24 November 2004.
[39] At the Shilin County Party School, for instance, a bonus of 300 yuan is paid for each published article, or more depending on the level of the journal. Interview 70, 28 November 2004.
[40] Interview 37, 24 November 2004.   [41] Interview 37, 24 November 2004.

renwen shehui kexue hexin qikan mulu suoyin), which is an authoritative, nationally unified list of the 500 most prestigious academic journals in China. In Chinese academic circles, only publications in one of these journals are taken seriously. Exactly one of these 500 journals is published by a party school or academy of administration: the *Journal of the Central Party School* (Zhonggong dangxiao xuebao).[42]

Like regular academic journals in China, the editors of the many journals in this field have considerable editorial freedom, and they select articles for publication almost entirely on the basis of academic merit and not on the basis of political correctness. However, there is a general norm of ideological orientation – i.e. the acceptance of CCP rule and the political system that one would expect from staff in party schools anyway – and a more specific range of forbidden research topics in political and administrative science, such as the separation of legislative, executive and judicial powers. Forbidden topics are regularly updated, and editors are informed in central documents, by word of mouth or at meetings. In addition, like all publications, the content of the journals is monitored by the party's propaganda department and the government news publishing bureau that are a journal's 'responsible department' (*zhuguan bumen*). Editors do not necessarily give preference to authors working in their own school, although the majority of the articles published in the Yunnan journal, at any rate, are from the province itself.[43]

TEACHING: DEGREE PROGRAMMES

As discussed in chapter 3, education at party schools consists of two very different categories. Short-term courses provide non-degree training, while long-term courses teach for formal degrees, mostly through the correspondence department. At the Yunnan Provincial Party School, the latter was almost completely separate from the party school proper with its main offices and teaching facilities at a different site in the centre of Kunming. The correspondence department was set up in 1983 and in 2004 taught more than sixty thousand students all across the province.[44]

A relatively small number of degree students are also taught on-site, although their number is currently much lower than in the early nineties. The Yunnan Provincial Party School is severely hamstrung in its ability to offer on-site degree education, because its degrees are not recognized by the

---

[42] URL literature.chinacdc.cn/CSqikan%5Cccss.htm (last accessed 2 March 2007).
[43] Interview 37, 24 November 2004.   [44] Interview 1, 1 April 2004.

National Degree Committee. In 2004, the school intended to apply to the State Council's degree committee for recognition of master's degree programmes in five disciplines in 2005, but realistically thought that only one of these (scientific socialism) would have a chance. However, once one discipline would have been recognized nationally the school would become a 'first level degree point' (*yi ji xuewei dian*). Adding further disciplines would henceforth only have to be approved by the provincial rather than the National Degree Committee.[45] Despite these difficulties in gaining recognition for its degrees, the school already offers a three-year minority master's programme for eight minority students, all county-level leading cadres. This *xuewei* course is taught in conjunction with the National Minorities University and teachers from Beijing regularly come to Kunming to teach on this course. Such joint degree programmes have become very common across the party school system. Not only have they proved an effective way around the National Degree Committee's very strict quality assurance procedures, but they have also helped party schools gain valuable experience for subsequent applications for independent recognition of degree points.[46] Hubei Provincial Party School, for instance, started joint degree programmes in 1994, gaining independent recognition in 2003.[47]

By contrast, on-site teaching for non-recognized *xueli* postgraduate (master's) degree courses, both full-time and part-time, is well-established at the Yunnan school. A full-time master's takes two years and is taught in the disciplines of philosophy, economics and scientific socialism. Part-time courses – targeted at students who remain in employment while taking the degree – take three years. Disciplines include economic management, administrative management and law. Each class has between forty and sixty students who come to the school three times each semester. The majority of the school's on-site higher vocational and undergraduate students study for non-recognized degrees in administrative management or economic management. These courses are mainly targeted at minority students as part of Yunnan's continued drive to nurture an indigenous cadre corps for minority areas; rather similar, in fact, to the long-term training and degree courses for cadres from Xinjiang and Tibet at the Central Party School. To this end, both admissions criteria and examination standards are set

---

[45] Interview 1, 12 December 2004   [46] Interview 1, 1 April 2004.
[47] See Hubei Provincial Party School (Hubei Shengwei Dangxiao), 'Base oneself on the norms Emphasize special characteristics: do a good job declaring degrees and training graduate students' (Lizu guifan Zhuzhong tese: zuohao xuewei shenbao yu yanjiusheng peiyang gongzuo), 26 May 2006, online at yjsy.ccps.gov.cn/docs/dfyjs/191.aspx (checked on 25 June 2008).

at lower levels than they would have been for non-minority degree programmes. Most importantly, minority students on special minority cadre degree programmes do not have to sit an entrance examination at all. Instead, their names are put forward by the organization department in their locality after a thorough 'appraisal' (*kaohe*) in which political and ideological quality is the most important consideration, and in addition command of Chinese, 'cultural quality' (i.e. education) and ability at work are taken into consideration.[48]

To compensate for the minorities students' lack of adequate educational background, a remedial (*yuke*) extra semester is added to special minorities' degree programmes prior to the start of the regular two-year degree programme. The need for such a remedial semester is routinely put in civilizing terms: minority cadres have to be taught how to be civilized Chinese, which includes a proper command of the Mandarin Chinese. According to two teachers at the Yunnan Provincial Party School:

> The class that I am responsible for (higher vocational class for minorities in economic management) lasts for two-and-a-half years. It has as its goal both to train and to raise the cultural quality (*wenhua suzhi*) of minority cadres. This is mainly because the level of education of minority civil servants is relatively low.[49]

> The level of Chinese language of many minority students is relatively low. To protect the interests of minorities, we first train minority students and only then have them take the entrance examination, to protect their interests... The number of minority cadres in Yunnan who have been trained is about 2,000 up to now. We have traced students back on inspection tours and their reactions have been relatively positive. The vast majority of students got a promotion, and some of them have already been promoted to become leaders of prefectural autonomous regions.[50]

TEACHING: NON-DEGREE TRAINING COURSES

As the school's main occupation, non-degree cadre training courses take up the bulk of the school's resources. Since 2000, cadre training has been much more emphasized by the Centre. As a result, the number of students at the school increased rapidly from about one thousand a year in the nineties to one thousand a semester (or two thousand a year) in 2003. Cadre training has grown not only in terms of number of students, but

---

[48] Interview 41, 25 November 2004.
[49] Comment by teacher during Interview 37, 24 November 2004.
[50] Interview 37, 24 November 2004.

also in the variety and number of training courses offered. In the spring semester 2004, when I did my first stint of fieldwork, the school ran the following in-plan courses:
(1) 16th advanced study class no. 1 for leading cadres;
(2) 14th advanced study class no. 2 for leading cadres;
(3) 16th class for young and middle-aged cadres;
(4) 6th training class for female cadres;
(5) 1st training class for county and office level minority cadres;
(6) 7th training class for civil servants in office;
(7) 7th training class for theoretical backbone cadres;
(8) Training class on 'the 2003 *Law on Administrative Licences*';
(9) Training class on 'county/office level civil servants and electronic government'.[51]

All the above courses were for leading cadres of county and office level (*xianchuji*), except the first, which catered for the higher level of prefecture and provincial department (*ditingji*). The curious habit of numbering the courses makes it possible to see how much cadre training has grown in recent years. Clearly, the two advanced study classes and the class for young and middle-aged cadres have been long-standing features at the school, and, if we assume that these classes are offered once a year, have been the mainstay and core of cadre training since at least the early nineties. All of these are targeted at leading cadres or people who are being groomed for a promotion to a leading cadre position. At the other end of the spectrum are the final two unnumbered classes that were organized ad hoc, in response, no doubt, to a requirement for such training in the annual provincial cadre education and training plan. The other classes are all of more recent vintage, but, given the fact that they are numbered, nevertheless are intended to be a regular feature of the school's offerings. These new courses attest to a strategy of broadening the reach of cadre training by adding courses aimed at more specific groups of cadres rather than simply adding more classes of the long-standing, generic variety. These categories of cadres are felt to be in need of more specialized attention, either because of their more specific needs (theoretical backbones, i.e. teachers at lower-level party schools and cadres working in the propaganda system; non-leading civil servants), or else because of the risk that they are neglected or under-represented in generic training classes (women and minorities).

---

[51] Interview 1, 1 April 2004.

To give a better idea of what exactly cadre training consists of, I present below the topics covered in these courses in 2004 as summarized to me by Professor Duan Eryu, the school's head of education. *Training courses for leading cadres* cover three main areas. First, study of the work of the party and state Centre. This includes study of the 'Three Represents' (contemporary background, historical significance and scientific content and nature) and the relationship between the 'Three Represents' and the road of socialism with Chinese characteristics. Other aspects of the study of the work of the Centre include current philosophical trends, the current state of society and the economy, emphasizing that the development of the state is the first task of party rule in order to let the country prosper. Here training also pays attention to several problems in the comprehensive construction of a developed society. The second main area of training is on the situation of Yunnan province, including the deepening of reform in Yunnan, problems of completing a socialist market economy, and the connection between economic and social development in Yunnan and the development of human resources. The third main area of training for leading cadres is party building. This includes building a ruling party that operates at the forefront of the current age, reform and completion of the party's leadership and methods of rule, and research on the relationship between the party and the masses under conditions of party rule. In short, the topics of study of leading cadre training involve the main questions China and the party are facing in any domain, both foreign and domestic. The study methods emphasize linking theory and practice and self-study of original material such as books and articles. Other methods are lecturing, individual guidance by teachers and discussions between the students. Lectures are given not only by teachers here at the school, but also by officials from party and government and external specialists.

Training courses for *young and middle-aged cadres* focus on more basic skills, such as computer use, English and leadership science. Courses for *female cadres* are basically the same as those for young cadres, but also include Marxist views on women, international women's organizations and movements, the image and style of female leading cadres, problems of women's development, and the psychological adjustment of female cadres. Courses for *minority cadres* focus on the following: raising the leadership capacity of minority cadres, issues in the construction of minority cultures in Yunnan, Marxist minorities theory and progress in Yunnan province, current religious work in Yunnan, minorities and religious problems in countries neighbouring Yunnan, and research on the system of autonomous rule in minorities areas.

Courses for *civil servants* include non-leading cadres, non-party cadres and cadres of one of the eight democratic parties, although the latter two also receive training at the academy of socialism. These courses cover both theory and administration. As far as theory is concerned, topics include the theoretical accomplishments of the party, management capacity, administration according to the law, global outlook, the image of public servants, the thought of the 'Three Represents' and Deng Xiaoping's thoughts on administrative management. Regarding administration, topics are the theory and practice of administration, the deepening reform of administrative management, current trends in the development of science and technology, administrative policy making, public policy, electronic government, the rule of law in government, assessing the achievements and efficiency of government, and the correct view of achievements in one's official career.[52]

One might expect that such courses are taught on the basis of strictly regimented curricula, set at the Centre and faithfully copied across China. In actual fact, quite the opposite is the case. Although the main mission of training remains 'unifying thought' (*tongyi sixiang*) – i.e. to bring cadres' work across the administration into line with central demands – local party schools are nevertheless proud of their own training courses and are given considerable leeway to teach them as they think best suits local conditions. The objective of training courses is not to teach a dead curriculum or to prepare students for examination, but better to prepare cadres to carry out their job in a way that both conforms to central priorities and is in tune with local conditions. Cadres are leaders of important organizations, and the party in its training recognizes that they have to be trusted with very considerable freedom. Traditionally, Leninist democratic centralism and Maoist strategy gave party cells and army units the autonomy to carry out their tasks as they thought best suited the circumstances. This spirit is again alive in the relationship of the party with its cadres: the Centre only establishes and imposes the principles that all have to abide by; it does not want to micro-manage its most trusted personnel or confine them to a Foucauldian panopticum. As we saw in chapter 2, when party schools were re-established with the reopening of the Central Party School in 1977, teaching was very much limited to the regurgitation of ideological dogma. The trauma of the Cultural Revolution and the factional struggle among the Party's top leaders were anything but conducive to pedagogical innovation, while the teaching staff also simply did not have the background to

---

[52] Interview 1, 1 April 2004.

do so. The glaring irrelevance of instruction at party schools to the challenges of reform and modernization was criticized and targeted during the modernization of cadre training that started in 1993, with the explicit aim of uniting administrative 'theory' and 'practice'.[53] As the head of education in Yunnan explains:

> Cases are derived from the teacher closely following the media and from his or her own research. In class, the main objective is to teach students how they should deal with real issues and practical situations, and the cases are the way to do that by discussing them and achieving consensus on the right way to deal with them. Obviously, the students will have knowledge about the topics taught, but teachers specialize in one specific one and their knowledge is the latest and goes deeper, and in this research is essential.[54]

The contents of what is taught on short-term training classes can best be described as a hybrid that reflects the ambiguities and contradictions of the Chinese administration. Yet both general political content and more applied aspects of the curriculum are infused with the need to explain and impose orthodoxy and uniformity. Teachers at local schools base their lecture notes and teaching materials in large part on their understanding of central documents and teaching materials at higher-level schools, usually simply by checking the website of these schools and reading their publications. Frequent meetings of school administrators ensure that central preferences are followed across the system and that policy initiatives at the Centre remain in tune with developments in the localities. The most important of these meetings is the year-end conference of all heads of provincial schools in Beijing (*Quanguo dangxiao xiaozhang huiyi*), and the larger five-yearly National Party Schools Work Conference (*Quanguo dangxiao gongzuo huiyi*). Provincial schools are bound by the decisions made at these meetings when drawing up their teaching plans for the coming year.[55]

Classes on general ideology therefore include what one might expect: Marxism/Leninism/Mao Zedong Thought, Deng Xiaoping Theory and of course the 'Three Represents', with a clear shift away from old orthodoxy to new elaborations. Classes quite often start with the assertion that the older theories still have some validity despite the fact that they cannot explain or guide everything that is happening now. Beyond the mandatory ideology classes, other content of training courses is much more recognizable to someone working in a university outside China. There is, for instance, a

---

[53] Wibowo and Fook 2006.
[54] Field notes 2 April 2004.   [55] Interviews 94 and 95, 28 April 2007.

very heavy emphasis on law. Law is a rapidly expanding instrument of rule that limits and obscures the processes of political decision making by men and women and imposes a uniform mould of rules that everybody has to play by. As has already been explained by the head of education in Yunnan, the emphasis on law rather than simple ideological orthodoxy is in fact a key instrument in restraining the use and abuse of power by officials, not only to fight corruption, but also, and more importantly, to make cadres more of an instrument of the political decisions made at higher levels rather than the political decision makers themselves. However, at the same time it is also important not to over-emphasize the role of law in administrative practice and cadre training: as we shall see in chapter 6, students at the Yunnan Provincial Party School still attach little importance to legal knowledge.

Another discursive formation that administration and, by extension, cadre training taps into is 'social science', or, to borrow a phrase much favoured by the British Labour Party, 'evidence-based policy'. Many classes spend considerable time on presenting and explaining the findings of research conducted by the teacher or others, and elaborating how this research can be relevant to administration. Obviously, there is considerable self-censorship here and boundaries that one cannot cross, but teachers, particularly the older and more respected ones, often do not shy away from pointing out some of the real problems highlighted by research caused by inadequate or non-existing policy. Nevertheless, many lectures are usually predictable expansions on new legislation, policy priorities and slogans. The ample use of PowerPoint presentations often only helps teachers in simply reading out a fully prepared lecture. This is still often found very useful by cadres to whom this is the lifeblood of their work and career. However, lecturers who simply regurgitate existing legislation, policy or ideology are criticized by students, who find this a waste of time. Good lecturers also draw extensively on their own research or experience, particularly where lectures are about implementation or experiences with current policy priorities. Nevertheless, students often find it difficult to see how the knowledge of teachers can be relevant to their work. Teachers in turn often comment on the difficulty of establishing credibility with their students, who are often of the same age or older, and have much more practical experience.

The format of lectures and seminars is quite similar to what one may expect at any university both inside and outside China. However, the students are not just students. They are cadres, and sometimes quite senior ones, which obviously informs both their relationship with the teachers and the conduct of classes. This is linguistically marked by using the term 'xueyuan' rather than the normal 'xuesheng' for student. Often, classes look very similar to official meetings or conferences, with the ubiquitous red banners, waitresses pouring hot water and, of course, smoking in class. As happens in meetings, students often freely answer calls on their mobile phones.

An example of the newer style of teaching that emphasizes dialogue and attention to the cut and thrust of daily administrative headaches was a 'teacher–student exchange' (*shuangxiang jiaoliu*) session for county-level cadres that I attended at the Yunnan Provincial Party School in April 2004. The session was intended to sum up the experiences and lessons learned by this class at the end of their two-month refresher training at the school.[56]

The chair of the day (one of the students it seems) emphasises that the idea is not to give speeches, but to exchange ideas, and is part of the school's teaching plan. The atmosphere in the class is much more informal than during lectures. People smoke, and more freely walk in and out of the classroom to go to the toilet, fill up their cups, or receive a call. Students sometimes talk in their own local dialect instead of Mandarin to the extent that some of the other students sometimes comment that they have no idea what the speaker is saying. However, all speakers still get a round of applause after their speech.

At the beginning the chair asks for a person to start with a question. There are no volunteers. Then, he says, let's do it by group then, let each group of students find a representative who will introduce the main questions raised during discussion sessions held by the group during the course. Again no one volunteers, until one person, possibly the oldest student, kicks off with a very long speech with many questions, rhetorical or real, points and sub-points, all neatly highlighted in the very best tradition of CCP bureaucratic speechmaking.

Other speakers then follow. A government county head from Qujing prefecture comments that the time for study, exchange of ideas and reflection here has been too short. You are just getting to know the teachers and your fellow students and then you have to go. He argues for lengthening the study period to three or even four months, and gets lots of laughter and support for this.

All speeches strike me as quite frank. They highlight the problems the speaker has in his (all speakers are male) county, even if this goes against the grain of central policy. One example that came up is the implementation of the shareholding system for state enterprises. The speaker quite directly said that this in fact amounts to full privatization, instead of, as the Centre says, the retention of the socialist

---

[56] Such sessions are by now a standard part of cadre training courses in party schools. For a document from the Central Party School on how to conduct such sessions, see Sun Huirong, 'How to develop teacher–student exchanges' (Ruhe kaizhan shuangxiang jiaoliu), no date, online at www1.ccps.gov.cn/xinwen.jsp?daohang_name=%E8%BF%91%E6%9C%9F%E8%A6%81%E9%97%BB&daohang_uri=/jqyw/index.jsp&content_uri=/root/jqyw/1113791305062 (checked on 27 June 2008).

character of enterprises. Other examples are the lack of constructive policies to deal with agricultural problems [*sannong wenti*], or the unfairness of the unequal development between the coastal areas and poor, inland, remote and minority areas such as Yunnan. Other speakers also criticize the centralization of the tax system.

There are six teachers present, but only the economics professor gets to talk after the students have spoken. The others just basically sit there, but that is also, as the chair says, because most questions were about economics. The economics professor acknowledges the frank opinions aired by several students regarding the inapplicability of national policies. However, these policies should nevertheless be adhered to. This holds for the shareholding system for state enterprises, and even more so for the contract system for agricultural land. The latter is a basic policy of the country and will never change. Privatization of the land would quickly widen the income gap between rich and poor and violate the socialist nature of China's society.

At the end of the session, the head of the party school, who had been present for the duration of the session, also gives a speech. He emphasises the importance of county-level development as the cornerstone of China's development strategy. In this, each county should find its own specialized sector. He also stresses the importance of the adherence to national policies.[57]

This class highlighted some of the main dilemmas of cadre training and the administrative setup as a whole. The students were leaders of counties in one of China's remote and poor areas and at the sharp end of some of the real and persistent problems that China is facing. To them, discussions during training at the party school were an opportunity to vent some of their frustration about central policies and the lack of central support that would enable them to create solutions to these problems. The teachers, on the other hand, had to stick with the orthodoxy regardless of what they themselves might think, a good example of how Leninist principles prohibit the free flow of information between the grass roots and higher levels, and clearly also a pointer to how these principles limit the extent of reform of cadre training at party schools, despite possibly the best intentions.

The student–teacher exchanges also exemplify the spirit of openness that generally should prevail in cadre training at party schools. To this end, the ethos of party schools de-emphasizes as much as possible status, rank and power, creating a level playing field for all participants, whether they are famous professors, senior cadres or recently promoted recruits. By making students of all ranks live and eat together, the school tries to be an environment strictly set off from normal life in the society around

---

[57] Field notes 15 April 2004.

it. Everybody is just a student or a teacher and anybody can learn from anybody else. This, of course, can only be partially successful as students tend to spend most of their time with other students in their class who are of equal rank. Nevertheless, as we shall see in chapter 6, the school also manages to be a place where new relationships and statuses are forged rather than old ones reinforced. At the school, cadres not only have the opportunity to 'recharge their batteries' intellectually, but also socially, an experience that reinvigorates both the formal institutional arrangements and informal relationships that make the party-state work.

According to the few accounts that are available, a similar situation pertains at the Central Party School. A 2001 article in *Shidai chao* (Trends of the Times), based on a visit to the Central Party School in Beijing, mentions that when students enter the school gates, no special privileges are given: indeed, all again become party 'comrades' regardless of how important their positions are. This is called the 'three transformations' (*sange zhuanbian*): from work to study, from individual family life to collective life in school, and from leading cadre to ordinary student.[58] The transformative quality of training at a party school is especially pronounced for recently recruited or promoted cadres on a young and middle-aged cadre course. According to the same article, such courses divide students up in small groups where they 'go through criticism and self-criticism and a thorough analysis and inspection of their work and ideological state since taking on leading cadre positions, in order to sort out problems, find deficiencies, seek origins and promote improvements'.

No special privileges are supposed to be extended to teachers as well. A 2007 article in *Nanfang zhoumo* (Southern Weekend) that is also based on a visit to the Central Party School, highlights the candour, inquisitiveness and interaction between teachers and students in classes, including classes on special issues such as the SARS crisis and public health, or the lessons from the 1959 Lushan party conference, the latter of which became cause for heated discussions on inner-party democracy and supervision. Teachers are well aware that their students are high cadres, including those who are destined to become central leaders in future years, and that the majority have university undergraduate degrees, while more than 30 per cent nowadays have postgraduate degrees. Moreover, teachers are routinely evaluated by the students, who reportedly pull no punches in their comments. However, the article adds that the openness at the Central Party School also has a negative side. Students know that they are being monitored and

---

[58] Wang Yueping, 'Inside the Central Party School', 2001.

evaluated by the representatives of the Central Organization Department present in their classes and that speaking out will not hurt prospects of gaining a promotion. In some classes, the competitiveness apparently led to factional division between left-wing and right-wing cadres to the point that the teacher was no longer able to teach the class normally.[59]

The above two journalistic accounts of training at the Central Party School were intended to convince the reader of the seriousness and importance of cadre training. Perhaps surprisingly, they have done so as much by highlighting the modern spirit of openness and debate as the continuities with the past: the disciplinary and transformative use of criticism and self-criticism in small groups that was a cornerstone of the Maoist tactics of creating revolution and socialist transformation (Whyte 1974). Interestingly, the more recent 2007 *Nanfang zhoumo* article uses the same tactic to add a more critical note. Presenting cadres at the Central Party School as self-promoting careerists whose competition sometimes leads to factional splits, the article makes an only slightly veiled reference to the disastrous political competitiveness and factionalism between Chinese students during the Cultural Revolution (Shirk 1982; Chan 1985).

Regardless of whether one wishes to emphasize reformist modernity or socialist tradition, it is clear that cadre training is about more than its curriculum: it is an experience that produces *cadres* and their unique culture of power, not mere administrators. In chapter 6, I will return to both the formal and informal aspects of cadre training as a formative and transformative experience, but in the next chapter we will first turn to some of the changes that have been wrought by neo-socialist marketization and state building.

---

[59] 'Deciphering the Central Party School: already 1/3 of students from younger and middle-aged cadre courses have been promoted to provincial-ministerial rank' (Jiemi Zhongyang Dangxiao: Zhongqingban xueyuan yi 1/3 jisheng sheng-buji), *Nanfang zhoumo* 8 November 2007, online at news.qq.com/a/20071108/001619.htm (checked on 23 June 2008).

CHAPTER 5

Marketization and centralization of cadre education and training

CENTRALIZATION, THE POLITICS OF QUALITY AND
'INTERNET MARXISM'

In the previous chapters we have seen how in the eighties minimum degree levels were made mandatory for employment in a particular level of post, and millions of incumbent cadres were forced to obtain the required degree. An astounding expansion of the number of degree holders in the course of just a very few years ensued. Party schools and other institutions set up tailored correspondence courses that earned pupils the required degree certificates but were nevertheless quite different from the formal degree courses at regular schools and universities. For local cadres, especially in rural areas and the less developed parts of China, correspondence degrees were often the only way to overcome the disadvantages of their background and earn a chance of promotion. Conversely, correspondence courses have been a financial lifeline that allowed many party schools to continue operating.

The proliferation of degree courses across party schools has been criticized on a number of grounds. Despite a fixed curriculum and a tight control over the examinations, the quality of correspondence degrees is increasingly deemed to be unacceptably low. As became clear when the Hainan Provincial Party School's 'diploma wholesale shop' (*wenping pifa dian*) was exposed in 2004, there has been often serious inflation of party school degrees up to the point of the outright sale of degree certificates.[1] Concerns over the quality of correspondence courses had already been voiced explicitly in the landmark 2000 *Decision on the strengthening and*

---

[1] See 'Hainan dangxiao lanfa wenping diaocha: weigui ban ban shouru 1600 wan yuan' (Investigation in the reckless issuing of diplomas by the Hainan Party School: 16 million yuan income from organizing classes in violation of the regulations), transcript from TV broadcast 'economic half hour' on the CCTV economy channel, no date, online at news.sohu.com/2004/07/02/14/news220831461.shtml, 2 July 2004 (checked on 21 March 2007); Huang Yong, 'Hainan dangxiao 'pifa' wenping' (Hainan Party School sells diplomas 'wholesale'), *Zhongguo qingnian bao* 16 June 2004, online at www.gmw.cn/01wzb/2004-06/20/content_45710.htm, 20 June 2004 (checked on 21 March 2007).

improvement of party school work in the twenty-first century.[2] Increasingly, the proliferation of such degree certificates sat uneasily with the new status and weight that the party schools were given in the nineties, and section seven of the 2000 *Decision* was intended to deal with this problem. In this section, the party Centre announced the establishment of a quality inspection setup specifically for party schools. The *Decision* also required that proper examinations be set for short-term training courses, which pupils would have to sit in order to be issued the course completion certificate that they needed to satisfy the pre-promotion training or period retraining requirement. For master's degree certificates, the *Decision* required at least two years of full-time study of a regulated curriculum and an oral thesis defence at the conclusion of the course. For other degree certificate courses taught as correspondence courses, the *Decision* demanded a much stricter systematization and standardization of enrolment, teaching and examination. Finally, the *Decision* also envisioned a gradual expansion of the number of establishments that have the right to confer *xuewei* university master's or doctoral degrees under the guidance of state departments responsible for educational degrees and graduate studies, and assigned special responsibility for this task to the Central Party School.

In fact, concerns about correspondence courses ran so deep that a special policy document regarding the Central Party School's operation was issued in 2001, the *Programme for educational reform in the Central Party School's Correspondence Academy*.[3] This document specifies the lack of uniformity of quality of correspondence education across the nation, including examination standards and the quality of teaching. The document details a range of measures, such as setting up a nationwide quality control system, improvement in teacher training and certification, the creation of a credit point system to allow for greater student choice, the tightening of the examination system and a greater use of distance learning methods. The programme also insists that education in party spirit should be a mandatory course on every degree programme. Correspondence education, too, is party school education and should be a way to improve the work style of the party, the administration and cadres: in other words, correspondence education ought to be more than just a way to raise the educational standards of the cadre corps, and should be an instrument in eradicating the

---

[2] See chapter 2.
[3] *Zhonggong Zhongyang Dangxiao Hanshou Xueyuan jiaoyu gaige gangyao*, issued on 23 November 2001; reprinted in *2002 Zhonggong Zhongyang Dangxiao hanshou jiaoyu nianjian* (Yearbook of correspondence education of the Central Party School), Beijing Zhonggong Zhongyang Danxiao Chubanshe, 2003: 10–12.

widespread evils of corruption, power abuse and the lack of ideological or moral awareness.

In a sense, the unease over correspondence education is just one aspect of the rift that has opened up between the Centre and developed areas on the one hand and the less developed parts of China on the other. From the perspective of the Centre and the developed coastal provinces, correspondence education was a mid-eighties Dengist measure to rid the administration of leftist stalwarts and to bootstrap the cadre system into the modern era. However, ten or fifteen years on, the administration in these developed areas recruited almost all its new cadres directly from among university graduates and no longer needed the basic, substandard degree education offered by party schools. Insofar as their cadres needed more education, this ought to be master's or even doctoral degrees that were fully competitive in the labour market. In other words, cadres should obtain real *xuewei* degrees, either from regular universities or from other recognized establishments for higher education.

According to the 2000 *Decision on the strengthening and improvement of party school work in the twenty-first century*, the solution for the lack in quality of *xueli* degrees was to encourage party schools to seek the right to confer such full academic degrees. Only higher education institutions recognized by the degree committee of the State Council (*Guowuyuan xuewei weiyuanhui*) have the right to confer *xuewei* degrees. In the nineties, these institutions did not include party schools and schools of administration, except for the Central Party School in Beijing (but excluding its correspondence academy). In its assessment of an educational establishment, the degree committee mainly looks at the quality of the teaching staff and the quality of their research.[4] However, as of 2007, only the Central Party School and a dozen or so provincial party schools offer recognized *xuewei* degrees, and obtaining the right to confer such degrees is only becoming harder with each passing year.[5]

As we saw in chapter 4, at the Yunnan Provincial Party School, as no doubt at many other provincial schools, administrators expressed the

---

[4] Interview 34, 19 April 2004.
[5] Interview 93, 27 April 2007. One provincial school that had gained the right to confer recognized master degrees is the Fujian Provincial Party School. As part of their programme of 'disciplinary strengthening', the school had invested heavily in the quality of its research to bring its academic disciplines in line with the 1997 requirements of the National Degree Committee. The school's success is clearly presented as a model for other schools to follow, and it earned itself the honour of an article to boast of its achievements in China's leading high-brow daily newspaper, the *Guangming Ribao*; Lin Shushun 'Shengji dangxiao xueke jianshe tanxi' (Analysis of disciplinary construction at a provincial party school), *Guangming Ribao* 1 April 2005, online at theory.people.com.cn/GB/40551/3286724.html (checked on 11 September 2007).

ambition to gain this right, but also admitted to doubt that this would be a realistic option. Both correspondence courses and on-site courses continued to teach for *xueli* degrees, for which, in Yunnan at least, there still was considerable demand: in 2004, less than half of the leading and ordinary cadres in Yunnan had a university degree.[6] In Qujing prefecture, for instance, although demand for undergraduate or vocational *xueli* degrees among leading cadres had dropped considerably in recent years, the demand among ordinary cadres, including non-leading civil servants and employees in enterprises and public services organizations, was still considerable.[7]

However, at the Centre the ambition to phase out *xueli* degrees has only become stronger. When I interviewed administrators of the Central Party School's Correspondence Academy in December 2006, I was quite surprised to learn that the academy's correspondence degree teaching would in fact be discontinued completely. In the developed coastal areas, I was told, there is little demand now for basic higher vocational and even undergraduate degrees and these programmes would no longer be offered. In addition, regular universities now offer more and more degree programmes specifically targeted at cadres, often in collaboration with local party schools, a development that I also witnessed in Yunnan. Instead of correspondence degrees, the Central Party School would concentrate on recognized master's degrees, for which there is high demand due to the competition between cadres for promotion. After its abolition, staff at the Central Party School's Correspondence Academy would be redeployed within the school. The leadership of the correspondence academy itself expected to be asked to contribute to non-degree cadre training, using its expertise in distance learning and its existing extensive contacts with high-quality lecturers available in Beijing. However, in subsequent conversations and other interviews administrators at the Central Party School told me that most of the academy's staff would in fact be used to strengthen the school's commercial branch, an issue that I will return to later on in this chapter.[8]

Using direct satellite or Internet links, former staff at the correspondence academy could also help strengthen the school's 'lectures for the whole

---

[6] Interview 1, 12 December 2004.   [7] Interview 54, 16 November 2004.
[8] Interview 90, 21 December 2006, and interviews 94 and 95, 28 April 2007. The formal announcement of the termination of the Central Party School's correspondence degrees happened in November 2007, see 'Central Party School announces termination of correspondence degrees' (Zhongyang Dangxiao jiao ting hanshou xueli), *Nanfang zhoumo* 28 November 2007, online at news.sina.com.cn/c/2007-11-29/103814413534.shtml (checked on 23 June 2008).

party' (*quandang jiangke*) by high leaders or scholars based in Beijing. Such 'Internet Marxism' (*Yintewang Makesi zhuyi*) is a growing addition to the normal training programmes at local party schools, and the school's distance learning network centre periodically posts guides of forthcoming programmes on its website. 'Internet Marxism' is part of what is called the 'transformational development' (*zhuanxing fazhan*) of party schools and cadre training in which higher degree work and on-the-job training have priority. The creation of 'web-based party schools' (*wangshang dangxiao*) is an increasingly important element in the party's ambition to provide specific and specialized training for cadres at all levels, and to make life-long learning a normal aspect of all cadres' jobs.[9]

Like other elements of this transformational development, the effort to get rid of *xueli* degrees and the development of 'Internet Marxism' are driven by a strongly centralist and even elitist agenda. Local party schools, especially those in the less well-off parts of the country, are considered less than fully equipped to deal with the increasingly sophisticated demands of China's administration. As in other policy areas, the reaction of the Centre has been to bypass local governmental institutions and direct matters from the Centre.[10] In addition to the impatience with conventional cadre training displayed in policy documents, a centralist attitude also came across very clearly in the interviews with the Central Party School's Correspondence Academy.

Central work is better because of the much broader pool of teachers one can draw on in Beijing, and because teachers (academics or high cadres) here have a broader exposure and deeper knowledge than in the provinces. A professor in a provincial school may be a professor but he will draw on knowledge gained only in the province. It is a bit like a scholar talking about America who has never been there... I understand that in places like Yunnan they have their special circumstances and that may mean that they will make the transition four or five years later, you have to adapt to local circumstances. And income is an issue, but that will mean that these schools have to get more support from the finance department of their local government, they have to rely on their own resources [*zili gengsheng*]... At the Central Party School income is not an issue, we are mainly

---

[9] See Li Qihong, 'Wushi, kaifang, chuangxin: ganbu jiaoyu peixun gongzuo xin moshi' (Concrete matters, opening up, innovation: the new model of the cadre education and training work), *Lilun dongtai* 1743 (20 May 2007): 34. The Internet has, in fact, long been an important tool in teaching, research and administration across the party school system, of which several examples have been given throughout this book. For an article on the uses of web-based learning in party schools, see Jiang Yuxiang, 'Wangluo jiaoyu zai dangxiao de yingyong (Applications of web-based education at party schools)', *Xuexi Shibao* 22 July 2005, online at www.studytimes.com.cn/txt/2005-07/22/content_5921749.htm (checked on 11 September 2007).
[10] See for instance Mertha 2005.

concerned with guaranteeing quality. We get ample support from the Centre, in this we are different from local schools. Local schools will have to solve their own problems.[11]

This agenda originates at least in part at the Central Party School itself, which very early on had gained the right to confer *xuewei* degrees. Moreover, the Central Party School receives generous funding from the central government and thus does not have to rely on teaching correspondence degrees for financial survival, despite the fact that this was a very large and profitable operation. The only concession to China's poorer areas is that the policy of replacing correspondence courses with programmes for recognized *xuewei* degrees would be applied 'flexibly'. In most areas, recognized programmes will only be offered for master's degrees, while party schools will be allowed to continue their *xueli* programmes for higher vocational or undergraduate degrees as long as there is demand. Students applying for recognized degrees will all have to take the national entrance examination set by the Ministry of Education, which many cadres will find very difficult, if not impossible, to pass. The admissions criteria and course requirements for full-time or part-time *xueli* degrees are much less demanding, and in particular the absence of mandatory English is a strong attraction to cadres who need a degree purely to further their career within the bureaucracy. For this reason, even the Central Party School expects to continue offering certain residential master's level *xueli* degree programmes.[12]

Nevertheless, there is strong central pressure to continue the build-up of recognized degree education at (provincial) party schools that both conforms to the government's standards and preserves the unique party nature of education at party schools with the aim of building up a special brand and form of party school graduate education. At a discussion meeting in May 2006, party school representatives admitted to many problems, including a lack of qualified academic staff that are respected in academic circles in China, a lack of more practically oriented disciplines, a lack of innovation in the content of courses, and a lack of autonomy in student admission, funding, course administration and courses on offer, all of which restrict the scope and range of student enrolment.[13]

The gradual spread of recognized degree education in party schools across the country is aimed at the needs of China's new stratum of

[11] Interview 90, 21 December 2006.   [12] Interviews 94 and 95, 28 April 2007.
[13] Hou Dianming, 'Summary of a discussion meeting on the task of graduate student teaching on recognized courses across the national system of party schools' (Quanguo dangxiao xitong xuewei yanjiusheng peiyang gongzuo zuotanhui jiyao), online at yjsy.ccps.gov.cn/docs/qt/173.aspx (checked on 1 July 2008).

well-educated and ambitious younger cadres mainly in the highly developed parts of China. However, unless they take a part-time degree course, these cadres in many cases will have to resign from their jobs to become full-time students. Upon graduation they have to enter the job market afresh in the hope that a party school recognized master's degree will help them get a better job. Many students on party school courses are therefore not necessarily cadres, but simply recent university or higher vocational school graduates wishing to take a graduate degree that may help them gain relative high-level entry into the administration. Meanwhile, in other areas not even the second-rate *xueli* correspondence degrees from the central school are on offer any more, and often all that remains there are third-rate degrees from the correspondence academies of the local provincial party school. Clearly, this development not only helps raise the educational level and quality of China's new cadre corps, but also threatens to deepen the rift between the more and less developed parts of China. However, local initiative seems at least in part to bridge this gap. Local party schools have found ways to offer recognized degree programmes that do not depend on direct central recognition. In Yunnan, as in many other provinces, party schools started teaching courses certified by, for instance, the university extension department of regular universities, thereby enabling local students to obtain real recognized degrees.[14] The Yunnan Provincial Party School set up modest collaborative master's programmes with the National Minorities University in Beijing and the Macao Technological University. The highly entrepreneurial party school of Qinlin urban district in eastern Yunnan had joined up with Yunnan Normal University. Although the degrees under the latter programme were still *xueli* degrees, the degree certificate had the seal of both the provincial committee for cadre education and training and Yunnan Normal University affixed to it.[15] In Shilin county in central Yunnan, the party school had been offering higher vocational degree *xueli* classes in collaboration with the Central Radio and Television University since the early nineties. More recently, even this county-level school set up master's recognized degree classes with Yunnan University.[16] As it will only get harder to gain independent recognition, the trend of setting up joint degree courses is bound to strengthen in the years to come.[17]

---

[14] When I mentioned this practice to academics or administrators in Beijing, many refused to believe that such a thing was happening, because it was against the regulations to do so without the prior approval of the National Degree Committee.
[15] Interview 67, 18 November 2004.   [16] Interview 70, 28 November 2004.
[17] Interview 93, 27 April 2007.

GEOGRAPHY AND POWER: EXCHANGES, MODELS AND ADVANCED EXPERIENCES

We already have seen that bureaucratic rank, level and jurisdiction are inseparable from the world of cadre training. Party schools only train cadres of a particular rank and within the jurisdiction of the administration that they are part of. Typically, cadres receive training at a school or centre one level higher than their own. Training itself thereby strongly reinforces both the vertical lines of authority within the bureaucracy and the horizontal boundaries of the jurisdiction of a particular level of administration. By gathering its subordinate cadres at a central location for training, the administration at a particular level reinforces the fact that, ultimately, these cadres belong to and are supposed to be loyal to that administration and not to the lower-level locality or institution that they happen to be working in.

Party schools are thus important centres in their jurisdiction of what I would like to call the party's administrative civilization: a combination of advanced knowledge, ideological discipline, normative and moral guidance and access to the power, wishes and desires of the leadership of the administration that one belongs to. This role of party schools extends beyond the training and education they provide, or the research that staff at party schools conduct for local administrative bodies. Teachers, particularly the older and more respected ones, often get asked informally for their opinion, advice or assistance in helping to sort out problems that former students run into.

A student of mine became party secretary at a rural township. Villagers at either side of the border between two counties had a conflict over water, and this student asked me how to handle this. I suggested that he handle the issue according to the law. He checked the autonomous regulation but could not find a legal basis to solve the problem, but in the end found a legal basis in China's water law, which said that only counties can set up agreements on water resources. The agreement between the two villages therefore had no legal basis. This voided that agreement and also solved the problem.[18]

Personal student–teacher relationships forged at the party school knit together the community of cadres working within the jurisdiction of the administration that the school is part of. Furthermore, a significant number of students at party schools are in fact part of the party's so-called 'theoretical backbone' (*lilun gugan*) that includes teachers and staff at lower-level

---

[18] Interview 2, 2 April 2004.

party schools.[19] Teacher–student relationships at party schools therefore also informally weld together the system of lower-level party schools within an administrative area, relationships that are often more important than formal bureaucratic guidance. In the course of my fieldwork I had ample opportunity to witness the strengths of these informal ties as my main contact person, the head of education at the provincial school, used his relationships with former students to arrange visits and interviews at lower-level schools across Yunnan. Furthermore, lower-level schools make funds available to their teaching staff for sabbatical visits to higher-level schools, again an opportunity to create personal relationships that may come in very handy later on. Teachers from higher-level schools are also regularly invited for guest lectures in lower-level schools. In the case of lecturers from the Centre lecturing at the Yunnan Provincial Party School, the audience often consists of teachers at local party schools from all around the province.[20] When viewed from within, the system of party schools (and, as we will see in the next chapter, the administration as a whole) often operates more as a cluster of hierarchically embedded networks rather than an impersonal bureaucratic hierarchy.

The relationship between school teachers and cadres is also reinforced at a more formal level. Party schools are sensitive to the problem that their teaching often has insufficient bearing on the realities of cadres' day-to-day work, and require from their teaching staff that they serve an extended period of time in the field in a non-executive appointment at a local government or other administrative agency. This practice, called 'linked positions' (*guazhi*), not only teaches teachers things they would otherwise never learn – 'to connect theory and practice' as it is often put in Marxist terms – but also creates relationships and loyalties with that locality and its cadres that often last an entire career. This applies particularly to younger teachers who have often been recruited straight out of college. Older teachers often have considerable prior administrative experience and do not need 'linked positions', but likewise maintain their relationships with places of previous employment.

The flow of information, students and personnel is only partially conditioned by relatively straightforward vertical bureaucratic links and the network of social relationships that these create. One of the first things that struck me when I started my research was that cadre training involves

---

[19] Training theoretical backbone cadres (including those working in the propaganda apparatus) is routinely mentioned in policy documents as one of the core tasks of party schools, particularly those at the central and provincial level.

[20] Interview 69, 27 November 2004.

a great deal of mobility. Indeed, the very efficacy of training seems to be predicated on travel or temporary residence elsewhere, which is why all institutes involved in training have ample facilities for lodging large numbers of often very demanding students. Such travel goes far beyond what is needed to receive normal training at the school in one's jurisdiction. Both students and teachers commonly travel far and wide to party schools, universities, academies and other institutions across the country and indeed abroad. Teachers at the Yunnan Provincial Party School, for instance, could apply for sabbatical leave of a semester or a year, which they typically would try to spend at a famous university, often in Beijing, for instance the Central Party School, the National Academy of Administration, Peking University, Tsinghua University or the Central School of Nationalities. These sojourns were not arranged through vertical administrative relations, but by individual agreement. Conversely, as we saw in the previous section, well-known teachers from higher-level institutions frequently give guest lectures or even teach whole classes at lower-level institutions.

Such academic travel is predicated on the notion that superior and more modern knowledge is hierarchically and spatially distributed, a hierarchy that explicitly also extends to the developed nations, with the US at its apex. In the words of an experienced teacher at the Yunnan Provincial Party School:

QUESTION: Do teachers have the opportunity for further training?
ANSWER: Yes, they do, for instance they can go to another university for further study or as visiting scholars. Normally, they go to Fudan University in Shanghai, or the Central Party School or the National Academy of Administration in Beijing or such like. Their training there lasts a few months, half a year or at the most a full year.
QUESTION: What exactly do they do there?
ANSWER: For instance, they listen to lectures of high-level professors, serve as assistants to professors with the right to supervise PhD students and join their research projects. One of the teachers at our school is a visiting scholar at the National Academy of Administration. He studies with a teacher who has studied in the United States, and serves as his assistant. We do not have any teachers who have been sent abroad for study, but we have made short-term study tours, mainly to Europe, Australia and to neighbouring countries of Yunnan.[21]

The Yunnan Provincial Party School does not, as yet, have the academic stature to forge direct relationships with the US, and has to limit its aspirations to national schools and to Southeast Asia, Europe and Australia. For

---
[21] Interview 2, 2 April 2004.

instance, the school has an ongoing relationship with Macao Technological University that brings teachers from Macao to the school, while students from Yunnan can take a degree in Macao, although their instruction except the final oral examination takes place at the school in Kunming.[22] At the other end of the spectrum, the Central Party School in Beijing has fostered extensive foreign links, and routinely sends whole classes of students abroad for a few weeks of study, especially to Japan, Korea, Singapore, the US, Canada and western Europe. Academic staff and administrators also have opportunities to go abroad on delegations, as visiting scholars or to take a further degree.[23] In 2007, more than two thousand scholars, businesspeople and politicians from abroad came to the school for a visit or to give a lecture.[24] Delegations of high-level school administrators routinely travel abroad seeking opportunities to expand foreign exchanges and collaborations.

The spatial projection and conflation of modernity, administrative civilization and academic excellence has spawned an incredible range and density of exchanges, off-site training courses and study tours, and, as more funds are poured into cadre training, each year brings yet more. The Yunnan Provincial Party School routinely sends groups of students to other party schools for short-term courses coupled with inspection tours of local enterprises and other examples of desirable development. Some of these training classes are free of charge as part of mandatory support provided by developed areas to developing areas,[25] others fall outside the assistance plan and have to be paid for.[26] The Beijing Municipal Party School is mainly a recipient of students from other, less developed parts of China and even from Vietnam. However, the Beijing school also sends students to Shanghai, to learn about the latest developments in economics and finance, and to Georgia in the US.[27] Similar arrangements exist at lower levels of the administrative ladder: Yiliang county in Yunnan sent four hundred cadres to Shanghai in 2004 and had started sending individual cadres to Guangdong province for temporary non-executive appointments as early as 1992.[28] According to the head of educational affairs of the party school in Qujing prefecture in eastern Yunnan:

[22] Interview 27, 16 April 2004.   [23] Interviews 94 and 95, 28 April 2007.
[24] Sun Xiangdong, personal communication, 6 May 2008.
[25] Cadre training as part of mutual support between different parts of the country is coordinated by means of regulations of the State Ministry of Personnel; Interview 93, 27 April 2007.
[26] Interview 1, 12 December 2004.
[27] Interview 93, 27 April 2007. On American impact on China's administrative reform, including cadre training and education, see Tong and Wang (2005).
[28] Interview 69, 27 November 2004.

After full-time study on the training course here has been completed, students go on an inspection tour for half a month to places like Zhejiang, Shanghai, Guangzhou or Shenzhen, mainly for inspection and to attend classes. After class, students visit enterprises and villages. The students' expenses are borne by their work unit, while those of the teachers from here who accompany them are paid for by our school. Our teachers also have to pay fees for sitting in on the lectures. Two years ago we went to Shenzhen, where we had requested lectures from eight teachers from the Shenzhen City Party School, four on theoretical knowledge and four on enterprise management. Finally, there was one week when the students carried out party spirit analysis. The students wrote their own summary of their experiences that were discussed in their group. After that followed an exchange of views for the whole class that was attended by leaders of our school and leaders of the organization department here.[29]

Significantly, the party schools that students are most frequently sent to are not located in the nation's administrative centre Beijing – the Central Party School is not involved in any such programmes at all[30] – but in the areas where China's market-driven economic reforms have progressed the farthest: Shanghai, Zhejiang and Shenzhen. Schools in these places cater for large numbers of such students from all over China's less developed areas, an arrangement which, one would imagine, is also a significant source of income quite apart from the possible gratification that comes with the confirmation of being one of the centres of China's administrative civilization. In Shanghai, these students are kept separate from the normal student-cadres and are reportedly looked down upon, in time-honoured Shanghainese fashion, as poor country bumpkins (Tran 2003).

Almost all party schools regularly send inspection delegations to foreign countries. The Yunnan Provincial Party School, for instance, sent delegations first to Australia and more recently to four western European countries. However, more important is the growth in the number and visibility of training programmes that partially or wholly take place at a foreign university or other institutions, such as schools of government. The best known (at least in China) and possibly the earliest of these involved the Central Party School and the Kennedy School of Government at Harvard University. From the early 2000s onward, this programme enabled selected younger county-level cadres to spend half a year at Harvard in a programme specifically tailored to their needs after a period of preparatory training in Beijing. The success of this programme has spawned several other programmes of this kind in countries such as the US, Canada, France, Sweden and the UK.

[29] Interview 68, 18 November 2004.   [30] Interview 93, 27 April 2007.

As a rule, international cadre training programmes are not run by party schools themselves, but by the organization department at the Centre, a province or lower levels as part of their cadre education and training programmes. Competition for places on such a programme is quite often very keen, not only for the opportunity to travel abroad (about which Chinese cadres take an increasingly jaded view), but also for what it will do for one's future career prospects. The establishment of these programmes has been much facilitated by the enthusiasm of international organizations and foundations, foreign governments and foreign universities. Particularly in the case of national programmes, most, if not all, of the funding often comes from foreign donors or partners, who see these programmes as an opportunity to have an impact on the modernization of China's administration and the new generation of Chinese leaders, and to establish invaluable personal and institutional relationships with the Chinese government.[31] Programmes for provincial governments in China are often taken on mainly for the income that they generate, and students are as a rule trained entirely separately from regular students. Chinese cadres who come to a famous university in a developed country in the West are therefore treated in a very similar fashion as cadres who have been sent on a training programme at a party school in, for instance, Shanghai or Shenzhen in China itself.

DIVERSIFICATION AND MARKETIZATION

Both domestic and international training trips are part of the Centre's strategy of marketization by increasing the number of institutions and ways to deliver cadre training. The current requirement is that cadres receive minimally three months of training every five years, but such training should be flexibly adapted to their specific needs and objectives, rather than be solely provided by the conventional standard programmes at party schools. However, it is probably wise at this point to emphasize that programmes of training for individual or groups of cadres remain firmly part of the cadre education and training plans of all governments in China, and the coordinating and supervising role of the organization departments and bureaus of personnel remain intact. Marketization and diversification should therefore not be interpreted as a loosening of the grip of a government or party committee on the cadres within its jurisdiction, or

---

[31] The University of Oxford, for instance, decided in 2006 to subsidize a training programme of high-level cadres when it became clear that the international donors' and the Chinese contribution together would not be enough to cover the full costs.

as incompatible with the strongly centralizing trend discussed earlier in this chapter. In fact, several recent policy initiatives in the use of off-site training programmes have strengthened the grip of the Centre, arguably at the expense of local administrations. Examples discussed earlier in this book are the decision to train county party secretaries centrally at the Central Party School in the course of the tenth five-year plan (2001–2005) and, even more ambitiously, the establishment of the three new cadre academies for 'experiental learning' in Shanghai, Jinggangshan and Yan'an, and most recently (2006) the academy for economics and management in Dalian.

Despite these centralist initiatives, the main thrust of the marketization of cadre training has been to allow for a greater diversity of providers of training in modern management skills and other forms of non-ideological training. Cadre training has become a very profitable market for some of China's universities. At the three best-known universities in Beijing (Peking University, Tsinghua University and Renmin (People's) University) large numbers of cadres spend periods of anywhere between one to several weeks on training programmes tailored on demand specifically to their needs.[32] Especially since 2002, such training has grown exponentially. In 2006, Tsinghua's School of Continuing Education taught 120 classes, each with on average fifty cadres in it, and the School expected to teach 150 classes in 2007. Such 'high-end training' (*gaoduan peixun*) caters for groups of cadres from a specific province, prefecture or city administration, or sometimes a central government department. As with the international cadre training programmes, getting a place on a programme at a prestigious national university is a privilege given only to selected individuals, usually cadres with potential for promotion to a higher rank, or else those who have recently been recruited and await their first appointment to a leading position.

Training at prestigious universities is virtually devoid of political content, and the curriculum usually focuses on subjects such as management and leadership skills, economics, city planning or law. Although cadres in China now normally have at least a BA or MA degree, many have majored in the sciences or engineering. Training with a focus on management and the social sciences is therefore much needed in their preparation for leadership.[33] Like local level training courses and *xueli* education, training programmes in Beijing have created a very active secondary market in

---

[32] The following paragraphs are based on Interview 86, 16 December 2006), Interview 92, 27 April 2007, Interview 97, 30 April 2007, and interview 87, 19 December 2006.
[33] Interview 97, 30 April 2007.

teachers. The academically strong schools and departments can, of course, rely on their own staff to teach core courses, but the many additional subjects and topics that specific delegations request can often only be catered for by paying a teacher from another department in the university, or even from another school or government department in the city, to teach specific sessions. In this regard, schools in Beijing have a distinct competitive advantage over academic institutions outside the capital: nowhere else is the potential pool of specialist teachers as rich and diverse as in Beijing.

In selling their wares, the schools rely not only on word of mouth, repeat business and simply the reputation of their university, but also have developed elaborate websites to attract customers. Departments employ full-time staff to market, design and support training courses. The clients that departments deal with usually are the organization department or personnel bureau of a particular local government. They negotiate a specific programme of training for a specific delegation of cadres at a specific price, usually including board at a university guesthouse or hotel nearby. Although cadre training is principally a money-making undertaking, an additional benefit is that trainees become alumni of sorts of the university. The enduring relationship between trainees and university is considered an important intangible asset that may serve the university well in the future, and this consideration may well lead a department in certain cases to decide not to charge the full market price for the training of government cadres. At Tsinghua's School of Continuing Education, for instance, training courses for personnel from private enterprises cost one thousand yuan per person per day, while government cadre courses were charged at lower rates that also took into account how poor or well-off their area was.[34] As we have seen, very similar arguments are made by foreign universities, governments and sponsors in discussions about setting up or subsidizing foreign training programmes for Chinese cadres.

In all three universities, the school of public management or public administration is an important provider of such training courses. Other providers may include the business school and the department of continuing education. At each university, little cooperation or coordination exist between different schools and departments, although centralized accounting at each university ensures that departments cannot use the income from training courses to freely build up their own slush funds ('small treasuries', *xiao jinku*) beyond the oversight and control of the central

[34] Interview 97, 30 April 2007.

university administration. Departments and schools pay a certain percentage of their income from training courses to the central administration, and also have to submit brief annual reports about their training activities, while at Peking University the Centre of Continuing Education has formally to approve the curricula of training courses before they can be offered.[35]

However, party schools are not necessarily passively watching central initiatives and regular universities encroaching on their traditional territory, and the largely unhappy experience of provincial and lower-level party schools in Yunnan is clearly only one side of the picture. While schools in more remote and poorer parts of the country have only limited options, those in affluent and developed parts of the country have themselves entered the new market for cadre training and other kinds of education.[36] The party school of Beijing municipality (a province-level party school), for instance, was not only confident that it would be able to retain 60 to 70 per cent of regular training for Beijing cadres, citing its staff's direct exposure to and knowledge of Beijing's specific circumstances as its edge in the competition with regular universities. The school also made considerable headway in turning itself into a diversified provider of higher education to organizations and individuals both inside and outside the administration. Surprisingly, an area that has become one of the school's strengths is the provision of short Chinese language and culture courses for foreign students. Conversely, they also offer foreign language training for Chinese preparing to go abroad. The school also claimed to organize management courses for large companies in the Beijing area. As a result, the Beijing school was on a financially solid footing. In 2006, only one-third of the funding for its total annual budget of 120 million yuan came from the normal budgetary allocation from Beijing municipality, the rest came from 'self-raised' (*zichou*) funds, including outside-the-plan courses, the rental of facilities, and fee income from *xuewei* and *xueli* degree students.

The perhaps most unexpected operator in the emerging market for cadre training is the Central Party School itself. In 2005, the school opened its commercial branch, called the External Training Centre (*Duiwai peixun zhongxin*). Quite openly, the new centre aims at offering training courses for cadres who otherwise would never have been able to gain acceptance on one of the school's regular courses. In this way, such cadres can have at least some of the prestige associated with the Central Party School.

---

[35] Interview 87, 19 December 2006, and Interview 92, 27 April 2007.
[36] In Russia, the transition to postcommunism has had a similar, albeit much more profound, impact on the higher party schools of the Soviet era; see Huskey 2004.

Even the most vaunted source of Maoist revolutionary glory and Leninist career opportunities, it appears, is now for sale. In 2007, the school expected greatly to expand cadre courses offered through its External Training Centre. Teaching staff released from their duties because of the phasing out of non-recognized *xueli* degree teaching would be re-employed on training courses offered by the Centre. Deftly adapting to shifting national policy, the school ensured that employment and loss of income from *xueli* education would be compensated for by expansion in a new market.

According to two administrators at the school who I interviewed on this point, the school knows full well that it has to exercise considerable care here. Unlike regular universities, the school does not simply advertise its services far and wide. Recruitment on commercial courses is done exclusively through the organization and united front departments of the CCP, and its courses are available only to cadres of at least *chu* (county) rank, and not to employees of private enterprises.[37] However, according to the *South China Morning Post*, very short, six-day courses at the Central Party School aimed specifically at businesspeople are in fact on offer commercially. Agents across the country recruiting students on these courses openly advertise the opportunity to meet very senior former government officials and to learn from the horse's mouth about the CCP's ideas and plans. Reportedly, the six-day course costs 6,800 yuan; by 2006, already 10,000 students had taken such a course.[38]

Since 2002, the marketization of cadre training has led to a proliferation of course providers across China, and governments, organization departments and other organizations can now choose from a highly diverse supply. Marketization has also had the, perhaps unintended, effect of turning party schools themselves into more diverse and open providers. Much of this is surely only for the better, and governments can now tailor training much more to the needs of a professional managerial cadre corps. Political training continues to be the terrain of conventional party schools, but here too, they face competition from the standardized revolutionary outings to the new cadre academies. However, both Central initiatives and the market mechanism favour schools and governments in China's developed regions. Party schools in poorer areas do not have the local resources to turn themselves into more diverse providers of higher education. As local party

---

[37] Interviews 94 and 95, 28 April 2007.
[38] *South China Morning Post* 24 April 2006. Possibly, these commercial courses for businesspeople are not organized directly by the school or its External Training Centre, but through an independent provider. This would explain why the two administrators of the school remained silent on this point.

schools deteriorate and the central requirements of the quality and quantity of cadre training continue being raised, governments in these areas will be forced to spend more money on off-site training programmes at prestigious institutions elsewhere, further adding to their already very precarious financial situation. To be sure, mechanisms exist whereby poorer areas are given free or subsidized training elsewhere, but the extent of these provisions will have to be raised considerably to keep up with the development of China's neo-socialism.

The booming industry that off-site cadre training programmes have become is predicated as much on the new wealth of China and the increased solvency of the Chinese administration, as on the cheapness of travel and the convenience of long-distance communications that are familiar drivers of globalization processes anywhere (Castells 1996). However, national and international study tours and training programmes also draw on long-standing Chinese administrative practices, such as study tours by individual leaders or leadership delegations or periodic meetings at higher administrative levels for coordination, policy dissemination and the enforcement of conformity to higher-level wishes. However, most striking are perhaps the similarities with the Maoist practice of establishing advanced models (such as the famous Dazhai agricultural brigade or the Daqing oilfields in the sixties). During the Maoist period, models illustrated by example what a leader wished to achieve. Models were faithfully studied by visiting delegations from across the nation, and they were supposed to emulate the famous example upon their return home. International and national programmes for cadre training can thus be read as a specifically Chinese (and Maoist-Leninist) way that globalization processes play out in the context of China's market reform and opening to the west. They are, in other words, as much a part of the unfolding pattern of Chinese globalization as, for instance, the new Chinese migration or the flow of international capital in and out of China (Pieke, Nyíri, Thunø and Ceccagno 2004). As I have shown in this section, the outcome of at least this aspect of Chinese globalization has not been a weakening of the Chinese government, the Communist Party, or communism, but a modernization of Leninist administration and, if anything, a strengthening of central control. Currently, large numbers of Chinese cadres routinely partake in pilgrimage-like trips across the nation and abroad to the sacred sites of China's revolution and market reforms and the world capitalist system, thereby also impressing upon these cadres the message that China's new administrative civilization is somehow spawned by economic success and exposure to the west. Most importantly, it reinforces the notion that modernity is unequally spatially and hierarchically distributed; by necessity, modernity is to be found elsewhere, to be studied, emulated and, ultimately, surpassed.

THE EROSION OF LOCAL PARTY SCHOOLS

The rapid growth of a whole range of expensive training facilities and off-site programmes has come at price, even apart from their financial costs. The main reason that the Centre has encouraged the diversification of cadre training was dissatisfaction with the quality and variety of training provided in traditional party schools, particularly at the local level, and it is indeed there that the pain of the reforms is felt most. The national and provincial party schools and schools of administration are full-fledged institutes of higher education and research, in addition to their specialized function of the provision of short-term main courses. Provincial schools are to all intents and purposes smaller versions of the central schools, which includes the important right to independently confer degrees. However, at lower levels of the administrative hierarchy this right no longer exists, and it would be a mistake to think (as I did initially) that prefectural and county-level schools are simply lesser copies of the provincial and central schools. Sub-provincial party schools are a different world from the prospering, even pampered establishments at the Centre and provinces. Indeed, reality at sub-provincial schools presents a picture that is in many respects similar to other local state organizations. Budgetary constraints, leadership neglect, the ubiquity of the use of connections, tokenism in performance and even downright corruption make one understand why the central authorities have lost much of their patience with local party schools and have resorted to the combination of centralization and marketization to insert vitality and relevance in cadre training.

One of my interviewees, a teacher at a Yunnan prefectural school, had recently gone so far as to publish an article in the *Journal of the Yunnan Provincial Party School* about the degradation that he witnessed around him. In the article, he observed that:

Currently, several problems exist in cadre training that cannot be ignored. Judging from the author's investigation, they mainly manifest themselves, firstly, as uneven development. In economically backward areas, the strength and measures taken for cadre training are insufficient. Secondly, the work done is not real. Several areas only care about writing the final report and numbers. Most of what has been laid out in annual work plans is not carried out; annual reports do not match reality, and in several cases even are baseless fabrications. Thirdly, cadre training's loud thunder brings little rain. Much is said and written, but little is actually done.

The erosion of local party schools

Fourthly, in the form and content of training problems of monotony, dullness and inflexibility continue to exist. Training still consists of cramming and spoonfeeding, lacking the vitality and liveliness that it needs. Fifthly, in several places, the problem exists that cadre training only goes through the motions. Sixthly, by not emphasising the actual impact of training and only paying attention to the process, cadre training is not concerned with quality or results and is a waste of time and money. This is as far as training provision is concerned. In addition, many cadres lack enthusiasm about the training they receive. A minority of cadres even thinks that getting on as cadres principally depends on connections and a firm backing. Knowledge and ability are secondary; they therefore think that participation in training is a waste of time. Participation in training is often imposed by higher levels and not done on one's own initiative, and is something that one just has to put up with. Furthermore, there are also cadres who tend actively to participate in training, but who attach more importance to degrees and diplomas than to learning and knowledge; they take professional study, of culture, technology, economics and law, seriously, but treat lightly theoretical study of knowledge about the party, world view, outlook on life and faith in ideals. Their study goal is either just a paper certificate, or else to accommodate temporary requirements, and therefore do not do their best to raise their own overall quality. (Dong Yaming 2003)

During visits to the prefectural schools in Qujing and Honghe and the county-level schools in the urban district of Qilin and the counties of Yiliang and Shilin, all in Yunnan province, I came away with very mixed impressions indeed. Sure enough, all schools had an organizational setup that was a trimmed-down version of higher-level schools, much like other government and party departments at all levels are built on the same template. All schools also fulfilled their core task of teaching short-term main training courses for cadres of the rank appropriate to a school at their level, and organized teaching for correspondence degree courses.

Funding at levels below the province tended to be much less generous than higher up. All schools had responded to the lack of funding by active involvement in the market for degree courses. As discussed in chapter 4, they could only do this by organizing the coursework for degrees of other higher education institutions, capitalizing on their assets (buildings, teaching and administrative staff) and proximity to potential students. One other common adaptation to restricted funding was to merge not only the party school and the academy of administration, but also the local academy of socialism into one institution, a practice frowned upon by higher levels, but probably unavoidable in the absence of targeted central subsidies. This strategy is illustrated in Photo 5.1, with no less than four different signs at

Photo 5.1 Entrance of the Qujing Party School

the entrance of the Qujing Prectural Party School (from right to left party school, academy of administration, academy of socialism, correspondence academy).

However, other responses to the financial realities of local government were perhaps less straightforward, and in several ways compromised at least in part the institutional integrity of such schools. From my limited exposure to just five local party schools in only one province it is obviously difficult to generalize, and indeed at all of the five schools I visited the situation was different. What they all seemed to have in common, however, is that the main financial constraint pertained to the recurrent budgetary allocation from the local government that pays for the salaries of permanent staff (*bianzhi*) and recurrent costs. At Yiliang county, for instance, the party school's budget had been consistently reduced in recent years, forcing the school to send many of their staff on early retirement, leaving only seventeen established staff (including a driver and three administrators), supplemented by external teachers hired for specific sessions or classes. Even so, the school's budget was not enough fully to carry out the tasks assigned

Photo 5.2 Classroom at the party school of Honghe Prefecture

to it in the county cadre education and training plan, and the school relied heavily on income from degree classes to make up the shortfall.[39]

Several schools that faced considerable hardship as far as their annual budgetary allocation was concerned actually occupied spacious new premises. In central and provincial schools, new buildings had been paid for with one-off investment authorized by the planning commission (now development and reform commission). Such projects had been approved under central pressure to strengthen the infrastructure of party training since 2002. However, at the Shilin County Party School self-generated income was the sole source of an investment of 3.2 million yuan in the school's new premises, attesting to the fact that, like so many other local government departments, local party schools were left to fend for themselves.[40]

---

[39] Interview 69, 27 November 2004. Of the student fees of correspondence degrees, the local school can only retain 30 per cent, with the rest going to the provincial and central schools whose degrees the school teaches.

[40] Interview 70, 28 November 2004.

During my interview with him, the head of the Shilin school summarized very candidly what the reduction in budget had led to. At the time of my visit to Shilin in 2004, the county's total budget for cadre training, including such items as expensive inspection and study tours in other parts of China, was two million yuan. However, from this, the party school only received the salaries for its twenty-one staff, the teachers of whom earned a monthly salary of about 1,600 yuan, and forty yuan per main course student per day, a sum that was just enough to cover the cost of their lodging and food. With twenty-one staff and two thousand main course students trained on average for seven days, the total budgetary allocation to the school could therefore not have been more than one million yuan per year. At the same time, the school's total self-generated income (*chuangshou*)[41] was also about one million yuan, of which it could retain and spend about 300,000 yuan,[42] which paid for all other costs, including running the school's office, the maintenance of buildings, equipment and fees for external teachers. The budgetary allocation from the finance department was in fact so low that three of the teachers supplemented their salary with commercial businesses they had set up under their wife's name. Unheard of at higher-level schools, the teacher with the largest business went as far as refusing to join the party, because he felt that this would restrict his freedom in taking care of the business.[43]

Despite its tight budget, the school's contribution to cadre training was important in Shilin, whose Stone Forest only fifty miles from Kunming is a major domestic and international tourist attraction. The fact that two thousand students had taken main courses in 2004 constituted a sharp increase compared to the about five hundred students in the past. The chief explanation for this rise was that cadre training very heavily emphasized the skills required by Shilin's exposure to the outside world: proper Mandarin Chinese (especially important because many local cadres were

---

[41] *Chuangshou* ('creating income') is a pervasive practice within the Chinese state sector. An institution's created income falls outside the regular budget of that institution (and is thus termed 'extrabudgetary') and can be used at its own discretion. Since 2000, the extrabudgetary income of administrative departments and governments has been brought under more direct central control and is now more of a separate funding stream than invisible treasuries completely beyond the scrutiny and control of higher levels as reported on in studies of county administrations in the nineties (Pieke 1996: chapter 4; Wong 1997; 1998; Whiting 2001). Like other departments, party schools first had to transfer their self-created income to the finance department of the higher-level government and then received a fixed percentage back as a separate, 'extrabudgetary' allocation. Furthermore, expenditure from both in-budget and extrabudgetary income had to be approved by the government's finance department. Interview 70, 28 November 2004, and Interview 69, 27 November 2004.

[42] Interview 70, 28 November 2004. [43] Field notes 28 November 2004.

members of non-Han minorities), computer skills, electronic government and English.[44] While this particular school was fully engaged in teaching both main courses and degree courses, in other respects it was at risk of becoming somewhat of an empty shell. Not only was its staff increasingly attracted by the glittering prizes on offer in China's booming market economy, but the main courses taught at the school were predominantly aimed at improving cadres' linguistic and administrative skills with little attention paid to ideological training.

An even more interesting and extreme case of the impact of the market economy on a bulwark of socialist governance was the party school of Qilin city district (a county-level administration) in Qujing prefecture in eastern Yunnan, where capitalism came in the form of the commercialization and privatization of education. In Qilin district, the party school no longer even had its own building: since 2003, it had become simply a sign at the gate at the Qilin district vocational upper middle school.[45] The latter was a semi-private undertaking, and showed all the signs of success: very large, ostentatious premises, well-equipped classrooms, a very comfortable meeting room and a well-rehearsed routine to receive outside visitors. The school mainly catered for the rapidly growing market for vocational training and education, in addition to local government contracts. These contracts did not only include the party school, but also short-term courses for farmers who had been evicted from their land to make room for the district's development zone funded under the national government's programme to open up the west (*xibu da kaifa*). These courses trained farmers before they joined government teams of contract workers that were sent to work in the developed coastal areas in Fujian and Guangdong.

In Qilin, cadre training – and in fact the whole party school – thus had become fully enmeshed with the commercialization of the educational sector. The party school's responsibilities included both short-term (five days) main courses for local township (*zhen*) and street (*jiedao*) cadres of section or deputy section (*zhengke* or *fuke*) rank, main courses for deputy office (*fuchu*) level cadres in the urban district, and *xueli* degree courses of the Yunnan Teachers College, the Central Party School and the Provincial Party School at the middle vocational, upper vocational and undergraduate level. Because the party school only received an annual budget of 100,000 yuan and six staff from the district government, most of the teaching was

---

[44] Interview 70, 28 November 2004.
[45] See their brochure 'A short introduction to the national level keypoint vocational school the *Qujing City Qilin District Vocational High-level Middle School*' (Guojiaji zhongdian zhixiao *Qujing Qilin qu zhiye gaoji zhongxue* jianjie).

done by hiring in teachers from the prefectural party school, from Yunnan Teachers College, or from elsewhere in the area.[46]

From my interviews at the school it remained unclear what exactly the incentive structure was that made the party school's tasks attractive to the middle school, but obviously the arrangement was part of a wider web of relations and transactions between the local government and the school's leadership. What is clear from this example and the previous one is that the financial constraints of county-level governments made operating fully independent party schools a very difficult proposition. As in many other policy areas, central government requirements put a great strain on county governments, while the same central government simultaneously reduced their fiscal autonomy and sources of extrabudgetary income. In the case of party schools, considerable creativity has been applied to come up with workable arrangements that would allow party schools to be in effect cross-subsidized by commercial activities going beyond the profitable degree teaching that had already been an important source of income for a long time. In sum, even in cadre training, the ideological heart of Leninist governance, the impact of market reforms was increasingly felt, and, as so often, this happened first and most visibly at the lowest levels of government.

However, financial constraints are not the only contributory factor to the erosion of local party schools. As we have seen in chapter 2, policies since 2000 have quite deliberately allowed for competition between different providers of cadre training in an attempt to break down the monopoly of party schools. The effect of this was clearly visible at the prefectural party school in Honghe in southern Yunnan during my visit in 2004. According to the signs outside the school's main entrance, the party school doubles up not only as the academy of administration and the school of socialism, but also as the school for minority cadres of whom there are many in this southern frontier area. However, unlike the provincial party school or even the prefectural school in Qujing, these multiple signs turned out to be just that: mere signs. The school itself only occupied itself with party school cadre training and teaching for various degree courses, but had little to do with the organization of the various forms of non-party cadre training that fall under the headings of the academy of administration, the school of socialism and the school for minority cadres. Instead of being a comprehensive institution for all aspects of cadre training, the school merely provided teachers, classrooms and boarding facilities if requested by other local administrative agencies.

---

[46] Field notes 18 November 2004.

Training of non-CCP leading cadres, the prerogative of the school of socialism, was fully in the hands of the CCP's United Front Department. During my visit, the 'sixth non-CCP leading cadre training class' was just underway, and it was quite revealing how little the school's administrators knew or cared about it, despite the fact that many of their teachers (including one of the deputy heads of the school herself!) had been enlisted to teach specific sessions. Yet this, as a non-CCP cadre course, was the responsibility of the school of socialism, which was, as in all other prefectures in Yunnan, part of the party school's remit. The deputy head of the united front department, who was in charge of the course, explained the role of his own department and that of the school of socialism as follows:

Each year at the beginning of the year, the cadre education committee of the Honghe prefecture party committee draws up a cadre training plan, and each year this course must be offered. This falls under the united front department's own plan that we coordinate with the cadre education committee. Their general plan incorporates the united front department's own plan. The cadre education committee's plan is shaped from top to bottom. After a course is over we have to submit a written report for filing. The responsibility to draw up the [united front department's] education plan lies with our cadre section, after which we consult and report to the school of socialism. As a final step, it is examined and approved by the cadre education committee. QUESTION: Why do you offer the course here [at the party school]? ANSWER: This is a school for cadre training, their focus is on adult training. The emphasis of training organized by the government's personnel bureau is professional training, but much of this course is about inculcating political theory... We have contact with the school of socialism, because our training tasks are the same. Our training is also a task in the school of socialism's own training plan, and they provide their classrooms free of charge. It is their task to make sure that they consult with related departments.[47]

It is quite interesting that in the above quote the head of the united front mentions that the fact that this course is also part of the party school's educational plan as a reason for organizing the course here. However, on the very next day I interviewed a deputy head of the party school, who explained the lack of involvement in the organization of the course exactly because it was not part of the school's plan. Clearly, the language of bureaucratic planning was employed very differently by these two informants to describe and rationalize the reality of the school's uncomfortable position in the local administration.

A similar situation existed regarding other types of training as well. Categorical courses for female cadres, for instance, although taught at the school, were considered the women's federation's responsibility and not

---

[47] Interview 78, 1 December 2004.

part of the school's plan. As far as minority cadre training was concerned, more cooperation between the school and the government's minority committee existed, and the school helped the committee in finding teachers and designing the courses. However, under the prefectural cadre education plan minority cadre courses continued to be considered principally the responsibility of the prefectural government's minority committee. As a result, the committee liaised directly with the party's organization department in selecting students and with the government's finance department to obtain funds. Interestingly, no mention of the party's united front department was made, whose involvement in minority work was much less than with non-CCP cadre work.[48] In the case of training courses that are part of the academy of administration's remit, the situation was even more extreme. Disagreements with the government's personnel bureau had led to the almost complete removal of all courses from the party school's premises. Instead, the personnel bureau had made alternative arrangements with other schools in the area and only a few novice civil servant training courses were held at the party school.[49]

Marketization, budget constraints and central policy are eroding the institutional integrity of party schools. This has had a particularly adverse impact on low-level party schools that, unlike national and provincial schools, are very small institutions that have been consistently starved of funding. Furthermore, smaller local party schools find it increasingly hard to compete in this market because cadre training now emphasizes professional over ideological skills. Public universities, large party schools and other institutions for higher learning are much better equipped to provide such training than the small and understaffed party schools in counties and prefectures. A final reason that local party schools are losing out in the market is that cadre training and education have become somewhat of an item of conspicuous consumption. As in many companies in the capitalist west, training has become a way to award and incentivize employees, and is as much a way of tying them to the company as to equip them with new skills and knowledge. Against that background, the local party school quite simply is no longer up to it as far as China's increasingly demanding cadres are concerned.

---

[48] Interview 85, 2 December 2004; see also Interview 80, 2 December 2004, and Interview 78, 1 December 2004.
[49] Field notes 1 and 3 December 2004; Interview 80, 2 December 2004.

CHAPTER 6

Cadre training, cadre careers and the changing composition of China's political elite

As this book has shown, the training and education of cadres are essential elements of China's cadre management system. The recruitment, promotion, placement, assessment, further education, remuneration and discipline that shape the careers of Chinese cadres are all punctuated by frequent participation in a plethora of training courses specifically designed for the political and professional needs of cadres. Equally important, the pursuit of educational qualifications, from middle vocational all the way to doctoral degrees, and public examinations for specific posts increasingly determine the twists and turns of an individual's career.

In this final substantive chapter I will analyse some of the many connections between cadre training and education, the cadre management system, cadre careers and, ultimately, the composition of China's ruling elite. I will first discuss the expectations, experiences and opinions of cadres about the role of education and training in their own work and career development, followed by a discussion of the fit – or lack thereof – between the realities of cadres' daily work and the party's requirements and ambitions. I will then turn to an analysis of the career paths of leading cadres in Yunnan, and the impact that recent reforms in cadre management had at the time of my fieldwork in 2004 and 2005. In the final section I will turn to the implications of the rise in the status of professional training and qualifications and the composition of China's cadre corps. Although I do not believe that professional, less ideologically committed cadres necessarily spells the death of socialism, the emergence of such a stratum of expert cadres nevertheless has profound implications for the relationship between the party, the administrative system and individual cadres. Furthermore, the prioritization of professional qualifications and knowledge also potentially increases the tension between expert cadres and the more traditional kinds of cadres who in many places are still the backbone of the party's rule. The current very heavy emphasis on and investment in cadre training, I argue, are in part intended to resolve the ago-old Maoist problem of the tension between expertise and ideological merit. Training attempts to instil socialist virtues into professional experts, while raising the educational and professional qualifications of more traditional cadres.

CADRE TRAINING AND EDUCATION: EXPECTATIONS AND EXPERIENCES

The good sides of coming here to the provincial party school are, first, your thinking and ideology undergo a definite change; second, you learn about new circumstances and information; third, you make new friends and these new relations will help you in your work later on. And the standpoint of some of the teachers is also worth taking note of. All five times that I have received training were arranged by the organization department... It is a requirement of the job... The most valuable aspect of studying is that, although we study in our spare time when we are working [literally, when we are at lower levels, *zai xiamian*], this is not as systematic. But up to now there has been nothing that's been taught here that I didn't already know. It's just that they teach more systematically and completely here.[1]

The informant I am quoting here tried to give a positive but realistic picture of what training at party schools meant for him as a party member and a career bureaucrat. His comments fairly represent the sentiments and opinion of the majority of cadres who I interviewed. However, having said that, among my informants a range of opinions was represented. A few informants thought that the training they received at party schools was useless, often because they were not fully committed to their official duties anyway, or because they had very frequently been through many similar training classes in the past, or else because they attended a course at a low level school with bad or uninteresting instruction. At the other extreme were those informants who had just been promoted to their first leading cadre position. They tended to be extremely positive about their training, especially valuing the 'theoretical' parts of the curriculum: their eagerness to become a good cadre translated effortlessly into a desire to immerse themselves into the policies, laws and ideology that together constitute 'theory'.

None of the informants questioned the importance and use of ideological knowledge. They all believed strongly in the necessity to study ideology in order to build their 'party spirit'; at the same time, they did not necessarily treat this ideology as something that they had to believe in at a fundamental and deeply personal level. Time and again, ideology was presented as useful

[1] Interview 29, 16 April 2004.

and important. Ideology was knowledge that had to be studied, understood and learned in order to do their job in the way that the party expected and demanded. In other words, 'theory' in the context of cadre training and administrative work is an adaptable framework of ideas that guides the generation of bureaucratic action. Theory is a *pragmatic* and organizational ideology that is neither simply learned theoretical knowledge nor a deeply felt individual belief or set of shared cultural assumptions. Instead, it operates in between these two extremes, and can best be characterized as a habitual disposition that, paradoxically, is deliberately acquired and maintained. In this context discussions about the truth or falsehood of this ideology were completely pointless. Leading cadres are professionals who are paid to believe the most recent version of the party's orthodoxy as far as it is necessary to understand and produce the language of the administration and to carry out their job according to the wishes and desires of the 'higher levels'.

The importance attached to theory, ideology and up-to-date knowledge was borne out by the results of the questionnaire survey of cadre-students at the Yunnan Provincial Party School in 2005. Respondents were asked which aspect of their training course they valued most and which they valued least. The most useful aspect of the course was judged as 'latest knowledge' (38 per cent) followed by 'basic theory' (26 per cent), 'the ability to carry out one's job' (19 per cent) and 'administration according to the law' (13 per cent). Cadres clearly first and foremost expected to be informed on recent developments, policies and research in China and abroad. However, perhaps most telling about these findings is the fact that, despite the central leadership's commitment to the rule of law, cadres at the Yunnan Provincial Party School still ranked legal knowledge much lower than its supposedly old-fashioned Leninist counterpart 'basic theory' (see Table 6.1). Conversely, when asked which aspect of the course they found the least useful, only 7 per cent of respondents answered 'basic theory', again attesting to its perceived relevance. Contrary to what teaching staff at this school and many others routinely said in interviews, computer use, electronic government and public relations skills were deemed to be the least useful (see Table 6.2).

The emphasis on theory, knowledge, study and learning not only reflects a blend of Leninist democratic centralism and a technocratic commitment to modernization and 'scientific' rule, but also reveals a certain continuity with China's Maoist past. Mao, perhaps more than any other revolutionary Communist leader in China, believed in the power of ideological study in shaping 'correct' thinking. Yet the end product of Maoist and contemporary

Table 6.1 *Opinion on most useful part of course*

	No.	%
Basic theory	91	26.3
Latest knowledge	131	37.9
Ability to carry out one's job	64	18.5
Administration according to the law	45	13
Image building	5	1.4
Electronic government skills	8	2.3
Other	2	0.6
Total	346	100

Source: Yunnan Party School student survey 2005

Table 6.2 *Opinion on least useful aspect of course*

	No.	%
Basic theory	12	6.9
Latest knowledge	7	4
Ability to carry out one's job	13	7.4
Administration according to the law	3	1.7
Image building	63	36
Electronic government skills	20	11
Other	57	33
Total	175	100

Source: Yunnan Party School student survey 2005

ideological study could hardly be more different. The current pragmatic, bureaucratic and unreflexive quality of ideological commitment contrasts sharply with the revolutionary zeal cultivated and expected of cadres and activists during the heydays of Maoism in the fifties and sixties. This pragmatic quality of ideology often revealed itself in the remarkably bland statements informants came up with when asked what the party's ideology meant for them personally. To quote the same informant that I started this section with again:

I became a party member in 1986. At the time I was deputy head of a middle school. To be precise, my understanding of the party was insufficiently deep, I myself found that I was only just qualified. At the time, people mobilized me to contribute my wisdom and ability to the country. Nowadays, my understanding of how to be a Communist Party member in reality means to do some things for the masses, to restrain yourself, a plain and simple ideology. I have also studied some theory myself.[2]

Clearly, despite very frequent training at party schools, years of active duty have rubbed the edges of this informant's personal version of socialism, leaving only a general commitment to public service. Yet this is not to say that ideology is therefore unimportant, and the survey revealed that cadres themselves certainly did not think so. The emphasis on learning and knowledge in official discourse as the key to responsible and modern rule had spilled over in my informants' attitude to the education or training they received at party schools. Indeed, the value of knowledge has become so deeply ingrained in China's cadres that almost all informants expressed the need and relevance of education and training, not only to gain promotions or to better understand central policy and ideological developments, but also genuinely in order to do their job better. Central stock phrases were routinely invoked to express the hope and expectation that education and training would help them deal more 'scientifically' with the often intractable problems of local administration. Yet when pushed for examples of the use of the knowledge gained during training, replies were not terribly convincing.

Six months after I started working in a township I came up against the following issue. A few years earlier, land had been appropriated to build a new road, and some money was still owed to the local people. Because of the financial difficulties of the local government, there were insufficient funds for full compensation as a lump sum, so the government came up with a compensation scheme with annual payments of twenty per cent, resulting in full compensation in five years. Yet in January of this year [2004, FP], due to financial difficulties, although the county once again could only repay ten per cent, they had not informed the local people who were living along the road. So a misunderstanding arose among the people, they found it hard to accept that the standard of repayment had been lowered, saying they did not insist on the money, but that they demanded a statement. We began compensation work in the morning and had to persist until the afternoon when the people finally gradually began to understand. The masses agreed that the compensation fund would be taken away, but stated that they wanted to raise the situation with the higher authorities. In this matter, I think that is was not good that we did not give prior notice to the people of the lower standard of compensation, but only dealt with it afterwards; I also felt that I lacked the work methods to convince the masses. In the end, we had to work through our own

[2] Interview 29, 16 April 2004.

relatives. We used family and personal connections to resolve the contradictions, and only gradually was the problem resolved. I very much need thought work methods, I need to improve and update my knowledge.[3]

On the whole, cadres are very appreciative of the opportunity for training at a party school, which to them is also a way to understand better what the most recent political trends are at higher levels. However, quite often cadres were more than a little impatient with the limits of party training. It was often felt that many teachers had little to say about the practical aspects of leadership and administration, and often could not sufficiently relate the contents of a lecture to the issues and problems that their students would have to face again upon return to their job. However, this problem had just as much to do with the very nature of party training as with the quality of teachers. As we have seen, despite the profession of the unity of theory and practice, cadre training first and foremost remained a matter of the transmission and imposition of orthodoxy. Teachers were under constant scrutiny by a hierarchy of party institutions that started with the school's educational affairs bureau and ultimately ended with the Politburo in Beijing: they simply could not stray from the party line in their recommendations and suggestions.

Cadres at party schools respond to training like critical consumers. Such an attitude implies a certain passivity and deliberate lack of full involvement: cadres expect to receive a systematic treatment of the most recent and important ideological, policy and legal trends. Despite all the recent talk on innovative and interactive teaching methods in cadre training, this attitude of cadres translates into a clear preference for traditional teaching methods, especially lectures and seminar classes. In the 2005 survey of cadre-students at the Yunnan Provincial Party School, lectures as a method of training was consistently regarded as the best teaching method irrespective of gender or rank. Of the 350 respondents, 132 (38 per cent) identified lectures as the best method, followed by seminar classes (105, or 31 per cent) and case analyses (86, or 25 per cent). Exceptions were cadres of the lowest (*fuke*, or deputy section) and the highest (*zhengting*, or full provincial department) rank present at the school. Among those with *fuke* rank, 46 per cent found seminar classes the most useful. Those of the highest *zhengting* rank found case analysis (50 per cent) or simulation exercises (50 per cent) the most useful form of training and lectures the least. Except *zhengting* cadres, all ranks clearly found simulation exercises the worst method (see Table 6.3).

[3] Interview 6, 4 April 2004.

Table 6.3 *Students' opinion on teaching methods*

	Best method		Good method		Not very good method		Worst method	
	No.	%	No.	%	No.	%	No.	%
Lecture	132	38	105	34	37	17	42	22
Seminar classes	105	31	107	35	39	18	28	15
Case analysis	86	25	81	26	70	33	12	6
Simulation	21	6	14	5	69	32	110	57
Total	344	100	307	100	215	100	192	100

Source: Yunnan Party School student survey 2005

Training at a party school is valuable not only because of the formal teaching provided. Indeed, many informants mentioned that the opportunity to mix with a variety of other cadres was equally as important. Trainees value the opportunity for formal and informal discussions with other students, and learning from each other is often more important than learning from teachers.

My training class has seventy-three students. There are many opportunities for socializing and discussion. Everybody is from different work units and areas, so we can draw on each other's strengths and complement our weaknesses in conversations and discussions, increasing the depth of our reflection on issues. This kind of socializing is rather informal, and I also talk with students of other classes, but not as much as with students from my own class.[4]

Formal discussions take place regularly, usually at least once a week in the afternoon when there are no lectures, and are organized by the groups (*zu*) that make up a class (*ban*). Classes and groups play an important role in the life of students at the party school. Each class has assigned to it a teacher who acts as the head of class (*ban zhuren*). The head of the class is responsible for communication between the school's administration and the students, organizing events, keeping student attendance at lectures and ultimately reporting about student performance. Unlike class heads, the head of a group is one of the students and the events organized by the group have to do just as much with formal learning as leisure activities, such as sports matches, trips or simply just meals outside the school. Very importantly, the classes and groups coincide with the temporary party branches and small groups that tie all party members among the students

[4] Interview 11, 5 April 2004.

and staff into the party hierarchy under the school's party committee. The branches and groups play a role in study and leisure activities, and in party organizational and investigation work. From the students' perspective, the blending of the formal and informal in the functioning of temporary party branches and groups adds an important dimension to party membership, driving home the message that party membership is important if one wants to be a fully functioning member of the administration. At the party school, cadres learn (again) that the party is more than a professional organization, but a way of life that quite deliberately blurs the distinction between the public and the private.

With the exception of just a very few students, all informants reported having an extensive network of acquaintances among their fellow students.

I speak with other students but do not make many friends, friends are too precious, friendship must follow from the feelings of the two people involved. I frequently interact with people from my own class and also often from my own home area... That's because they are *laoxiang* [people from the same area] with a common language and similar opinions about issues. There are frequent common activities, such a trips or ball games. In addition, I also have acquaintances from other areas. My own class has twenty-one students, they all have the same profession and they all take the same classes. After graduation, I will stay in touch with some of my fellow students and other acquaintances, both from my own area and from other prefectures in Yunnan.[5]

As this informant suggests, even more important than the social activities organized by classes and party branches are the many forms of socializing that take place outside formal settings. Socializing with people outside one's class often takes place on the basis of common area of origin or ethnicity. In at least one case, these networks had attained a considerable degree of formality.

I have contact with students from my own prefecture and county and in my own class. Although the students in my class are not from the same minority, we are very tolerant of each other. If you do many things together you get along without constraints. I already knew the students from my own prefecture because I met them in the course of my work. One from among the students from my prefecture who was already here is responsible, he is called 'director' [*lishi*]. He is responsible for registering the students from our prefecture, getting people together and setting up leisure activities in order to promote the bond [*ganqing*] between them.[6]

Networks and social activities on the basis of common origin at the school play an important role in reinforcing and extending the hierarchically embedded communities of cadres that, as we will see in the next section,

[5] Interview 3, 3 April 2004.   [6] Interview 6, 4 April 2004.

are an important component of the CCP's mode of governance at the local level. This function is likely the reason that such networks and activities are tolerated at party schools. Although area of origin and ethnicity are accepted aspects of the social life at school, the party is also concerned that they could undermine the solidarity of all cadres and the role of the party as the core of cadre identity. Cadres should remain principally *party* cadres and not become local leaders with an independent power base. Activities of party branches are therefore promoted. In fact, at the Yunnan Provincial Party School it was formally forbidden to organize sports teams on the basis of ethnicity.[7] Party branches were the preferred principle in setting up teams, although sometimes teams were drawn from students from the same area of origin.

Study or training at the party school is a valuable opportunity to socialize with people from other areas as much as one's own. These people may not be immediately relevant to one's work now, but could become important contacts after a future promotion and appointment at a higher level. This aspect of cadre training is brought out in especially sharp relief at smaller local party schools where the quality and relevance of instruction often leaves something to be desired. As we saw in chapter 5, in my own fieldwork the Honghe Prefectural Party School was the clearest example of a troubled local school, and several students and teachers who I interviewed there minced few words. One seasoned teacher presented a particularly candid assessment of the attitude of students and the quality of instruction, and it is worth quoting him at some greater length.

In my opinion it is possible to raise [students'] professional capacity, but it is very hard to solve ideological problems. Some leading cadres suffer from the Chinese official's mentality of only thinking about their own department, and they still believe in fate, relying on the outcome of fortune-telling to determine their enthusiasm for study. They lack the attitude of serving the people, serving the taxpayers... Students on main training courses do not have to sit an examination, and students on main courses for young cadres only have to cultivate their relationships with their teachers and fellow students, because getting a good evaluation is all they need. More than half of the students on main courses ask for leave all the time... In class mobile phones ring constantly, and each time you ask them to shut off their mobiles only a few students genuinely comply... QUESTION: Why do students cultivate relationships? ANSWER: To recommend each other for promotions and to help each other get transferred to good departments and areas. Some cadres say that relationships are a production force [*guanxi shi shengchanli*]. If it were proper public relations it would indeed be a production force, but for some cadres using connections in reality is a private transaction. QUESTION: So

---

[7] Interview 8, 4 April 2004.

what is the use of cadre training in such a situation? ANSWER: Because of these problems the Centre has initiated a transformation of work style, and as a result a considerable number of changes have emerged in cadre training work... Informal organization in the main courses comes about because of professional or personal needs. Of course there are also students who demonstrate a good attitude [biaoxian], but they are a minority. Once the management system has been improved it will be better. Originally management was already very strict, but then it loosened up, causing the problems mentioned above. We do have a system, but it is not strictly enforced. The system is stuck on walls, spoken about, and then locked away in a drawer and not put into practice.[8]

This unflattering picture of cadre training at local party schools is at odds with the genuine enthusiasm that I encountered among many students at the provincial school in Yunnan. However, the attitude of students in Honghe highlights the fact that cadre training at all party schools serves an important function, no matter how good or bad the teaching is. At the end of the day, at all schools cadres attend the short-term training because they have to, whether or not they appreciate the training they receive. Even at the worst schools cadres will pick up updates on current policies and legislation, and often gain from the discussions in class. They may also very well gain from training in certain skills, in particular the use of computers. However, as with so many other courses and schools around the world, the most important gains of education are not in the curriculum, but in the experience. Cadre training is an experiential realization of belonging to the party or state apparatus. It is thus a form of socialization and exercise in community formation in which even boredom and wasted time serve a function: it makes cadres feel they are different, set apart from the public, and are special in their belonging to something most people are excluded from. Equally important, in cadre training students learn as much from other students as from their teachers, and the relationships formed during training are an important lubricant of the administrative system. Much time during training courses is spent talking, smoking, eating and drinking and playing sports with other cadres, establishing and cultivating relationships that may not only help getting transferred to a good job, but also make the solution of some future problem at work perhaps only one mobile phone call away. Non-vocational political training is especially well suited for this, because it is only here that cadres meet others who are not normally employed in their own specialized area. In this sense, the very lack of substance and generality of ideological training allows cadres from across the administration to meet, live, work, eat and drink together.

[8] Interview 76, 1 December 2004.

Cadre careers 151

Viewed from this angle, party schools are much more than the austere guardians of ideological orthodoxy and party discipline. Party schools are, in fact, rather similar to households. As Janet Carsten has shown, the materiality, co-residence and commensality of households not simply reflect but actually *produce* kinship relations (Carsten 1997). Similarly, cadre training at party schools supplements and reinforces the formal structures of the party and government. Ideological training gives cadres a common language and a set of tasks. These in turn facilitate the growth of informal communities of cadres that shape cadre careers and lubricate the functioning of the institutions of governance.

CADRE CAREERS

The career of many leading cadres in Yunnan at the provincial level or below follows a well-established pattern. Initially, cadres are recruited into the administration as high school or university graduates, often after working for a period of time in a non-administrative career such as teaching. Identified as people of promise, these bright young graduates are one day invited over for a conversation at their local (county or urban district) organization department. Starting them initially in non-leading cadre positions, the organization department subsequently selects some of them for the crucial career step of promotion to the lowest rung on the leading cadre hierarchy (i.e. deputy section (*fuke*) level). The organization department then rotates them in several jobs at that level before promotion to full section (*zhengke*) level.[9]

When I interviewed He in 2004 he was a full-time second year master's student of economics at the Yunnan Provincial Party School. In 1992 he had graduated from Yunnan Normal University. In that year, a total of twenty-six students from his native county in Kunming city graduated from Yunnan Normal University. At the time, the local Communist Youth League needed new cadres at the township level and recruited four people from among these twenty-six graduates. He was one of them. His post as a youth league official in a township and his second appointment in the county organization department were at ordinary cadre level, but in 1998 he was promoted to *fuke* rank, taking up the post of party secretary of a township discipline inspection committee. In 2000 he was promoted to *zhengke* rank and was given the job of party secretary of the county's youth league.[10]

---

[9] Stig Thøgersen's 2004 research in Xuanwei county in eastern Yunnan corroborates this pattern and several other findings from my own research reported on in this section and the next (Thøgersen 2008).
[10] Interview 17, 10 April 2004.

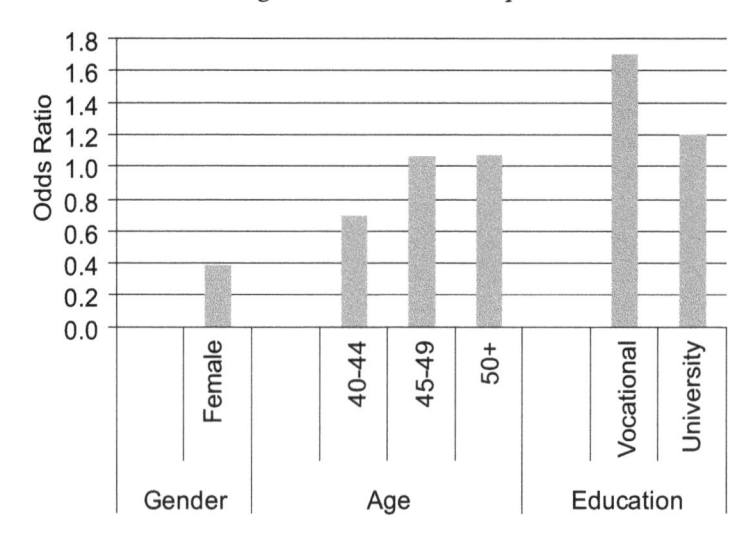

Figure 6.1 Odds of rank mobility by gender, age and education
SOURCE: Yunnan Party School student survey 2005

Such posts at *zhengke* level give cadres the opportunity to demonstrate their worth at direct executive responsibility, usually culminating in a stint as full head or party secretary of a town or township. If successful enough, these cadres are then slated for further promotion to deputy office (*fuchu*) and full office (*zhengchu*) rank, at which point their career management is taken over by the organization department of the prefecture. For a selected few, this pattern eventually repeats itself with promotion to deputy department (*futing*) and full department (*zhengting*) rank and management by the provincial organization department. At each level, a cadre usually serves in several posts of the same rank; only in exceptional circumstances is a cadre made to serve more than two terms (each previously three years and currently five years) in the same position.

During an individual career, changes in rank are usually upward, although downward mobility (demotion) also occurs. In the 2005 survey, we asked about jobs and ranks in the five-year period before the survey, and analysed the impact of background variables, including gender, age and education, on the chance (or technically odds, with odds of 1 being neutral, a figure below 1 indicating negative odds, and a figure above 1 indicating positive odds) of being promoted or demoted, defined as the difference in rank between the first and the last job in that period.

As we can see from Figure 6.1, the most salient finding was that women were more likely to remain at the same rank in the five-year period than men, while conversely men were more likely to be promoted: the chance (odds) of a promotion for a woman in our sample during the five-year period was 62 per cent less than that of a man,[11] translating into 32 per cent of women and 51 per cent of men gaining a promotion. The percentage of demotions in our sample was much smaller than that of either promotions or no change, and was about equal for both sexes (15 per cent for men and 12 per cent for women).

Second, education has a positive impact on a cadre's career prospects. Interestingly enough, the impact of a pre-university 'vocational' (*zhongzhuan* or *dazhuan*) degree is considerably stronger than that of a university degree. Having a vocational degree increases the odds of a promotion by 70 per cent, a university degree a mere 20 per cent.[12] This confirms that, in Yunnan at least, having a vocational degree is now almost a prerequisite for an official career, whereas a university degree will definitely help, but is (not yet) uniformly expected.

Third, among men, the more upwardly mobile gender, promotions are much more common early on in their career. As is shown in Figure 6.1, the odds of promotion are actually 25 per cent *less* for the 40–44 cohort than for their juniors, and only recover somewhat to 7 per cent for the oldest two cohorts (45–49 and 50+).[13] In the youngest age group (younger than forty years old), 59 per cent of respondents ($N = 161$) had gained a promotion. Conversely, in the middle age group (40–44 years old), only 42 per cent had been promoted in the previous five years.[14] This finding confirmed the impression from several interviews, when respondents complained that it was extremely difficult to gain a promotion beyond a certain age. Due to the age restrictions imposed on promotions, cadres who had not made it to *chu* level at forty or so should realistically no longer expect a rank

---

[11] This result is statistically significant at the $p < 0.05$ level.
[12] However, it should be emphasized that these results are not significant at the $p < 0.05$ level, most likely indicating that education has only a supplementary impact in explaining the odds of promotion. The lack of statistical significance indicates that the result could have been a matter of mere chance, and is a common issue with small sample sizes.
[13] However, as with education, these results are not statistically significant at the $p < 0.05$ level.
[14] Later on their professional life, chances of promotion among our respondents increased again, with 50 per cent of the forty-five- to forty-nine-year-olds and a full 61 per cent of those of fifty and over having experienced promotion. However, this finding means little, as most of the older respondents would have been from the classes for the highest ranking cadres at the school. In other words, they would have been mostly those cadres in these age categories who had already made the crucial promotion from *chu* to *ting* level, while the ones who had not made that promotion would be much less likely to return to the party school for retraining. This is a clear case of sampling on the dependent variable. Given that the same selectivity also applies to at least some respondents in the younger age cohorts in our sample, the drop in promotions among the forty- to forty-five-year-olds is even more remarkable.

promotion. The bottleneck created by these restrictions is a strong source of dissatisfaction among cadres, who feel that they still have their best years ahead, yet are not given the chance to realize their potential. The same bottleneck effect was not apparent among women in our sample, which may have been caused, among other things, by the fact that women were much less likely to be promoted in the first place.

However, even for the relatively few who make it through the career bottleneck by gaining a promotion to *chu* or even *ting* level and see their career develop well into their early or even mid-fifties, career progression eventually plateaus at a particular level. A tell-tale sign of this is when a cadre after a few years at a particular level fails to gain appointment to a 'number one' post (*yi ba shou*), usually the head or party secretary of a particular area (i.e. township, county or prefecture).[15] When further promotion is not an option, the individual will continue to receive new postings as head or party secretary of bureaus at the same level in the area under the jurisdiction of their organization department. At some point, an appointment to a post without direct executive responsibility, for instance in the local people's congress or people's consultative conference, is usually the signal that a particular individual should prepare for retirement, usually at the age of sixty, serving out his or her days at the current bureaucratic rank and jurisdiction.

At the earlier stages of a career, a certain degree of specialization is not uncommon, although even then the first few posts often have very little to do with the newcomer's educational background or previous work. It is striking that many mid and late career cadres are used for their general leadership qualities rather than their specialist knowledge or experience, particularly once a cadre has served a stint in a 'number one' post and thus has proven his or her political, in addition to merely professional, credentials.[16] Many cadres are moved freely between different functional areas of the administration (propaganda, economic management, finance, education, rural affairs, and so on), often requiring substantial training and on-the-job learning each time they take on a new post. Furthermore, organization departments treat all parts of the administration as one chessboard. At different times, cadres may work stints in posts in the party, the government, the people's congress, the people's consultative conference, the judiciary or mass organizations (principally the youth league and the women's federation).

---

[15] Interview 29, 16 April 2004.
[16] For a similar conclusion regarding provincial leaders, see Bo 2002, pp. 116–117; for township cadres, see Thøgersen 2008: 418.

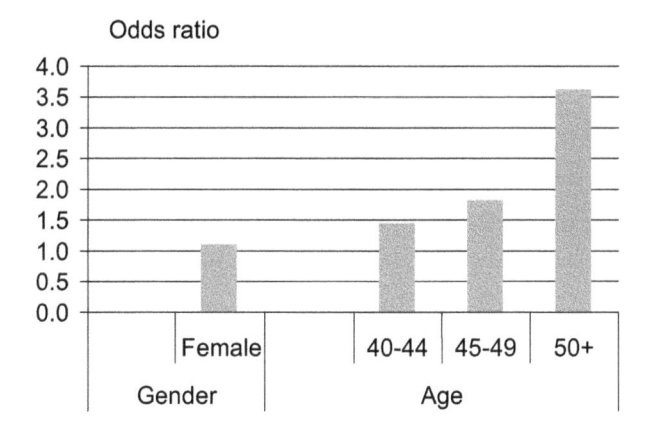

Figure 6.2 Crossover of units by age and gender
SOURCE: Yunnan Party School student survey 2005 ($N = 210$)

These findings from the interviews are confirmed by analysis of our 2005 survey. By comparing the first and last employment in the five-year period before the survey, we calculated the odds that respondents had moved between a party, government, people's congress, people's consultative conference, mass organization, service organization or state enterprise.[17] While the majority (about 60 per cent) of both men and women had stayed in the same part of the administration (which we will refer to as 'unit' below), the chance of cross-unit mobility rose markedly with age. Over 70 per cent of women and 50 per cent of men of fifty years and older worked in another part of the administration at the end of the five year period from where they had started out. In Figure 6.2 we present the odds ratio for crossover of units. Women have a 9 per cent increased likelihood of a cross-unit shift during the five-year period when compared against men. Increasing age is associated with increasing probability of cross-unit shift (the results show a 46 per cent excess at age 40–44, 82 per cent at age 45–49 and a 3.6-fold excess at 50 or over.[18]

From these findings we conclude that, at the level of governmental practice, there continues to be a very deliberate lack of separation of powers, despite elaborate institutional arrangements that might give another impression. This also is a vivid testimony of how cadre management is a

---

[17] For the sake of completeness, we also included 'joint venture' and 'private enterprise' as options in the survey, but only one respondent reported having moved to a joint venture and none to a private enterprise, which is obviously to be expected of a sample of cadres at a party school.
[18] However, only the last of these is statistically significant at $p < 0.05$.

key manifestation of the party's exercise of its leading role across all formal institutions of governance, including, of course, the party itself.

When I interviewed Li at the Yunnan Provincial Party School in 2004 he was fifty-four years old. He was undergoing his eighth training stint at the provincial school since his appointment in 1983 as head of his home county in Dehong prefecture. Li originally had only received lower middle school education because of the Cultural Revolution, but as a member of the Achang minority, a few years later he had been given the chance to study Chinese language and literature for two years at the Yunnan Minority Academy. After graduation in 1975, Li was allocated to work in his county as party secretary of a village office [*cungongsuo*] and then as a journalist before his first leading cadre posting as deputy head of the county propaganda department. In 1983, Li was promoted again and served three terms as head of the county. According to Li, his chief responsibility in this post was to ensure ethnic stability, as most of the people in the county were, like he himself, from the Achang minority. However, his abilities must have been greater than that, because in 1993 he was appointed county party secretary, which is fairly unusual in minority areas where this post tends to be given to an outsider and member of the Han majority. In 1995, he was promoted to deputy head of Dehong prefecture, serving seven years in this post before being moved to the post of deputy head of the prefecture's people's congress.[19]

The career of cadres I encountered at the Yunnan Provincial Party School started at the earliest in the very last years of the pre-reform era. Their background and outlook is therefore different from the first cohort of local leaders in China with direct personal experience of the pre-1949 revolution or the earliest stages of socialist transformation. They are also different from many local cadres who were recruited in the heyday of Maoism in the sixties and early seventies. The latter were often poorly educated, having been selected more for their 'redness' then their 'expertise'.[20] As Andrew Walder has shown, in the post-Mao years education has become the most important determinant of recruitment into both the party and the cadre ranks (Walder 2004: 201–205). In my research even cadres from minority areas who had been given special allowances in their recruitment and promotion had at the very least a lower middle school and usually a middle vocational degree upon recruitment. Nevertheless, despite the

[19] Summarized from interview 15, 8 April 2004.
[20] On the transition between cadre cohorts, see Lee 1991. In the eighties, the pre-reform generations were rapidly eased aside. For instance, Xueguang Zhou, using survey data from 1987, found that political cadres already had higher educational levels than ordinary, non-political administrators (Zhou 1995: 458). Richard Madsen captures the difference between the two cohorts well by calling the former 'Communist gentry' and the latter 'Communist rebel'; see Madsen 1984, chapter 9; Chan, Madsen and Unger 1992.

Table 6.4 *Father's and mother's most recent occupation before retirement*

	Father's Occupation		Mother's Occupation	
	No.	%	No.	%
Worker	29	11.6	45	16.9
Villager	67	26.7	104	39.1
Civil Servant	96	38.2	53	19.9
Management	15	6	6	2.3
Professional	26	10.4	25	9.4
Military	8	3.2	0	0
Other	10	4	33	12.4
Total	251	100	266	100

Source: Yunnan Party School student survey 2005

emphasis on formal education, surprisingly many cadres interviewed were from a relatively modest background, usually children of local cadres or school teachers, rather than middle-class professional backgrounds where one might expect a very heavy emphasis on educational achievement (see Table 6.4). This was also reflected in the 2005 survey. Almost 40 per cent of the fathers of respondents were or had been cadres, while more than a quarter of the fathers and almost 40 per cent of the mothers were villagers. Clearly, the cadre corps in Yunnan province tends to be a relatively closed elite with new recruits coming mainly from rural backgrounds. We should, of course, not over-interpret the relatively modest number of cadres from the working or middle classes, which after all are still relatively small in a poor province like Yunnan. However, at the very least it is clear that there is not, as yet, a tendency for middle-class urban children to break into the administrative elite.

In my own fieldwork, the younger generation of this type of cadre from rural cadre or school teacher backgrounds were particularly well represented among the full-time degree students resident at the Yunnan Provincial Party School, many of whom were also from a minority background. To such cadres, recruitment in the administration was a highly prized opportunity for upward mobility, including the opportunity to live in the county town. This holds in particular if the new recruit was from a relatively remote or deprived area – of which there are still plenty in Yunnan – where alternative career opportunities in entrepreneurship and business are often still very limited. Such cadres identify very strongly with the administration and the party, and often find it inconceivable to even think about possible career opportunities outside the administration. Being a cadre to them is more than just a calling, job or career. Being a cadre, particularly a leading cadre, informs almost everything that they do and think in a way that runs much deeper than explicit ideological indoctrination. Yet this is not the same as being a loyal instrument that simply and unquestioningly does what the party tells it to do. In interviews and informal conversations, leading cadres displayed a keen knowledge of how to strike a fine balance between going along with the wishes and commands of the 'higher levels' (*shangmian*) and exercising their own judgement. Indeed, as we have seen in previous chapters, such a 'unity of theory and practice' is in fact what the party expects from its leading cadres. Rather, the almost complete assimilation of their role as leading cadres often expressed itself in an almost offhand acceptance that they had given up to the party their independence to make their own choices about their career. Serving the party as a cadre is not so much an ideological commitment or calculated career move, but a habitual orientation that deeply moulds one's sense of personhood.

My future plans? Whether you are promoted or have to stay where you are, when you are a Communist Party cadre there is little point in thinking about that. You just put all your energy in the actual job you have to do and gain the support from the masses and recognition from the organization department. As for the issue of promotion, that is decided by the organization department.[21]

In this quote, it is particularly telling that the standard Maoist reference to 'the masses' is immediately followed by and thus in effect glossed as 'the organization department', or, in other words, the local party committee. To leading cadres, the local party committee is not only the concrete manifestation of the party and its power to discipline, reward and punish, but also the focal point of a local community of cadres of their own rank. This is not only true of ranked cadres in a post within the central administration of their own area, for instance as head or party secretary of a government bureau. Cadres who have been posted to serve in a subordinate area away from the central administration behave very much like expats. Their spouse and child often continue to live in their flat in the central town or city, with the cadre on such an outside posting commuting back and forth on a weekly or sometimes even a daily basis.

In an earlier publication, I showed that there are interlocking localist and hierarchical dimensions to cadres' sense of belonging (Pieke 2004:

[21] Interview 29, 16 April 2004.

529–530). Cadres are recruited from among the best and brightest in an area, and for them, serving the party includes service to their native place. Furthermore, serving the party means to work and often live together with other cadres of equal rank and from the same place: from the perspective of cadres, the party and its administration are not faceless institutions, but a community of peers of equal rank serving in and largely from the same jurisdiction. Yet this community and jurisdiction are at the same time embedded in a larger jurisdiction one bureaucratic level higher: townships are part of a county, counties are part of a prefecture and prefectures are part of a province. Not only does this higher level place its own cadres in the top positions in the localities that fall under its jurisdiction (minimally the party secretary, full head and head of discipline inspection) to serve as its eyes, ears and hands. Just as importantly, ambitious local cadres hope and expect that, one day, they will be promoted, leaving their local area and its community of cadres, to become a member of that larger, but otherwise very similar, jurisdiction and community. Because a cadre's original area is a part of, and hierarchically subordinated to, this new jurisdiction, cadres who are promoted in a sense never really leave their native area, but simply see the area they belong to expand first to include a county, then a prefecture and ultimately a whole province.

However, we should be careful here not to unduly simplify matters. At each level and locality the cadre corps does not simply consist of people who have all made their careers at lower levels in the same area, eventually earning a promotion to a job at a higher level of the administration. Although most likely the majority of cadres in a locality share such a background, they are, as we have just observed, supplemented by non-local cadres of senior rank who occupy a handful of key posts in the locality. These non-local cadres have been appointed by the organization department to serve as the agents of the higher-level administration, and serve for only a limited, fixed term after which they leave for posts elsewhere and are replaced by fresh appointees.[22] A further third group of cadres at a particular locality and level are younger ones who as a rule are better educated and

---

[22] In 2006, article 5 of the *Temporary Regulations on the Avoidance of Posts for Party and State Leading Cadres* (Dang-zheng lingdao ganbu renzhi huibi zanxing guiding, 6 August 2006, online at news.xinhuanet.com/politics/2006-08/06/content_4926400.htm (checked on 1 July 2008)) for the first time formally and officially forbade leading cadres, including minority cadres, to serve in their own native area. Until then, the People's Republic of China had not had a strict 'law of avoidance' like Imperial China that forbade government magistrates from serving in their native place. However, administrative practice already strongly discouraged native place service for the most senior officials, and especially for the party secretary. Even at the provincial level, for the whole period of 1949 to 1998, only one-quarter of first party secretaries and 38 per cent of governors were provincial natives (Bo 2002: 45).

are considered more promising. These cadres have been recruited to start their career directly at this level eventually to take them at least one and possible two or more hierarchical levels higher. David Goodman's research on elites in Shanxi province has shown that the mix between external appointees, entrenched local cadres and fresh, upwardly mobile recruits destined for bigger and better jobs elsewhere can vary very considerably depending on bureaucratic level and locality. This factor is very likely to have implications for the cooperation (or lack thereof) between hierarchical levels and is an important factor in the well-documented variability in central policy compliance between different areas in China (Goodman 2001).

With the connection between areas and hierarchy the party's orchestration of cadre careers achieves a powerful fusion of habitual localism and universalism. As they move up the hierarchy, cadres continue to be local cadres, rooted in their own native place, but the logic of promotion and job rotation expands, translates and co-opts their loyalties and attachments to more encompassing areas and larger communities of cadre-peers: promotion quite literally expands cadres' horizons of their service to the party. During my fieldwork at local party schools in Yunnan I was in an excellent position to observe this process in action. Cadres who are trained or educated at a party school are all drawn from the jurisdiction of the administration that the school belongs to. As we have seen in the previous section, to these cadres their stay at the party school helped them not only to strengthen and broaden personal connections with cadres from their own locality, but also to get to know cadres from other areas in the school's jurisdiction. Discussion sessions, extracurricular activities organized by the school's temporary party branches, and informal leisure activities all help cadres to build a broad range of informal ties that are both the lubricant and the glue of the administration. Crucially, these ties are not only with the cadre community in their area of origin, but also with the much larger community one tier up in the hierarchy. It is in this respect that cadre training makes perhaps its greatest contribution to the party's rule. Training at party schools helps cadres not only in their current job, but, if and when they get promoted, also in their future one, reinforcing and creating the hierarchically nested administrative communities of cadres that are the backbone of the Chinese administrative system.

However, it would be a mistake to think that individual leading cadres are completely passive and subject to the whims and fancies of the organization department and other departments of their party committee. Cadres are career bureaucrats who are as a rule highly motivated and ambitious to move up the ladder as fast as possible. In the literature on Chinese politics and the organizational role of the party, much emphasis has been put on the role of individual connections, factionalism and 'principled' particularism (Domes 1884; Nathan 1973; Teiwes 1993; Walder 1986); in fact, the concept of 'faction' is one of the principal tools of the China watcher's trade. Several times in conversations and interviews during my research allusions were made to the importance of connections to secure desirable appointments. However, never was I given specific examples of people or ways in which such practices might work. Instead, when talking about what drives appointment decisions and cadre careers, informants always spoke of the party, higher levels or the organization department without ever attaching to any of these a specific face or name. Time and again, interviewees professed to be largely powerless in influencing anonymous decision makers higher up in the bureaucracy on the future direction of their career.

In part this was no doubt caused by the constraints of interviews taking place in party schools. I was simply not in the best position to ask the right questions in this regard, and informants were most certainly not prepared to own up to illegal actions that they spent much time on denouncing during cadre training. The constraints of my fieldwork were such that in no way would I like to argue that the long-standing issues of favouritism, nepotism and factionalism are unimportant in the functioning of the Chinese bureaucracy, let alone the more recent problems with the purchase and sale of official positions (*mai guan mai guan*) and election fraud (*la piao hui xuan*).[23] However, the impact of 'connections' on cadre careers is not only a matter of straightforward nepotism, but is part of the institutionalized patronage of the CCP's 'neo-traditional' rule (Jowitt 1974; Walder 1986). A party secretary who grants promotions to subordinates rewards professional performance and loyalty to political associates rather than simply favouring his personal friends. As long as such promotions follow the established procedures, neo-traditional blending of procedure and patronage are simply part of normal bureaucratic practice. In sum, my interviews suggest that the party's grip on cadre appointment and the old *nomenklatura* system, whereby leading appointments are made at the next higher level, although it may not stop nepotism at

[23] I will briefly discuss these issues in the concluding chapter.

the local level, nevertheless prevents it from dominating the appointment process.[24]

Although my interviews provide only limited evidence of the direct use of connections for career advancement, many cadres had much more to say about two other ways to further their career beyond simply doing their job well, namely gaining further educational degrees and participating in training, and signing up for the public selection and examinations for specific jobs. The emphasis on examinations and formal education has had a very substantial impact on Chinese cadres, not only making the bureaucracy much more of a meritocracy than in the past, but also giving individual cadres ways to gain at least a measure of control over their own career. The proliferation of correspondence, part-time and full-time courses specifically designed for cadres documented in this book has enabled millions of cadres to gain the degree they need in order to earn the promotion they crave. My interviews are replete with examples of cadres who enthusiastically profess the use and importance of degree work in order to get ahead.[25] However, even here the hand of the organization department continues to be felt. Although cadres on correspondence degree courses sign up for these courses themselves, my interviews with full-time or part-time students on regular degree courses show that the latter are in great part merely another tool to manage the careers of promising local cadres.

Chen Jihong is a native of remote Diqing prefecture, which a few years ago renamed itself Shangri-la in the hope of attracting more foreign tourists. Chen's mother and father are both teachers at a village primary school. His brother is a farmer and his sister a teacher at a middle school. Chen graduated from Yunnan Agricultural University in 1993 majoring in rural studies, and was allocated the job of secretary to the people's congress in a township in his native area. Chen joined the party in 1995. Later the organization department transferred him to the

---

[24] It is also very likely that in this regard there is an important difference between the dynamics of careers at the local level compared to the Centre. The higher up the hierarchy one gets, the more cadres become 'politicians' and the less mere 'administrators'. Consequently, the careers of cadres of ministerial rank and higher are likely to be determined less by measurable performance and more by political reliability and loyalty. The very nature of the Chinese political system makes this a necessity. Leading cadres at local levels are subordinate to the party committee and organization department at one level higher. At the top, there is no higher administrative level. Career decisions are made by a small group of senior and current leaders who use the administrative organs of the Central Committee and State Council and election in the National People's Congress to appoint their supporters to positions of power around them. For a detailed discussion of the procedures and practices concerning top-level appointments at the 2002 sixteenth National Party Congress, see Bo 2006: 55–77.

[25] Admittedly, this is entirely to be expected since many of my interviewees were involved in degree study themselves and can be expected to emphasize this point.

office of the people's consultative conference in the county where he eventually became deputy head. At the time of interview, Chen was a full-time student of economics at the Yunnan Provincial Party School. He was selected onto this course by his organization department. The department also determined that he should study economics. The organization department receives a certain number of quota places each year and selects from among promising young cadres of deputy section rank with minimally a BA. The department usually identifies candidates by looking at the list of cadres in the area who have signed up for a party school correspondence course. According to Chen, studying full-time is a valuable opportunity to 'recharge the batteries' [*chongdian*], as it allows students to study much more systematically. Full-time study is also much more prestigious than a correspondence degree. Finally, students on full-time courses continue to receive their salaries, in addition to getting reimbursed for most of the costs of study. Chen said that he also had toyed with the idea of signing up for a master's course at a regular university, but realized that his English is too deficient to make that an option, and for his future career as a cadre it does not matter that he won't have a recognized degree anyway.[26]

CADRE RECRUITMENT AND APPOINTMENT

The large-scale provision of degree education to cadres has had more profound implications than merely raising the educational standard of the bureaucracy. In their study of cadre career mobility, education and party patronage, Bobai Li and Andrew Walder draw the important conclusion that the provision of adult education at party schools and elsewhere has enabled the CCP to avoid the technocratization of the regime's administrative elite, or, if I am allowed to extend their argument somewhat, what Robert Michels long ago called the 'iron law of oligarchization' (Li and Walder 2001: 1404; Michels 1915). Instead of increasingly recruiting highly educated graduates into the elite, the party focussed on young prospects with the right revolutionary credentials (class, party membership) subsequently educating them further: education was thus not a precondition but a consequence of elite status.

Although this pattern of cadre recruitment and education continues to apply, in recent years it has been threatened (or at least supplemented) by radically different policies for the recruitment and appointment of cadres. For instance, discontinuing the Central Party School's Correspondence Academy is a clear indication that the party is rolling back its decades-long reliance on the recruitment of cadres with modest backgrounds, and is stepping up the emphasis on achieved education as a precondition (and no

[26] Interview 30, 17 April 2004.

longer a consequence) of recruitment. Likewise, the introduction since the late nineties of democratic elections and public examinations for leading cadre positions has opened up further avenues for ambitious individuals to boost their career; potentially, they have profound implications for the composition of China's administrative elite. However, examinations and elections do not entail that the party has relinquished control over the management of leading cadres. After a public examination, the proposed appointee still has to go through rigorous investigation by the organization department and subsequent approval by the party committee. The co-optation of election, public selection and examination of cadres is, in fact, a prime illustration of one of the main themes of this book, namely how seemingly neoliberal changes have been incorporated in the neo-socialist Chinese party-state that continues to be based on Leninist principles, and it is therefore important to dwell on this in some more detail.

Since 2001, inner party democracy has become an increasingly important element in the party's neo-socialist strategy, a process that culminated at the Seventeenth Party Congress in 2007. As a result, the meaning of the existing term 'election system' (*xuanjuzhi*) in cadre appointments has started to expand, including not only the formal election by party congresses or people's congresses (Manion 2000), but also the increasingly rigorous procedures whereby a party committee or the standing committee of a people's congress selects candidates for either direct appointment or subsequent formal election by the party congress or people's congress. In the past, selection by party committees or standing committees tended to be dominated by a few or even just one powerful member, usually the party secretary. To counter this very common practice, in 2004 the party Centre issued a document that required party committees and standing committees to select candidates by a formal vote (*piaojuezhi*), thus in theory giving all members of the committee equal power.[27] These more recent forms of democratic appointment therefore do not amount to full democratic elections, but merely entail a more rigorous, transparent and competitive process whereby party committees select candidates for leading positions.

---

[27] The document in question is 'Methods for plenary sessions of local party committees of putting to a vote designated candidates and recommended candidates for principal positions in the leadership group of party committees and governments at the lower level' (Dang de difang weiyuanhui quanti huiyi dui xia yi ji dangwei, zhengfu lingdao banzi zhengzhi niren renxuan he tuijian renxuan biaojue banfa), issued in April 2004 by the Central Administrative Office (Zhongyang Bangongting), summarized in 'Reform of the cadre personnel system has yielded new results' (Ganbu renshi zhidu gaige qude de xin chengguo), *Dangjian yanjiu zongheng tan* (Talks about research on party building), Beijing: Dangjian Duwu Chubanshe, 2004: 117–118.

However, public participation in the nomination and even election of candidates is not ruled out, and experiments along these lines are likely to expand in the immediate future. Although there is as yet little documentation available, elections by party committees can reportedly involve vigorous campaigning by competing candidates, also involving sometimes very considerable expenditure on gifts and the entertainment of members of party committees, ways of canvassing votes (*lapiao*) that are a familiar aspect of elections in many democratic countries.[28] No doubt, this democratic turn in the CCP has been inspired by the success of the elections of village committees since the eighties and nineties (Alpermann 2001; Jakobsen 2004; Pieke 2004; O'Brien and Li 2006), and more recently the elections of urban neighbourhood committees and even township heads.[29] Elections, so the party has come to realize, help the party to increase its legitimacy and grip over local administration at the expense of local bosses who use cadre positions to build up their own power base and fortune. Democracy has become a way to increase the transparency and accountability of the administration, thereby strengthening rather than weakening the rule of the CCP.

As Stig Thøgersen has pointed out, direct elections put the prospects of career advancement on a radically different footing from the existing meritocratic system, and cadres often treat them with hostility. However, another new way of selecting candidates for posts, namely the introduction of competitive and open selection procedures that involve written and oral examinations, does exactly the opposite, formalizing and pushing meritocratic appointment even further (Thøgersen 2008: 418–423). Yet, as we shall see, incumbent cadres are not necessarily less hostile. Deng Xiaoping had already in 1980 called for the use of examinations to select and promote cadres, when he said that examinations could provide 'a sort of light ladder so they can come up more quickly, skipping some

---

[28] See, for instance, Niu Ansheng, 'The appointment system and the election system' (Weirenzhi yu xuanjuzhi), *Lilun dongtai* 1751 (10 August 2007), pp. 13–20. For some details on experiments with such appointments in Changzhi city in southern Shanxi, see 'Reform of the cadre system must hold firm to principles – an interview with Lü Rizhou, deputy head of the Shanxi Provincial People's Consultative Conference' (Ganbu tizhi gaige bixu jianchi yuanze, kuoda minzhu – fang Shanxi sheng zhengxie fuzhuxi Lü Rizhou), *Lilun dongtai* 1736 (10 March 2007): 1–10.

[29] For instance, in 2005 Sichuan province announced that all members of party committees in villages, towns and townships henceforth would be appointed by means of direct elections after experiments in 2004 that had already seen forty-five town and township party secretaries appointed through direct elections; see 'Complete public nomination and direct election of town and township party secretaries in Sichuan' (Sichuan xiangzhen dangweihui shuji quanmian gongtui zhixuan), *Dangjian yanjiu zongheng tan (2005)* (Talks about research on party building), Beijing: Dangjian Duwu Chubanshe, 2006, pp. 221–222. For a detailed study of one such election of township leaders in Sichuan in 2006, see Thøgersen, Elklit and Dong Lishen 2008.

rungs' (Deng 1984a: 306). However, only in the nineties were serious steps taken to realize this, initially in section 9 of the 1993 *Temporary Regulations on National Public Servants*, later followed by more elaborate regulation. When discussing selection by examination, both official sources and cadres themselves often invoke the parallels with the old imperial examination system.[30] It thus does not take all that much interpretive liberty to see that the party consciously seeks to tap into the memory of the imperial examinations to reinvigorate its right to rule: cadres who have been selected by examination are likely to command a culturally sanctioned legitimacy and authority far greater than the old, secretive and authoritarian *nomenklatura* appointments system.

In 1995 and again in slightly altered form in 2002 the party issued the *Regulations on the work of selection and appointment of party and government leading cadres* that provide the regulatory framework for examinations and public selection in cadre appointments.[31] Initially, examinations were used to select cadres in non-leading positions (referred to as 'public servants exams' (*gongwuyuan kaoshi*, or *gongkao*). In Yunnan, this was put into practice in 1995. Between that year and 1998, unified provincial examinations were organized. Those who passed the exam were given a certificate that entitled them to apply for civil servant positions in the province. This turned out to be unsatisfactory, because the content of the exams was not specific to the requirements of particular jobs. In 1998, the province shifted to competitive examinations for specific positions. Since then, each year individual government departments submit their hiring plan to their personnel office. These plans are then checked by the government staff department (*bianzhi bumen*) before the posts are advertised for examination. The examinations are held twice a year in January and August. A minimum of three candidates have to sign up for a particular post before the examination can take place. The great advantage of the examination method is that it has broken down regional boundaries, making it possible to recruit from a much larger pool and thus ultimately to hire better personnel.[32] In late 1999, the Centre took the much more daring step of using examinations for the selection of leading cadres as well, referred to as 'open selection and competitive appointment by examination' (*gongkai xuanba jingzheng*

---

[30] Interview 49, 11 December 2004.
[31] 'Regulations on the work of selection and appointment of party and government leading cadres' (Dang-zheng lingdao ganbu xuanba renyong gongzuo tiaoli), 2002, online at news.xinhuanet.com/ziliao/2003–01/18/content_695422.htm (checked on 25 May 2006). Both the 1995 and 2002 regulations are discussed in detail in Bo 2004.
[32] Interview 49, 11 December 2004.

shanggang kaoshi), or 'open selection' (*gongxuan*) for short.[33] Examinations for leading cadre positions are intended to assess the candidate's ability for leadership work and solving concrete problems: their focus is testing the 'ability and quality' of leading cadres.[34] Public examinations were in the first instance presented as just one of the methods for the selection of leading cadres in local party, government and 'other leading posts suited to public selection'.[35] However, this was quickly expanded to include positions at the Centre up to the department (*si*) and office (*chu*) level.[36]

My own interviews and conversations in Yunnan revealed that there are in fact two rather different types of examinations. The first consists of an organization department or personnel bureau publicly advertising one or more posts in their jurisdiction to be filled by public examination. Candidates are invited to sign up for an examination set specifically for one or more posts. All candidates, quite often more than one hundred, first

---

[33] The use of public selection and examinations are provided for in section 9 of both the 1995 and the 2002 versions of the *Regulations on the work of selection and appointment of party and government cadres*. According to article 49 of the 2002 *Regulations*, 'public selection' (*gongkai xuanba*) refers to external recruitment, whereas 'competitive appointment' (*jingzheng shanggang*) is limited to the relevant work unit or bureaucratic 'system' (*xitong*). Further elaboration on the provisions in these regulations is given in the 'Notice on the progress with the work on the public selection of leading cadres' (Guanyu jin yi bu zuohao gongkai xuanba lingdao ganbu gongzuo de tongzhi), Document no. 3 (1999) of the Central Organization Department, and the 2004 'Temporary rules on the work of public selection of party and government leading cadres' (Gongkai xuanba dang-zheng lingdao ganbu gongzuo zanxing guiding), issued by the CCP centre in April 2004. For an official statement on the background and utility of public selection, see 'CCP centre promulgates "Temporary rules on the work of public selection of party and government leading cadres" and other documents' (Zhonggong zhongyang banbu 'gongkai xuanba dang-zheng lingdao ganbu gongzuo zanxing guiding' deng wenjian), Xinhuanet.com 8 September 2004, online at news.xinhuanet.com/zhengfu/2004-09/08/content_1957579.htm (checked on 23 May 2006). For a short account on the introduction of selection and examinations, see Yang 2004, pp. 179–183. Unfortunately, Yang does not distinguish clearly between appointments to leading and non-leading cadre positions, leading him to overstate the speed and extent of the introduction of public selection.

[34] 'Appendix 2: Explanation of the circumstances surrounding the redrafting of the "Trial outline of the examinations for the nationwide public selection of party and government leading cadres"' (Fulu er: guanyu "Quanguo gongkai xuanba dang-zheng lingdao ganbu kaoshi dagang (shixing)" xiuding gongzuo qingkuang de shuoming)'. In Central Organization Department (Zhongyang Zuzhi Bu), *Outline of the examinations for the public selection and competitive appointment of party and state leading cadres* (Dang-zheng lingdaoganbu gongkai xuanba he jingzheng shanggang kaoshi dagang). Beijing: Dangjian duwu chubanshe, 2004: 52.

[35] Section 9, article 49 of the 'Regulations on the work of selection and appointment of party and government leading cadres' (Dang-zheng lingdao ganbu xuanba renyong gongzuo tiaoli), promulgated on 9 July 2002, online at www.people.com.cn/GB/shizheng/16/20020723/782504.html (checked on 30 June 2008).

[36] 'Appendix 2: Explanation of the circumstances surrounding the redrafting of the "Trial outline of the examinations for the nationwide public selection of party and government leading cadres"' (Fulu er: guanyu "Quanguo gongkai xuanba dang-zheng lingdao ganbu kaoshi dagang (shixing)" xiuding gongzuo qingkuang de shuoming)': 45.

sit a written examination. The 10 per cent or so who are allowed to pass are then called for an oral examination conducted by a panel of internal members and outside specialists. The panel then forwards between one and three names to the organization department for investigation, after which the party committee makes the ultimate decision.[37]

Since 1995, the scope of the examination method for the appointment of leading cadres has been expanded to include a very substantial number of leading appointments across the bureaucracy at the county, prefecture and provincial levels. In Yunnan, the first examination for 17 posts at the deputy provincial department level (*futingji*) was held in 1996. After 1997, the scale of such examinations was gradually expanded. In 2000, the Yunnan Provincial Organization Department opened up a total of 35 positions, again at the deputy provincial department level, to open selection by examination. In 2004, eight candidates from outside and 14 from inside the province were selected through open examination or application, again at the deputy provincial department level and including posts in functional units and mass organizations. By means of the examination system, candidates from universities in Beijing or with foreign PhDs have been offered three-year renewable contracts for jobs such as deputy dean of Yunnan University, deputy head of the provincial education department or the deputy head of the provincial legal office. However, at the time of my interview (December 2004), only three candidates had accepted the offer, and it was expected that some of the positions could not be filled.[38]

After the national *Notice on the progress with the work on the public selection of leading cadres* was issued in 1999, examinations in Yunnan were extended to the lower level of deputy office level (*fuchuji*) posts.[39] Public selection was originally only used for posts of deputy (*fu*) head, never the full (*zheng*) head of a department or government, as an obvious safety measure to avoid the appointment of cadres too junior and inexperienced

---

[37] According to section 3 of the 1999 *Notice on the progress with the work on the public selection of leading cadres*, the number of eligible candidates should be at least ten times as many as the number of posts advertised, while the number of candidates admitted to the oral exam should be five times as many as the number of posts. Finally, the number of candidates forwarded to the organization department for investigation should be around three times as many of the number of posts. In my own experience, posts are often advertised individually, with an exam specifically set for each.

[38] Interview 49, 11 December 2004. Functional organizations (*shiye danwei*) are those parts of the state sector that fall between administrative organs (*xingzheng jiguan*) and economic enterprises (*qiye*), such as hospitals, schools, research institutions, the media and organizations responsible for welfare, housing, sports, utilities, and so on (Lam and Perry 2001). Mass organizations are largely the leftovers of Maoist governance that function as the link between the administration and sectors of the public, such as the women's federation, the youth league or the official unions.

[39] Interview 49, 11 December 2004.

to be trusted with overall and final responsibility for decisions.[40] Although this is still the case with most appointments in Yunnan, it is not in fact required by the national regulations.

I encountered a rather different type of examinations while interviewing at the Yunnan Provincial Party School. Several students on one of the school's novice training courses (a requirement for cadres who have made a promotion to a higher rank) had sat the first open provincial examination in 2002. This exam was not intended to fill one or more specific posts, but to create a general 'talent reserve pool' (variously referred to as *houbei xuanren*, *houbei ganbu*, *chubei rencai*) of cadres qualified for appointments at the deputy provincial department level (*futingji*). Those who passed the examination were not immediately given a job, but would only be appointed if and when suitable jobs became available. In total, more than three thousand people signed up, of whom 1,420 passed, including members of the democratic parties or those without any party membership, and people from both inside and outside Yunnan. Although the main objective was to give bright younger people a chance, only those who had already held a post at the full office level (*zhengchuji*) or with at least three years' experience at the deputy office level (*fuchuji*) were qualified to sit the examination.[41]

Examinations for either specific posts or for entry into a talent pool provide bright, young and ambitious cadres with a faster career track than the normal patient promotion from one rank to the next. It also gives ambitious cadres more independence in planning and promoting their career, instead of simply having to wait for the next assignment from the organization department. Yet these examinations mainly function as an additional mechanism for the party and the state to manage the careers of cadres rather than being a fundamentally different approach. Candidates who have signed up are first screened, and only those who meet certain qualifications are eligible to sit the exam. As these qualifications include having worked as a cadre of a certain rank for a minimum number of years, and often in a specific area of expertise and/or location, only those people who are already in the system can participate.

However, although the exams are thus often limited to those cadres who would normally have been considered by the organization department or personnel bureau in a particular area anyway, this does not always have to be the case. Indeed, the stated purpose of open selection is to improve the composition of the leadership team, or to fill vacancies that would

---

[40] 'Notice on the progress with the work on the public selection of leading cadres' (Guanyu jin yi bu zuohao gongkai xuanba lingdao ganbu gongzuo de tongzhi), Document no. 3 (1999) of the Central Organization Department, section 2.
[41] Interview 10, 5 April 2004, and Interview 49, 11 December 2004.

otherwise be hard to fill or that require scarce expertise.[42] Particularly those parts of China that find it difficult locally to recruit adequately qualified cadres are now free to open up their examinations much more widely, creating the first beginnings of a regional or even national job market for administrative talent.

Selection and appointment to leading and non-leading cadre positions by public examination have spawned a genuine examination craze. Candidates spend weeks, if not months, with thick textbooks and manuals and in tutorial classes organized either privately or by the organization department in charge of the examination. These books and classes take them through the curriculum set for the exams and prepare them for the questions they might face in the interview. In fact, one of the stated objectives of public selection is to encourage cadres to study as a normal part of their life. For this reason, in 2004 the time between the announcement of a vacancy and the exam was shortened from a month to just ten days, giving candidates less time to bone up for one specific examination.[43]

The topics covered in the examinations are nationally unified. The examination consists of a written general examination, a further written examination specific to the job(s) to be filled, and an oral examination. Although the topics should be adapted to the requirements of the position, they nevertheless have to be drawn either from the pool of questions currently in use for the national examination, or from a pool of questions approved by the provincial organization department.[44] The new examinations for leading cadre positions reflect the Communist Party's continued Leninist

---

[42] 'Temporary rules on the work of public selection of party and government leading cadres', article 5.
[43] Interview 49, 11 December 2004.
[44] 'Temporary rules on the work of public selection of party and government leading cadres', article 16. In 2000, the contents of the leading cadre examinations were specified in *Trial outline of the examinations for the nationwide public selection of party and government leading cadres* (Quanguo gongkai xuanba dang-zheng lingdao ganbu kaoshi dagang (shixing)). In 2004 the Central Organization Department promulgated a new, final version of this document, which was given the status of law. Apart from a general expansion of the number of topics, the new *Outline of the examinations for the public selection and competitive appointment of party and state leading cadres* (Dang-zheng lingdao ganbu gongkai xuanba he jingzheng shanggang kaoshi dagang) also has a completely new section on the 'Three Represents', the new ideological orthodoxy since 2000. In the light of experiences in the first years, the outline now also emphasizes more the ability to deal with real problems over simple memorization and reproduction of facts, and aims better to assess a candidate's suitability for leadership. The general section on the examinations consists of five parts, namely theory, general knowledge, policy and law, problem solving and composition. Unsurprisingly, theory on the examination is weighed very heavily in favour of Marxism–Leninism, Mao Zedong Thought, Deng Xiaoping Theory and the Important Thoughts of the 'Three Represents'. It also features a section on Party history. However, the other sections on the exam are much less ideologized and include national defence, foreign relations, the economy, law, management, science and technology, and general history.

understanding of the role of cadres. With the party's self-ascribed transition from a revolutionary to a ruling party this is now expressed in a language that may seem less politicized that the 'red' versus 'expert' dichotomy in Maoist times. However, the ambition remains fundamentally the same. The party wishes to create a new cadre of leaders whose 'quality' is high in two respects: equipped with the knowledge and skills needed to manage an increasingly complex administration, and ideologically committed to the party and its mission.

Public examinations are thus an additional tool for the party to fine-tune and broaden the scope of the recruitment, deployment and promotion of its personnel. In most cases, it can hardly be argued that the examinations have suddenly opened the door to an administrative career to people that previously would not even have entertained the idea. Instead, examinations give ambitious people who are already part of the local pool of cadres a way to speed up the progress of their career, and a sense of autonomy and pride in their individual achievement.

Until last year, Zhang was the head of a township. In 2003, the prefecture opened up thirty deputy office level positions and three full office level positions for public examination. After the first round in 1997, 2003 was the second time that public examinations for office level posts had been held in the prefecture. According to Zhang, this method is gaining recognition because it is a step in the direction of a scientific, standardized and systematic procedure. The thirty positions had been advertised on the Internet, but only cadres already employed within the prefecture could apply. In the end, more than 1,900 people applied and only two posts could not be filled because they received less than ten applications. Zhang signed up for the post of deputy head of the prefecture's united front department. Originally, he had not planned to sign up because he was too busy at work, but then thought about it and figured the post of deputy head of the united front department suited his background as a university graduate and experience with work in the people's consultative conference and the organization department. In total, 118 people registered for the post. Eventually, Zhang was selected to take up the post, initially on a probationary basis.[45]

The continued role of the party is equally clear in the case of examinations not for specific posts but for the creation of a talent pool of 'reserve cadres'.

Chen graduated in archaeology from Peking University in 1986 and was allocated a job at the Yunnan Provincial Museum, where in 2003 he was made deputy head. In 1998, he was promoted to associate professor; he is currently preparing his application for promotion to full professor. In 2002, he took and passed the first provincial examination for deputy department (*futing*) reserve cadres. At the

---

[45] Summarized from interview 78, 1 December 2004.

time of the interview, Chen was participating in the seventeenth training class for deputy department reserve cadres, a class that included many of the examination's successful candidates, in preparation for active duty. As a reserve cadre, he was not immediately allocated a job at the appropriate rank, but continued in his old job at the museum, waiting for the provincial organization department to find him a suitable position.[46]

Only for a very limited number of posts, particularly ones that are hard to fill because they require specific qualifications or experience that are in short supply, are examinations opened up to applicants from outside the area, although even then usually only cadres of a specific rank and experience are eligible to enter.

Wang is originally from Inner Mongolia where his last post before he moved to Yunnan was head of a prefectural bureau. He has two BAs, one in mechanical construction and the other in industrial management, and worked as a teacher before joining a prefectural policy research office, which was his stepping stone into administration. In 1999, he signed up for the public selection of the position of assistant to the head of a prefecture in Yunnan, one of a total of twenty posts the prefecture opened up for national recruitment. The head of the prefectural organization department in Inner Mongolia was unhappy about him leaving, but in the end agreed. The post of assistant to the head of a prefecture is not part of the normal administrative setup [*bianzhi*] and is also not something that is likely to be a permanent feature of the prefecture's government. Nevertheless, he is still eligible for promotion if he gains the recognition of the higher level; if not, he will at least be eligible for another post at the same level; in fact, he could already have become the head of a prefectural bureau three years ago.[47]

In our 2005 survey, only 58 of 251 respondents in the previous five years had been appointed to a position by means of public examination, competitive selection, or direct recruitment, rather than the more traditional methods of formal election or appointment by a party committee or people's congress. However, these new ways of personnel recruitment and management nevertheless convey a powerful message, particularly when they are taken in conjunction with other changes in cadre recruitment and management discussed in this book, such as the emphasis on formal education as precondition of appointment at a particular rank, the shift at party schools from non-recognized to recognized degrees, and the strengthening and diversification of cadre training. Appointments and promotions will increasingly be based on an individual's excellence at learning, rather than habitual commitment to the local party apparatus, years of dedicated service and job performance. Selection will reward the ability to study and to

---

[46] Summarized from interview 10, 5 April 2004.   [47] Summarized from interview 13, 7 April 2004.

pass examinations, rather than solely depend on the opaque internal procedures of the organization department and party committee. Cadres can play a more proactive role in the progression of their career than in the past, and are increasingly rewarded for doing so. Waiting for the organization department's next assignment alone will no longer be enough: cadres will have to seek admission to relevant degree programmes, prepare for examinations and be on the lookout for job openings inside and increasingly also outside their own place of residence. In short, a local, regional and even national administrative job market will begin to supplement (but not replace) the party's Leninist methods of cadre management.

Under the impact of these changes in cadre recruitment and promotion, a new type of leading cadre is gradually beginning to populate the Chinese administrative system at the provincial and sub-provincial level. These cadres are characterized by a very high level of education, strong professional skills often obtained during previous employment in other areas or even altogether outside the administration, and fast-track promotion by means of public examination. Such cadres do not necessarily feel an unquestioning, life-long, localized and habitual loyalty to the party and the administration. These cadres' commitment to the party has been carefully crafted: it has been learned from books and at cadre training classes and is conditional on their success as career bureaucrats. This is how one of such cadres looked at his commitment to the party:

In 2002, Chen joined the party. 'In the past I did not have the opportunity because my father had a bad class label, but later my understanding changed, because the party's policies have relaxed. In 2001 I applied for membership and in 2002 I became a probationary member. In the past, the party's goals were straight Communism, very distant. Nowadays their goals are very realistic. Some are long-term, while others are more immediate and concrete goals. Our country's development is based on the idea that we have to build a relatively fair society. During my studies here at the party school, reading *Capital* has had a big impact. The development of man takes place over three stages, and our goal is to realize the comprehensive development of man. Although at the present stage this is not complete, we are working towards it. An ideal society will not become reality overnight, so we have to be more concrete and proceed step by step. Our goal is to realize a relatively free life for people. At the present stage we have to balance fairness and efficiency. We first talk about efficiency and only then about fairness. Too much emphasis on fairness will impede development. Development is a tool, people's happiness is the aim... It would not be right if China were to leave the Communist Party, but it also would not be right if the Communist Party would not reform and not keep up with the times... Now that the Communist Party is the ruling party its ruling force not only comes from the workers and peasants, but includes the whole Chinese nation.'[48]

This new type of cadre is a professional whose ultimate loyalty is to his or her own individual career, a career that she or he continues to promote independently from the plans that the organization department may have. This new type of expert cadre is in many respects similar to – and should perhaps be considered simply a part of – the rapidly growing stratum of career professionals in China (Hoffman 2006; Cucco 2008). Although in most cases their career plans do not extend beyond the limits of the administration, one informant who had already severed such local ties when he moved from Inner Mongolia to Yunnan (see above), seriously contemplated a lateral move into a career outside public administration.

At the time of the interview, Wang participated in a training class at the provincial party school, but admitted that he was not very interested and spent most of his time reading other books, mainly on law as he was preparing for a judicial exam. He did not plan to be a civil servant for the rest of his life: 'When you are a civil servant, you are not the master of your own time and there is little that you actually accomplish.' He reckoned that he could try his hand at another profession, and studying law meant that he was going with the trend of governmental rule by law.[49]

State employees and university graduates seeking employment in the private sector is a well-established pattern that in the nineties was often reported on as the 'going to sea' (*xia hai*) phenomenon. However, currently something more radical is happening. First of all, the more conditional commitment of the new expert cadres means that specifically *leading* cadres are also no longer bound to a life-long administrative career. Second, the administration is not simply being drained of talent, but is itself becoming an active player in the emerging labour market for professionals. Paradoxically perhaps, the party has gradually come to accept that, in order to realize its vision of itself at the head of a modern and professional administrative system, it will have to be prepared to allow market competition between administrative areas and other organizations in the public and private sector. Increasingly, the language and practices of (limited) contractual obligations enter the very core of the Communist Party's leadership, supplementing the (open-ended) Leninist principles of party spirit and party discipline.

It is very tempting to emphasize the implications of the rise of this new type of leading cadres. Yet however profound these may be, their progress depends in large measure on central policy making and thus the

---

[48] Summarized from interview 10, 5 April 2004.   [49] Summarized from interview 13, 7 April 2004.

vagaries of continued political support. Furthermore, the more radical implications of the reform of cadre appointment and promotion will only gradually emerge, and the great majority of cadres that I interviewed in 2004, including many younger ones, were still of a more conventional kind. Finally, and perhaps most importantly, we should be careful not to overstate the dissatisfaction and potential for conflict between what we could call 'conventional' and 'expert' cadres. By the 2000s, the earlier and much more divisive conflict between Maoist cadres appointed in the fifties and sixties on the basis of their political credentials and Dengist meritocratic cadres had already been unequivocally decided in favour of the latter. All cadres I interviewed had gained the educational degrees required by their rank and post; they were career bureaucrats who believed that promotions had to be won by performance, education and knowledge rather than political virtue. Furthermore, 'conventional' and 'expert' should be treated more as Weberian ideal types than categories of real flesh-and-blood cadres. Most cadres who I interviewed shared characteristics of both types. On the one hand, they all emphasized the importance to their career of gaining higher degrees, and of study and knowledge more generally. On the other hand, the career and ambitions of most were strongly rooted in their belonging to their local administrative hierarchy and community with little evidence of a more proactive, individual approach.

THE CHANGING COMPOSITION OF CHINA'S LOCAL ADMINISTRATIVE ELITE

In *The Intellectuals on the Road to Class Power*, Konrád and Szelenyi contend that after the 1956 uprising in Hungary, the Communist Party and the administration gradually recruited larger numbers of members and cadres from middle-class and intellectual backgrounds, leading to the formation of a dual elite of political loyalists, who did not necessarily possess high educational and professional qualifications, and professional experts, who did not necessarily strongly believe in the party's communist ideology (Konrád and Szelenyi 1979). In the nineties and early 2000s, in the sociological and political science literature a debate ensued on the possible relevance of this dual elite model for contemporary China. Was China's administrative elite simply becoming a technocracy (Lee 1991; White 1998), or, alternatively, had two different career paths emerged (Zhou 1995; Dickson and Rost Rublee 2000; Walder, Li and Treiman 2000; Zang 2001a; 2001b), or were political loyalists upgrading their educational qualifications while the administration also recruited larger numbers of college graduates?

It is not my intention here fully to enter the debate, which has become very technical and requires survey data and quantitative skills that greatly surpass the limits of my own modest survey and analytical abilities. I would like to limit my involvement to just a few observations. The first is that my survey data do not reveal any correlation between an 'expert' mode of appointment to a position (public examination, competitive selection, direct recruitment) and class (defined as either father's or mother's occupation). Clearly, new methods of appointment have no doubt increased the opportunities available to certain types of cadres, but have not (yet) led to a qualitatively different recruitment base for the Yunnan administrative elite. Second, educational requirements are clearly becoming much more important, but, and here I agree with Walder, these are being met both by recruiting new cadres with the needed qualifications and by providing opportunities for the further education of existing cadres. Third, the huge emphasis on cadre training that we have documented in this book is in large part a very deliberate effort to counter a tendency towards the growth of a dual elite: for political loyalists training provides the professional expertise they lack, while for expert cadres training immerses them in political orthodoxy. This effort may or may not, in the long term, be successful, but it does show that the potential elite's bifurcation, in the eyes of China's rulers at least, is a real issue.

The changes in the Chinese administrative elite are more profound than these rather bland observations would suggest. As I have tried to show in this chapter, gauging the technocratic or dual nature of the administrative elite is not only a sociometric but also an ethnographic issue. From the evidence of my fieldwork it seems unlikely that the changes in the cadre management system will result in the full and sudden replacement of one type of cadre by another; however, I have found some real changes in cadres' attitudes and above all career strategies. Very likely, the party will in the future recruit some of its leading cadres fully from outside the administration; they, and new recruits fresh out of university or graduate school, will be less likely to think of an administrative career as a life-long commitment that is hierarchically rooted in a particular locality. Yet the majority of cadres already in post will simply try to adapt to the new ways and criteria for promotion. It is exactly in these gradual changes in career strategies that I believe the reforms will have their most profound impact. Some of those who would have made a successful career in the past will find their ambitions thwarted, while others who in the past would have had little prospect may find their star rising. Selection by examination and an emphasis on study and formal degrees reduce the career prospects of cadres who have patiently worked their way up from modest appointments in township administrations. One informant with many years' experience as township and county party secretary in one of Yunnan poorest regions expressed this tension in his frustration with appointments gained by bookish upstarts; he had little faith in their ability to weather life in the trenches.

> Gaining promotion through examinations is one aspect of the reform of the cadre system, but involves only very small numbers, less than five per cent of all cadres... The examination and approval and the investigation they have undergone are quite strict, [but] cadres who have sat the examinations are very different in their way of thinking than the cadres who were originally in post. Reality has proven that a part of them are not up to the requirements of their post.[50]

In this context it is important to note that many of my informants felt ill-prepared for the new challenges of the reforms. Several had tried to enrol in a degree course at a regular university, but had either failed to gain admission or else were unable to complete the degree. In some cases they subsequently elected the second-best option, namely to study for a non-recognized correspondence or residential degree at a party school. Others had registered for public examinations, but had not been selected from among the sometimes several hundred hopefuls. Yet others said that they had considered degree work or examinations, but had given up the idea before they even started. They often thought that they would not have the time outside their busy work schedule, or else felt that they lacked the qualities to be successful, often turning instead to other, more conventional way of getting ahead.

Hu has considered signing up for the public examination for a suitable post himself, and would welcome the greater mobility and competition that this would bring, but in the end has not done so. Instead, in 2002 the Kunming city organization department selected Hu for a place on the full-time economics course at the provincial party school. After graduation later this year, Hu expects that the organization department will allocate him a new position commensurate with his educational background, work experience and special strengths.[51]

Cadres such as Hu have a lot to thank the party for and understand how important the strides are that the party has made since its near-demise during and immediately after the Cultural Revolution. To such cadres, their entire professional personhood is tied up with their local status of cadre and service to the party. With the reforms, the move away from promotions on the basis of political attitude to merit created a broad base of support for the party among its personnel at the sub-provincial level, many of whom were from a relatively modest background and had been

---

[50] Interview 29, 16 April 2004.   [51] Interview 17, 10 April 2004.

recruited from among the best and brightest in their area. The fusion of localist loyalties with universalist commitment to the party, backed up by a bureaucratic ethos of hard work, commitment and impersonal service explains much of the resilience of the CCP's rule, even during its bleakest period in the late eighties and early nineties.

However, as we have seen in this section, the recent rise of a new and much more heterogeneous stratum of expert cadres introduces an element of strain in the party's established local model of governance that is set gradually to become more acute. At this point, it might also be useful to add a few comparative comments on higher levels of the administration. My own research project on the administrative system focussed mainly on leading cadres at the township, county and prefectural level. Although I do not have systematic information on cadres at the provincial and central level, essentially the same procedures and practices are at work to determine the course of an individual career. Most cadres at the central level, for instance, seem to have started their careers as recruits either in centrally administered state enterprises, government or service agencies, party departments or the army, or else in higher-level provincial posts. Subsequent appointments and promotions rotate cadres to other posts at the same and higher ranks until ultimately their appointments qualify them for election to the Central Committee or State Council. As Bo Zhiyue has shown, in the pursuit of their career provincial and central cadres are acutely aware of the importance of educational qualifications. Like local cadres, they enrol in part-time degree courses at universities or party schools to obtain the higher degrees they need for promotion, usually in social science or humanities subjects more directly relevant to administration. As is to be expected, abuses of power and status are not uncommon. Busy leaders with little time or inclination to study dispatch a subordinate to take classes and sometimes even sit examinations, while others resort to the outright purchase of real or counterfeit degrees. These problems notwithstanding, formal education is evidently as important, if not more important, a factor in the careers of cadres at the Centre as for local cadres (Bo 2006: 80–87).

Bo also observes that since the nineties, degree holders in the humanities and the social sciences have become more prominent at the expense of scientists and engineers. This again resonates strongly with my observations at the sub-provincial level, where party schools exclusively offer degrees in the social sciences and the humanities, while my informants held degrees in a broad range of disciplines with no particular bias toward the sciences or the social sciences. To Bo himself this is grounds for arguing that the central leadership has evolved from the technocracy that it arguably was in the nineties (Bo 2006: 98–107). Although Bo may be right on strictly definitional grounds (formally, a technocrat is an expert in engineering or the sciences who puts his or her skills and knowledge to the solution of political problems), to me this merely reveals that the regime's understanding of which skills and knowledge are needed for leadership has evolved. What is more important is the continued value given to expert knowledge and formal education.

Although the eventual replacement of more conventional and locally rooted cadres clearly is the intention of reform, it may very well be that policy makers at the Centre in Beijing are insufficiently aware of (or at least attuned to) the potential dangers of this strategy. By design, the new expert cadres share the background characteristics of their superiors in the Centre and may be more inclined to comply with the wishes of a Centre that has become increasingly impatient with what it perceives as the intransigence and incompetence of local cadres. In this sense, the recent reforms of cadre management reflect the much more general drive to centralize government, especially since 2002, without, however, a clearly defined vision of a new role and structure for local government. No doubt, there is much wrong with local government that delivers too little and quite often openly preys on the local population.[52] However, simply to blame this on the low 'quality' of local officials might be politically expedient, but largely misses the point. Many of the chronic problems of local government are structural. The Chinese state continues to be highly decentralized, which gives local government at the same time too much to do and mainly local sources of revenue to pay for it. Local officials, especially in poorer areas, therefore have to scramble for resources not only for the many functions and services they have to deliver, but also often simply to pay their own salaries. In the absence of a fundamental reform of local government, simply replacing local cadres with better qualified – and possibly more pliant – experts is unlikely to make much difference.

---

[52] In the late nineties and early 2000s in particular, the central government embarked on a systematic campaign against the 'peasant burden' deriving from taxes and levies from local government, culminating in the very popular abolition of the agricultural tax on 1 January 2006. The most systematic account in English of the argument of the predatory nature of local rural government is given in Bernstein and Lü 2003.

CHAPTER 7

Conclusions: cadre training and the future of party rule

CADRE TRAINING, THE PARTY-STATE AND ANTHROPOLOGY

One of the most striking aspects of cadre training and education is how much it is suffused with a discourse on (if not an obsession with) modernity. At the most general level, this takes the familiar shape, common to all reform policies and a linear descendant of the CCP's May Fourth roots, of an unchallengeable belief that China should progress from a state of backwardness and weakness to one of strength and modernity. Of course, the reforms also buy off political discontent with the material fulfilment of the consumerist desires of middle-class life, but the key of the success of the reforms is that they have delivered, or promise to deliver, the completion of China as a modern nation – strong, unified and prosperous – that will at last right all the wrongs that China has suffered in the course of 150 years of humiliation since the Opium War in 1840. What makes this discourse on modernization irresistible to almost all Chinese is that differences in modernity also imply and justify inequalities in status and power: the discourse on modernity not only liberates, but also locks its subjects into a hierarchical vision of the world. The hierarchical nature of the Chinese concept of modernization entails that modernity is always elsewhere: modernization means trying to improve one's place on the ladder of modernity by trying to become like other, more modern places, people, institutions or nations.

'Quality', as the measure of modernity, provides a convenient discursive shorthand for modernity that collapses a range of dimensions of inequality (power, location, bureaucratic status, education and civilization to name only the most common ones) and issues (for instance environmental pollution, water shortage, disease, poverty, corruption, illiteracy, infanticide, migration) into just one variable. This not only has the advantage of simplicity, but also puts the blame for backwardness squarely on the poor and downtrodden rather than the structural factors that produce and reproduce inequality and exploitation. This truncated analysis in turn points to a clear and unambiguous course of action: in order to solve China's problems, the quality of its population quite simply has to be improved. That, in turn, can only be done by modernizing each and every aspect of China's troubled society and culture. Obviously, this modernizing will have to be done by those who are already the most modern, who in turn must be those people and institutions that are the most powerful, most centrally located, best educated and most civilized, and have the highest status. The discourse on quality and modernization is ubiquitous in the field of cadre training. Poor areas are deemed poor in part at least because the quality of their cadres is lacking, and the intransigence and autonomy often found among local cadres in these areas is simply a remnant of traditional thinking that has to be erased. The remedy is obvious. The quality of the cadres in poor and remote areas such as Yunnan province will have to be raised by educating and training them better, which not only means making them more like cadres in other developed places, but also strengthening their ideological and organizational ties and loyalties to the Centre.

The design and methodology of my project mean that my research has little to say about the impact that cadre training may have on the actual functioning of the administration. Does cadre training and better education make cadres less corrupt, more efficient and more amenable to the Centre? Are they more modern managers and better communists? Is China becoming a better and more humanely governed society that guarantees its people freedom and prosperity? These are important questions that I hope will guide future research on Chinese administrative innovation. However, an exclusive focus on just these intended outcomes would, in many ways, be missing the point. Following Foucault's lead in his discussion of the failure of the modern prison system, James Ferguson observed that the routine failure of rural development projects to produce 'development' masks the other things that such projects equally routinely do achieve: an expansion of the bureaucratic state and the depoliticization of politically contentious issues such as unemployment, failing services and poverty (Ferguson 1990: 254–256).

The ethnographic approach in this book – viewing the party-state just like any other aspect of society, namely a specific way of being with other people – has made it possible to discover many unintended effects of cadre training and education. This study has viewed the life of cadres within the institutions of the party-state as the immersion in a specific culture and a way of becoming a specific kind of person. Party schools are one of the key sites where cadres are steeped in the power cult and the cult of eliteness of the CCP. At party schools and other sites of cadre training, cadres acquire the necessary ideological and habitual commitment to the party and its mission, become part of networks and informal communities of fellow cadres, are trained in the professional skills and knowledge needed to run complex organizations, imbibe the formal and informal social skills and life style that come with power and position. Most importantly, they learn that they are different from – and indeed better than – ordinary Chinese. This latter lesson is also not wasted on the outside world, where the seclusion of party schools and lack of knowledge about what is going on there greatly add to the mystique of cadre power. Returning with knowledge of the latest policies and ideologies from the Centre, cadres have in a very real sense recharged their 'party spirit', exercising power nor simply as one-dimensional administrative post holders, but as members of a ruling elite and the embodiment of the party's organizational charisma.

Cadre training at party schools creates the personal and professional qualities needed of a cadre. Training achieves this not merely by the content of its teaching, but more importantly also by engineering a transformative experience of seclusion, study, reflection and residence at the school. In this sense, the work that cadre training does is rather similar, at least functionally speaking, to undergoing a rite of passage. As Victor Turner has shown, rites of passage create a separate liminal sphere set off from the structure of normal life in which the participants are stripped of their normal roles in preparation for the new roles that they will assume upon the completion of the ritual (Turner 1974). Cadre training at party schools likewise takes place in such an 'anti-structural' environment separate from normal life. At a party school, students are supposed to forget about their position, rank and normal obligations and privileges of family and work. Immersion in the Marxist classics serves a conversionary purpose: students will (again) discover the absolute, scientific truth of Marxism. After completion of their training, the students are supposed either to take on new, more responsible positions or to assume their old ones with a reinvigorated party spirit and a better set of skills. It is this transformative quality of party schools, preserved from the CCP's long tradition of cadre training, that continues to set it apart from mere professional or corporate training. Cadre training at party schools does not simply produce better administrators, it creates Leninist party cadres and Marxist believers.

Cadre training at party schools not only creates or reinforces the official reading of the party-state's power cult that is prescribed by the Centre's many policies, meetings and documents, but also more local and informal aspects that are every bit as important to survival in the party-state's labyrinthine institutional environment. In particular, during their stay at a party school, cadres get to know other cadres of similar rank from a wider administrative jurisdiction than the township, county or prefecture that they work in. This experience creates a sense of belonging to a community beyond one's immediate peers of the higher-level administrative jurisdiction. Translating formal vertical and horizontal administrative lines of command into human relationships, these experiences are a vital preparation for a promotion to a higher rank and appointment to a job in the administration one level up. In humanizing impersonal bureaucratic structures, such relationships also reproduce the delicate balance between localist particularism and centralist universalism that has been a long-time characteristic of the Chinese party-state. Many times cadre localism has proved to be a stumbling block for ambitious central initiatives. However, the roots of local cadres in the area where they were recruited and their embeddedness in a local administrative community have equally often helped the party-state survive in times of upheaval if not near-anarchy at the Centre.

At the level of fully intended outcomes, too, our investigation of cadre training has revealed much more than a straightforward effort to upgrade the administrative elite in contemporary China. Training continues to put a heavy emphasis on ideology, fostering a detailed understanding and conformity to the requirements and 'spirit' of the party centre. Cadre training expresses the party's insistence that cadres retain their role as a Leninist elite and moral vanguard. Just as long-serving cadres are given the opportunity through training and education to become better educated and better equipped for leadership, so are highly educated new recruits required to study and ultimately internalize the ideology of the organization that they have signed up to serve. Cadre training is thus the party's chief instrument to avoid cadres becoming apolitical technocrats who simply put their education and skills to the solution of administrative problems. However, the suffusion of such training with party ideology and the very fact that training is an unavoidable requirement the CCP imposes upon all cadres, party members or not, also reinforces the taken-for-granted acceptance among cadres of the role of the CCP as the ruling party.

This in itself is not new: from the party's earliest beginning, ideological training was used to forge ideological and organizational commitment to the party. However, for the first time in the CCP's history, this commitment can (or perhaps simply must) now *exclusively* be learned in the artificial context of training and study, with 'practice' for new recruits being limited to study tours to factories or farms, revolutionary tourism at the new cadre academies, discussions about specific cases during training sessions or at best an assignment to a temporary adjunct post in a local government. In addition, formal instruction to forge ideological commitment and conformity is increasingly assigned to specific institutions. The proliferation of non-ideological training programmes at schools and universities in China and abroad and the rise of individualized 'à la carte' training leave ideological study and immersion in the party's revolutionary tradition to party schools and the national cadre academies. There is every chance that the reliance on separate arrangements and institutions devoted to different aspects of training may in effect ghettoize ideological training, a minor requirement that has to be fulfilled rather than an intrinsic element of an integrated training package that includes all aspects of what it takes to be a good cadre.

The specialization of different aspects of training is largely intentional. Since the year 2000, policy making has reflected the Centre's impatience with conventional training at local party schools. Strengthening or establishing central institutions and the creation of a market for cadre training have been the main alternative approaches, in line with the more general project of the neo-socialist rebuilding of the party-state. As we have seen in this book, the strengthening, centralization and marketization of cadre training have many consequences. The attention lavished on cadre training in recent years that has been documented in this book goes well beyond any practical use that such training might have. The expenditure for cadre training has risen sharply not only in order to pay for better instruction, but also because training has become an item of conspicuous consumption, a way of rewarding cadres for their services and reinforcing their sense of being special and privileged. Well-funded party schools have become a powerful symbolic tool to assert the vitality of a reconstructed socialism and more generally the new administrative ethos that undergirds the CCP's claim to be China's legitimate ruling party. Central schools for cadres (the National Academy of Administration, the Central Party School and the four new cadre academies in Shanghai, Yan'an, Jinggangshan and Dalian) are flush with central funds. Other parts of China have also invested heavily in their local party schools, particularly at the provincial level and in large cities. This is most clearly the case with the party schools in Shanghai and Shenzhen. The ostentatious modernity of the party schools there and their role as hosts to pilgrimage-like study tours of cadres from all over China serve not only as a constant reminder that they are the developmental model for the rest of China, but also as their recognition of the fact that their new wealth and stability hinges on continued socialist rule at the Centre.

Marketization and centralization of cadre training have led to a proliferation and diversification of courses, exchanges, schools and programmes, and a general blurring of the boundaries between cadre training, other forms of training and regular secondary and tertiary education. In addition, Chinese governments and departments in search of ever-more excellent and prestigious training programmes increasingly send their cadres abroad for exploratory trips, short training courses, and even longer exchange visits or degree programmes. The commercialization of cadre education and training in China is beginning to produce some clear winners. A handful of well-endowed, prestigious and strategically located party schools and cadre academies have availed themselves of the opportunities to offer degree courses and training programmes that attract cadres from across the country. In addition, just as regular universities and schools have entered the market for cadre training, so have the prestigious and rich party schools used their competitive advantage to offer courses to a range of other customers, including businesspeople and even foreign students. Increasingly, cadre training has become just one of many services that educational institutions offer, whether they are party schools, universities, or other secondary and tertiary schools.

In this book, I have looked beyond the relatively narrow scope of cadre training itself, documenting new avenues for cadre recruitment and promotion as a vital component of the neo-socialist project that are creating the beginning of a regional or even national talent and job market. In the past, assignment to a top post in a subordinate locality, demobilization from the army or state job allocation after graduation from university were the only regular ways that outsiders got jobs and residence outside their native area. Currently, candidates for many jobs are recruited through open examination, advertisement and competitive application. As a result, younger cadres with excellent educational and professional qualification are beginning to look for professional jobs in China's burgeoning private sector; regional administrations and administrative departments find that they have to compete with other regions and departments and the private sector and to attract talent, particularly for positions that require a great deal of professional expertise. As these trends gain momentum in the years to come, we should expect an increasingly unified public–private market for professional talent to grow, enabling the richest areas to attract the best administrative talent, thereby even further increasing their advantages over poor and remote areas. At the same time, the life style and career expectations of professionals inside and outside the state sector will increasingly become similar, further encouraging the formation of an integrated middle class that includes professionals, managers, educators and private entrepreneurs.[1]

Despite the trend towards the marketization of recruitment in the party-state, I have shown that the CCP's local organization departments and party committees retain control over these new-style appointments, and that job entry exams are often only open to local cadres of a specific rank. Currently, we are clearly in a transitional phase that retains much of the old cadre management system. Despite many changes, the localism of cadres remains fundamentally untouched and local governments continue to have to rely on their own, local revenue base. It would therefore be a mistake to conclude that the marketization and centralization of the neo-socialist project are now complete. Across China, the more traditional 'honeycomb and web' pattern of hierarchically arranged decentralized local governments remains strong. Local administrations continue to be dominated by local cadres whose careers depend on their ability to balance the demands of the higher levels of the administration with local interests and sensitivities. Neo-socialist state building is, at present, still making only limited inroads in traditional administration.

Despite the persistence of the traditional autonomy of local governments, poorer regions of China already run the risk of lagging further behind in terms of governmental capacity. They simply cannot afford the expenditure needed to upgrade their administrative infrastructure to deliver needed public services, for instance in education, health or social insurance. At the same time, the central government continues to shy away from providing these services directly to the localities. Prefectural and particularly county party schools are often neglected and face financial difficulties similar to those in many other local government departments. These schools are the intended losers in the harsh market environment for higher education of which cadre training is becoming a part. However, the commercialization of cadre training and the central support and training provision apparently have not progressed far enough that local

[1] Sociologists in China such as Li Qiang at Tsinghua University and Li Peilin at the Chinese Academy of Social Sciences have for several years already been researching and debating the likelihood and extent of class stratification along the lines of developed capitalist countries. Given the continued importance of Marxist class analysis, this debate has been constrained by the fact that critics of the regime might use sociological evidence of the rise of class strata as an argument that the CCP has finally sold socialism down the river. Western studies on this issue are only just beginning to emerge, for instance Tomba 2004; Goodman 2008.

administrations feel they can do without their party school. For the moment at least, small local schools and their traditional courses continue to linger on shoestring budgets. The central emphasis on cadre training and the reform of the cadre system is still caught between centralization and neo-socialist marketization on the one hand and the traditional autonomy of local governments on the other. Only economically successful areas can actually afford to buy into the central government's vision of modern socialist governance, in addition to their competitive advantage on the emerging labour market for administrative talent mentioned earlier. The widening gap between rich and poor areas in China is therefore about more than economic growth and wealth alone: there is a real risk that poorer areas cannot partake in China's new, glossy socialism, and will not only economically, but also politically and administratively be left behind. In the absence of major budgetary transfers, the current limited neo-socialist rebuilding of the party-state translates poverty into governmental incapacity, thereby exacerbating rather than diminishing the gap between China's rich and poor areas.

THE FUTURE OF PARTY RULE AND DIVERGENT SOCIALISMS

Over the last twenty-five years China has overcome the contradiction between a capitalist economy and socialist governance, giving rise to the neo-socialism documented in this book. However, the conclusion that socialism in China is evolving into a robust form of governance that is qualitatively different from what preceded it should not make us ignore the fact that many weaknesses still remain: neo-socialism is very much a work in progress. Indeed, the very continuation of the rule of the CCP itself should not be taken for granted lest the party finds ways and means to address several of the problems have been discussed in this book: the incomplete reform of local government and the consequent autonomy of local cadres; the increasing gap in governmental capacity between rich and poor areas; the technocratization of the cadre corps and the untested quality of cadres' learned commitment to the party's ideology and rule. In addition, two others in particular should also be mentioned.

First, corruption. As Dali Yang points out, especially since 1998–1999, corruption has been battled on a number of fronts. Some of the most prominent culprits (and especially those who politically had fallen out of favour) have been exposed and mercilessly persecuted in anti-corruption campaigns. Much more importantly, the institutions of the party and the state that are supposed to combat official corruption have been strengthened and made more independent from the organizations and people that they are supposed to oversee (Yang 2004: 223–235). I would, in fact, interpret the latter as a prominent aspect of the neo-socialist state-building project. As the state's general capacity to control local administration increases, we should also expect its ability to contain corruption to improve. However, I also must agree with Melanie Manion that the current dual party–government institutional setup in anti-corruption work precludes a truly effective approach (Manion 2004: chapters 4 and 5).

Either way, it is unlikely that the battle against corruption will be won any time soon. Although neo-socialist state strengthening provides better instruments to contain more familiar forms of corruption in which official position is used for self-enrichment, it also encourages new forms of corruption in which wealth is used to obtain official position. In the nineties the practice of buying and selling cadre positions, including leading cadre positions, became increasingly widespread (Burns 2006: 51; Yang 2004: 182). According to He Zengke, a prominent researcher at the CCP's Central Compilation and Translation Bureau, a key liberal think tank, 'buying and selling of official positions' (*mai guan mai guan*) became widespread in the nineties, and has more recently become endemic. No longer are posts 'retailed' individually, but are often 'wholesaled' by the hundreds, usually shortly before the party secretary who controls official appointments leaves office. Furthermore, while the risks are still very low, prices have gone up, also because in cases that were investigated public funds now amount to 90 per cent of the money used to buy positions (He Zengke 2005: 368). According to He, the main reason behind the endemic nature of this phenomenon is the continued opacity of the appointment system that gives the local party committee and especially its secretary ultimate control over official appointments in his jurisdiction. He boldly concludes that until the principle of party control over appointments is relinquished, the problem of buying and selling official positions will not go away.

The Centre is well aware of this problem,[2] presenting the neo-socialist changes in appointments and promotions that were discussed in

---

[2] In November 2006, Zhang Quanjing, a former head of the central organization department, publicly spoke out against this form of corruption; see 'Former CPC official lambasts selling of gov't jobs', *The China Daily* 13 November 2006, online at www.chinadaily.com.cn/china/2006-11/11/content_730587.htm (checked on 13 November 2006). For the full text of the interview with Zhang Quanjing, see Xinhua News Agency news.xinhuanet.com/legal/2006–11/10/content_5311550.htm, 10 November 2006 (checked on 13 November 2006). Several references to the problem of vote buying are made in 'Reform of the cadre system must hold firm to principles – an interview with Lü Rizhou, deputy head of the Shanxi Provincial People's Consultative Conference' (Ganbu tizhi gaige bixu jianchi yuanze, kuoda minzhu – fang Shanxi sheng zhengxie fuzhuxi Lü Rizhou), *Lilun dongtai* 1736 (10 March 2007): 1–10.

chapter 6 of this book (public selection, examinations, elections) as solutions. However, these changes are unlikely to fully solve the problem as neo-socialism itself fuels the problem. Neo-socialism is premised on maintaining the Leninist principle of party rule, and remedies can only amend but not abolish the control of party committees over leading appointments. Furthermore, neo-socialist changes have much increased the attraction of official positions. Not only are official perks and salaries now much better than five or ten years ago, but many opportunities for self-enrichment continue to exist, either legally or illegally.[3] Lastly, the attractiveness of official positions coupled with the increased scope given to formal elections within party committees is giving rise to corrupt strategies of canvassing votes associated with elections the world over. Although outright vote buying does not (yet) appear to be widespread, candidates reportedly often spend very considerable sums of money on gifts, banquets and other ways that are (just) within the rules to curry favour with their selectorate or electorate;[4] indeed, it seems only a matter of time before reports will reach us on similar practices in the much publicized public elections in townships and villages.

A second and to my mind equally important danger to the neo-socialist project is the party's tendency to revert to an old-fashioned totalitarian response when it feels threatened by external forces. Since 1989, the CCP has actually made very considerable progress in dealing with popular protest and freedom of expression as the government no longer aspires to control all thoughts and actions of the population. However, there are still certain boundaries that cannot be transgressed and, if that happens, the reaction has often been extremely harsh. More importantly, the party itself sometimes does not fully seem to trust the efficacy of its newer and more sophisticated forms of political control, reverting to a siege mentality in which all hostile forces are lumped together and uniformly excluded: Muslim, Tibetan or Taiwanese separatists, independently organized religions,

---

[3] A glance into the details of cadre income is given in a research report from the Fujian organization department, published in 2003 in the *China Investigation Report*. The report looked in detail at the legal and illegal sources of income of cadres. Even when limiting itself to legal sources, the report showed that there existed very wide discrepancies between different departments within the same administration, revealing that these departments were using much if not all of their discretionary incomes (for instance levies, fees and business ventures) to top up the nominal salaries of their cadres. In Fujian's Putian prefecture in the year 2000, the departments dealing with mineral extraction had the lowest average annual income (5,722 yuan), while the departments in the field of finance and insurance had the highest (12,957 yuan). Depending on the job, in the early 2000s being a cadre could therefore be a financially rewarding proposition even without the expected income from illegal sources. In more recent research, Christine Wong reached identical conclusions (Wong 2008).
[4] Conversation with Chinese researcher based in Hong Kong, 7 November 2008.

Chinese dissidents and foreigners calling for democracy and human rights. Recent examples that come to mind include the repression of the Falungong in 1999, the SARS crisis in 2002–2003 and the government's jittery reaction to the Tibetan riots just a few months prior to the Beijing Olympics in the summer of 2008. As the global recession deepens in 2009, the already very frequent protests of jobless workers and landless peasants are bound to increase steeply, further testing the party-state's neo-socialist resolve.

Fortunately, until now such episodes have been relatively short, but serve as warnings to foreign observers and the Chinese population alike. Despite several decades of administrative reform, the CCP itself still has far to go in evolving into a fully neo-socialist ruling party. Widely reported steps have been taken to broaden the party membership, including private entrepreneurs. More recently, in the run-up to the seventeenth party congress in October 2007, there was much talk about intra-party democracy. In order to avoid potentially very damaging totalitarian relapses, the party will have to continue to take such steps that will help it shake the hermeticism of its socialist past, ultimately becoming a pluralist arena of political debate and competition among a diverse elite composed of leading cadres, prominent intellectuals, high-level professionals and entrepreneurs. However, such a change runs the obvious risk of jeopardizing the party's organizational integrity and myth of Leninist infallibility, thus potentially undermining the very essence of the neo-socialist project. However, if past experience is anything to go by, the leadership will probably not want to think in such stark terms. Instead, it will opt for a strategy of small-scale experiments and incremental changes, pragmatically progressing and retreating as the political realities of the day dictate, without working from a clear blueprint for a radically different long-term future.

China's current trajectory of neo-socialist development combines many contradictory elements: reaffirmation of the Leninist organizational discipline, creation of a modern governmental bureaucracy, and neoliberal marketization all unfold in parallel. Despite their apparent incompatibility, these elements do add up to a society that not only works, but has also managed to steer a consistent course of unprecedented social, economic, cultural and administrative modernization. As I have pointed out repeatedly in this book, these contradictions are hardly an ideological issue: the point is not that capitalist avariciousness and individualism might necessarily undermine socialist collectivism and egalitarianism. By now, the CCP has shed its commitment to revolutionary transformation to the point that there is no perceptible ideological difference with neoliberal prescriptions for market-driven economic development. This is not simply a matter of the increasing vacuity of socialism as a political ideology. Socialist rule and neoliberal economic development have not merely come to tolerate and complement each other. I concur with David Harvey that in China neoliberal principles and practices are both predicated on and support the long-term sustainability of the Chinese party-state (Harvey 2005). Not only has successful capitalist development replaced revolutionary transformation as the party's mission, legitimizing and enabling continued Leninist rule. The CCP has also nurtured markets and patterns of globalization that have penetrated the very core of the party-state itself. What has emerged in China is an organizational and ideological fusion and synthesis of socialist and neoliberal principles.

As the general conclusion that follows from my work on the specifics of cadre training it might be good to dwell on this a bit more. As pointed out in the introduction to this book, it is almost customary to identify the party's power monopoly as the source of contradictions, an anachronism that will inevitably be swept aside by the force of historical necessity. However, in this book I have tried to approach the issue from the opposite direction, starting from the mounting evidence from research on contemporary China that the CCP's continued hold on power is not the problem that has to be solved, but the reason for China's remarkable combination of sustained rapid economic growth and political stability. This in turn points to the conclusion that the operational question should not be what is wrong with CCP governmentality, but rather what it is that the CCP has been able to bring to the table that has helped it to transform China.

The answer, in my opinion, is not hard to find: it is quite simply the continued organizational (rather than ideological) credibility of the CCP's Leninist leading role in society. As the undisputed ruling party, the CCP continues to draw on the 'charismatic impersonality' of Leninist party organizations (Jowitt 1992). As the infallible source of absolute truth, the party has an unchallengeable and almost mystical mandate to resolve contradictory trends and objectives by relating them to an unquestioned final and overriding mission and desire, no matter how vaguely defined. However, this organizational charisma is not simply a given quality that the party can draw upon at will. At the root of its survival as a Leninist organization lies the party's almost uncanny ability time and again to learn from its mistakes and act upon itself and its ideology. Approaching revolution and later rule as a learning process has given the party a virtually unique capacity for renewal, change and reinvention. Despite totalitarian appearances, the CCP in the course of its history has gone through many brushes with near-extinction – more often than not self-inflicted – each time to re-emerge with a clearer vision of how to tackle the many challenges that lie ahead. Perhaps the most unexpected aspect of China's rise after the 1989 debacle has been the party's success in re-establishing its leading role, not by suppressing all dissent or disagreement, but quite the contrary by allowing a remarkable scope of debate in society and within the party itself. In terms of political reform, the last fifteen years have seen remarkable proposals, experiments and legislation to strengthen the party's popular appeal and the administration's accountability and base in the rule of law; anything, in fact, that does not call for open and direct multi-party elections.

It would be a mistake to dismiss the party's willingness to experiment with novel ways of reinventing its Leninist organizational charisma as merely the desperate attempts of a regime that refuses to face up to the historical necessity of a full democratic transition. The party's success has not happened despite its socialist heritage, but thanks to it. The party's survival is predicated on its Leninist charisma which in turn needs ideologically prescribed goals. In other words, the key to the party's ability to renew itself and its charisma is its skill in redefining its mission to change China, creating a moving target that is always many years away. The party may have shed its revolutionary pretensions, but it still genuinely believes that it is the sole transformative agent that will bring to China deliverance from poverty and foreign humiliation. After the eventual failure of planned state socialism, the party fully bought into the neoliberal belief in the transformative power of the market, government streamlining and contemporary global modernity. However, unlike many other developing countries, the party's continued rule has enabled it to do this on its own terms, rather than those of western powers, international organizations and multinational corporations. It is here that the full implications of neo-socialism become clear. The Chinese Communist Party has not simply borrowed the neoliberal techniques of governance and market transition as adjuncts to continued socialist rule. The irony of neo-socialism is that it fully has incorporated the neoliberal reinvention of the economy and society in its recipe for China's future modernity. As such, the success of the neoliberal project in China is as much predicated on the continued rule of the party as neoliberalism has become a vital source of the renewal of the party's Leninist organizational charisma. Far from being at odds with each other, under neo-socialism Leninism and neoliberalism have indeed become one.

With the maturation of the symbiosis of Leninism and neoliberalism in the last twenty years, the party has felt increasingly secure in its ability to strengthen its hold on power in the context of capitalist economic development. It is here that the success of the efforts at modernizing the cadre system may have had their most important impact. The massive investment in cadre training and education that have been documented in this book have given China a corps of cadres that are incomparable to their predecessors of twenty years ago in terms of their educational qualifications, managerial skills and understanding of China and the world. At the same time, they continue in time-honoured Leninist fashion to be the loyal instrument of the party rather than politically neutral professional administrators, like civil servants in western democracies. The continued emphasis on political theory in the revamped cadre training and the role of party committees in decisions on appointments, promotions and demotions despite innovations such as elections and public selection of cadres are intended to guarantee that this continues to be the case. Neo-socialist reform of the cadre system has put the party's Leninist leading role in society itself on a more solid footing. This has given the party the administrative capacity, expertise and most importantly the confidence in the long-term viability of its rule needed to endorse experiments with further forms of participatory government and rule by law that are being proposed by intellectuals and advisors both inside and outside China. Perhaps counterintuitively, a strengthening of the CCP's rule *enables* further political reform in the direction of a more pluralistic and consultative form of benign neo-socialist dictatorship, while at the same time making the emergence of a full-blown multi-party democracy less likely.[5]

I would like to end this book with a few comments on the broader comparative picture that the CCP's neo-socialist reinvention fits in. It has become fashionable to point out that capitalism is not a one-size-fits-all economic model, but evolved the world over into very different systems of social and economic organization. In the recent literature on 'varieties of capitalism' (Hall and Soskice 2001; Crouch 2005) the 'Confucian' capitalisms in East Asia (Japan, Korea, Taiwan, Hong Kong and Singapore) play a paradigmatic role (Redding 1993). I would argue that contemporary mainland China is not simply a case of yet another East Asian 'divergent capitalism', but also the most important and most successful example of the *divergent socialisms* that have emerged from the ashes of the apparent

---

[5] Mark Leonard reaches a similar conclusion based on quite different material, namely his interviews with prominent intellectuals in China (Leonard 2008: 81).

uniformity of Cold War socialism, in Asia, Eastern Europe, Latin America and Africa.

Almost twenty years after the fall of the Berlin Wall, it has become clear that for more than fifty years the Cold War had blinded our vision. The bipolarity of that period made us forget that liberalism and socialism share the same roots in the eighteenth-century Enlightenment; in fact, I would argue that one cannot be a socialist without being a liberal, just as one cannot be a liberal without also being a socialist. Both are a vision to set humanity free from the yokes of serfdom, absolutism and exploitation. Just as socialism does not necessarily entail a negation of the market, so does liberalism in fact wish to set free and enfranchise both poor and rich. Both liberalism and socialism present paths to the equality, freedom and prosperity of a truly modern society that are in many ways complementary. With the benefit of hindsight, exclusivist readings of the two major ideologies of the twentieth century really started when Marxism arrogated the monopoly over socialism, turning a humanist ideology of liberation into the pseudo-science of class struggle, and opening the door to the increasingly totalitarian, violent and paranoid delusions of radical German communism, Leninism, Stalinism and Maoism. Ultimately, human life, freedom and happiness no longer counted; all that mattered was the vacuous concept of 'the revolution'. Their antagonistic language and practice alienated increasingly large numbers of potential sympathizers to a more humanist understanding of socialism, forging a grand alliance in the western world of capitalists, the middle class and the working class that rallied around new and equally combative and exclusivist readings of liberalism. The stage was set for a cold war so intense and absolute that, by the end of it, we had forgotten what history could be like without it. In the east, all we could see was postsocialism; in the west, history was thought to have reached its final conclusion.

In actual fact, of course, history has moved on. Despite globalization, the universalist pretensions of the neoliberal world order are being challenged in sites across the world both large and small. What emerges is a myriad of unorganized and messy new recombinations of bits and pieces of liberal and socialist ideas and practices. State socialism as an economic system may indeed be largely dead and buried, but socialism as a political system and ideology continues to morph and change in all kinds of societies, and will be highly relevant to the many challenges that will face humankind in the twenty-first century. Just in the last few years we have seen the reinstatement of Keynsian economics and the interventionist state under the pressure of the 2008 global financial crisis on the grand stage of international economic policy making, the first hesitant and selective engagement with the liberal world order in North Korea and Cuba, the neo-socialisms of China and Vietnam, the revolutionary socialisms of Nepal and India that now rule very substantial parts of both these countries, and the populist socialism of Chavez in Venezuela. The grand project of liberalism and socialism that started in eighteenth- and nineteenth-century Europe to bring a freer, fairer and more prosperous life continues.

APPENDIX I

List of interviewees

No.	Role	Position	Date
Yunnan Province			
1	administrative staff	Head of Education, Yunnan Provincial Party School (YPPS)	01/04/2004, 12/12/2004
2	teaching staff	Professor and Head of Department of Public Administration, YPPS	02/04/2004
3	degree student	undergraduate student of economic management, YPPS	03/04/2004
4	degree student	*dazhuan* student of administrative management, YPPS	03/04/2004
5	degree student	master's student of economics, YPPS	03/04/2004
6	degree student	undergraduate student of administrative management, YPPS	04/04/2004
7	degree student	undergraduate student of administrative management, YPPS	04/04/2004
8	degree student	student on minority preparatory class for undergraduates	04/04/2004
9	teaching staff	teacher of science and technology, YPPS	05/04/2004
10	training student	Deputy Head, Yunnan Provincial Museum	05/04/2004
11	training student	Deputy Head, Propaganda Department, Yunnan Normal University	05/04/2004
12	training student	Head, Office of Social Management, Yunnan Province Audit Bureau	07/04/2004
13	training student	Assistant to Head of Qujing Prefecture	07/04/2004
14	teaching staff	class monitor, female cadres training classes	08/04/2004
15	training student	Deputy Chair, Dehong Prefecture People's Congress	08/04/2004
16	degree student	master's student of scientific socialism, YPPS	10/04/2004
17	degree student	master's student of economics, YPPS	10/04/2004
18	degree student	master's student of economics, YPPS	11/04/2004
19	degree student	master's student of economics, YPPS	11/04/2004
20	training student	Head of Government, Lincang county	12/04/2004

List of interviewees

No.	Role	Position	Date
21	training student	Deputy Party Secretary, Jinggu Autonomous county	12/04/2004
22	administrative staff	Deputy Head, office of organization and personnel, YPPS	13/04/2004
23	training student	Deputy Head, office of organization and personnel, Yunnan Minorities University	13/04/2004
24	training student	Deputy Chair and Party Secretary, Yunnan Province Centre for Science and Technology Exchange	13/04/2004
25	training student	Deputy Chair, Kunming City People's Congress	14/04/2004
26	training student	Deputy Chair, Work Committee of Lincang Prefecture People's Congress	14/04/2004
27	administrative staff	Research Office, Yunnan Party School	16/04/2004
28	training student	Standing Deputy Head, Kunming City Party School	16/04/2004
29	training student	Deputy Party Secretary, Zhenxiong County	16/04/2004
30	degree student	master's student of economics, YPPS	17/04/2004
31	degree student	master's student of scientific socialism, YPPS	17/04/2004
32	degree student	master's student of economics, YPPS	17/04/2004
33	teaching staff	teacher at the Civil Servants Training Department, YPPS	18/04/2004
34	administrative staff	Deputy Head, educational affairs office, YPPS	19/04/2004
35	teaching staff	Head, Correspondence Teaching Section, YPPS	19/04/2004
36	teaching staff	teacher and class monitor, Training Department, YPPS	24/11/2004
37	administrative staff	Editor, Journal of the Yunnan Academy of Administration	24/11/2004
38	degree student	*dazhuan* student of economics, YPPS	24/11/2004
39	degree student	*dazhuan* student of administrative management, YPPS	24/11/2004
40	training student	Head, Research Office of Edible Fungi, National Supply and Marketing General Agency	24/11/2004
41	administrative staff	Deputy Head of Education, YPPS	25/11/2004
42	administrative staff	Deputy Head, General Office, YPPS	25/11/2004
43	administrative staff	Head, Training Department for Civil Servants	25/11/2004
44	degree student	*dazhuan* student of economic management, YPPS	25/11/2004
45	degree student	*dazhuan* student of administrative management, YPPS	25/11/2004
46	degree student	undergraduate student of economic management, YPPS	25/11/2004
47	training student	Head, Propaganda Department, Huaning County	26/11/2004

(*cont.*)

No.	Role	Position	Date
48	administrative staff	Standing Deputy Head, Yunnan Academy of Socialism and others	26/11/2004
49	administrative staff	Head, Public Examinations Section, Organization Department, Yunnan Province	11/12/2004
50	administrative staff	Public Servants Management Office, Personnel Bureau, Yunnan province	11/12/2004
51	teaching staff	teacher, Office of Languages and Literature, Yunnan Party School	11/12/2004
52	teaching staff	Associate Professor, Public Management Department, Yunnan Party School	12/12/2004
53	teaching staff	Associate Professor, Economic Management Department, Yunnan Party School	12/12/2004

Qujing prefecture

No.	Role	Position	Date
54	administrative staff	Standing Deputy Head, Qujing Prefectural Party School and others	16/11/2004
55	administrative staff	Deputy Head, Qujing Prefectural Party School, Qujing Prefectural Party School	16/11/2006
56	teaching staff	Head, Office of Marxism and Leninism, Qujing Party School	16/11/2006
57	teaching staff	Deputy Head, Office of Economics, Qujing Prefectural Party School	16/11/2006
58	teaching staff	teacher, Office of Economics, Qujing Party School	16/11/2006
59	teaching staff	Deputy Head, Office of Literature and History, Qujing Party School	17/11/2006
60	teaching staff	teacher, Office of Economic Management, Qujing Party School	17/11/2006
61	administrative staff	Deputy Head, Research Office, Qujing Party School	17–18/11/2006
62	teaching staff	Deputy Head, Office of Literature and History, Qujing Party School	17/11/2006
63	teaching staff	teacher, Politics Office, Qujing Party School	17/11/2004
64	teaching staff	teacher, Office of Party History, Qujing Party School	17/11/2004
65	administrative staff	Head, Educational Affairs Office, Qujing Party School	17/11/2004
66	teaching staff	Deputy Head, Office of Administrative Managment and Law, Qujing Party School	18/11/2004
67	administrative staff	Head, Qilin District Party School and others	18/11/2004
68	administrative staff	Head, Educational Affairs Office, Qujing Party School	18/11/2004

Yiliang county

No.	Role	Position	Date
69	administrative staff	Head, Yiliang County Party School and others	27/11/2004

Shilin county

No.	Role	Position	Date
70	administrative staff	Head, Shilin County Party School	28/11/2004

No.	Role	Position	Date
Honghe prefecture			
71	administrative staff	Section Head, Cadre Education Section, Organization Department, Honghe prefecture	29/11/2004
72	teaching staff	Head, Office of Party History, Honghe Party School	30/11/2004
73	teaching staff	Head, educational affairs office, Honghe Party School	30/11/2004
74	training student	Head, Industry and Commerce Association, Luchun county	30/11/2004
75	training student	General Manager, Passenger Transport Company, Gejiu City	30/11/2004
76	teaching staff	Head, Office of Administrative Management, Honghe Party School	01/12/2004
77	administrative staff	Deputy Head, Educational Affairs Office, Honghe Party School	01/12/2004
78	administrative staff	Deputy Head, United Front Department, Honghe Prefecture	01/12/2004
79	training student	Deputy Head, Development Planning Bureau, Mengzi county	01/12/2004
80	administrative staff	Deputy Head, Theoretical Education Section, Organization Department, Honghe prefecture	02/12/2004
81	administrative staff	Head, Personnel Section, Culture Bureau, Honghe prefecture	02/12/2004
82	administrative staff	Deputy Head, Honghe Party School	02/12/2004
83	teaching staff	Head, Office of Law, Honghe Party School	02/12/2004
84	correspondence degree student	undergraduate student of public management	02/12/2004
85	administrative staff	Head, Cadre Section, Minorities Commission, Honghe prefecture	02/12/2004
Beijing			
86	teaching staff	Associate Professor, School of Public Administration, Renmin University	16/12/2006
87	administrative staff	Deputy Party Secretary, Peking University	19/12/2006
88	teaching staff	Professor, National Academy of Administration	19/12/2006
89	teaching staff	Professor, Department of Politics and Law, Central Party School	20/12/2006
90	administrative staff	Deputy Head, Central Party Schools Correspondence Academy	21/12/2006
91	teaching staff	Professor of Public Management, National Academy of Administration	26/04/2007
92	administrative staff	Head, School of Public Management, Tsinghua University	27/04/2007

(cont.)

No.	Role	Position	Date
93	administrative staff	Head and Deputy Head, International Cooperation and Exchange Department, Beijing Party School	27/04/2007
94	administrative staff	Head, Office of Leadership Science, Central Party School	28/04/2007
95	teaching staff	Professor, Department of Party Building, Central Party School	28/04/2007
96	teaching staff	Professor and Head, Office of Sociology, Central Party School	29/04/2007
97	administrative staff	Deputy Head and Head, Continuing Education Department, Tsinghua University	30/04/2007

APPENDIX 2

Student questionnaire survey

The survey was carried out between September and December 2005 among all cadres who participated in a training programme at the Yunnan Provincial Party School. The questionnaire was designed together with Professor Duan Eryu of the party school, and administered by the class teachers (*ban zhuren*) at the school. The survey results were coded in MS Excel and analysed in SPSS. A full list of survey variables is attached at the end of this appendix.

A total of 490 questionnaires were distributed with 362, or 74%, valid returns. Three-quarters (74%) of the respondents were men and one-quarter (26%) were women. Around two-thirds of the participants were between the ages of 40 and 49 (65%). The age distribution for men and women was similar, with modal ages of 43 for men and 44 for women. There were seven ranks in the study population: below *ke*, vice *ke*, full *ke*, vice *chu*, full *chu*, vice *ting* and full *ting*. The largest category of respondents were of *ke* rank (171, or 47%), followed by *chu* (133, or 37%), and the highest rank *ting* (19, or 5%). The largest individual rank in the study was vice *chu* (93), followed by full *ke* (83); together they constitute 49% of respondents.

Variable codes Yunnan cadre training survey

Variable	Question
	1.1 Individual background
1	year of birth
2	sex
3	nationality
4	household status at birth
5	place of birth
6	place of residence
7	marital status

(*cont.*)

Variable	Question
8	party membership
9	year of joining party
10	military service
11	duration of military service
	1.2 Employment in the past five years
	First employment
12	rank of position
13	type of unit
14	level of unit
15	length of employment
16	method of appointment
	Second employment
17	rank of position
18	type of unit
19	level of unit
20	length of employment
21	method of appointment
	Third employment
22	rank of position
23	type of unit
24	level of unit
25	length of employment
26	method of appointment
	Fourth employment
27	rank of position
28	type of unit
29	level of unit
30	length of employment
31	method of appointment
	1.3 Education
32	educational status at first employment
33	current educational status
34	year of highest diploma
35	full-time/part-time course
36	currently taking a degree course
37	number of years of course
38	full-time/part-time course
39	reason for taking this course
40	main source of funding for costs of course
	1.4 Training received
41	name of current training course
42	duration of course
43	reason for participating in training course

Variable	Question
	1.5 Other short-term training received in previous two years
	First training course
44	name of course
45	cadre rank of course
46	work unit of training course
47	duration of training
48	reason for participating
	Second training course
49	name of course
50	cadre rank of course
51	work unit of training course
52	duration of training
53	reason for participating
	Third training course
54	name of course
55	cadre rank of course
56	work unit of training course
57	duration of training
58	reason for participating
	Fourth training course
59	name of course
60	cadre rank of course
61	work unit of training course
62	duration of training
63	reason for participating
	2 Opinion on training received on current course
	2.1 Opinion on the content of the course
65	most useful content
66	useful content
67	not very useful content
68	least useful content
	2.3 Opinion on methods of training
69	best method
70	good method
71	not very good method
72	worst method
	3 Participation in official recruitment by public examination
	First time
73	rank of position applied for
74	year of application
75	place of application
76	examination result

(cont.)

Variable	Question
	Second time
77	rank of position applied for
78	year of application
79	place of application
80	examination result
	Third time
81	rank of position applied for
82	year of application
83	place of application
84	examination result
	Fourth time
85	rank of position applied for
86	year of application
87	place of application
88	examination result
	4 Immediate relatives
	4.1 Father
89	present place of residence (prefecture)
90	current household registration status
91	nationality (ethnic group)
92	party membership
93	profession (before retirement)
	4.2 Mother
94	current place of residence (prefecture/city)
95	current household registration status
96	nationality
97	party membership
98	profession (before retirement)
	4.3 Spouse
99	year of birth
100	place of birth (prefecture/city)
101	sex
102	nationality
103	household registration status at birth
104	current household registration status
105	party membership
106	year when joining party
107	current profession
	4.4 Children
	First child
108	year of birth
109	sex

Variable	Question
110	lives at home
111	current educational status
112	current profession
	Second child
113	year of birth
114	sex
115	lives at home
116	current educational status
117	current profession
	Third child
118	year of birth
119	sex
120	lives at home
121	current educational status
122	current profession

APPENDIX 3

Glossary of Chinese terms

banshiyuan	办事员	office worker
beifen	辈分	generational rank
bu(ji)	部级	ministry (level)
Budui Fenbu	部队分部	Military Branch Department
caidanshi jiaoyu	菜单式教育	*à la carte* education
chu(ji)	处级	office (level)
chuangshou	创收	creating income; self-generated income
churen peixun	出任培训	novice training
Dalian Jing-Li Xueyuan	大连经理学院	Dalian Academy of Economics and Management
dangjian	党建	party building
diaoyanyuan	调研员	investigator
difang dangxiao bangongshi	地方党校办公室	office of local party schools
dushu ban	读书班	reading class
feidang ganbu; dangwai ganbu	非党干部; 党外干部	cadre without party membership
fenyuan	分院	branch academy
fu	副	deputy (of post)
fudaozhan	辅导站	teaching stations
ganbu jiaoyu peixun weiyuanhui; ganjiaowei	干部教育培训委员会; 干教委	cadre education and training committee
ganbu jiaoyu weiyuanhui (xiaozu)	干部教育委员会 (小组)	party leadership committee (group) for education
ganbu peixun	干部培训	cadre training
ganbu peixun guihua	干部培训规划	cadre training plan
ganbu xueyuan	干部学院	cadre academy; executive leadership academy
ganjiaowei bangongshi; ganjiao bumen	干教委办公室; 干教部门	cadre education committee or department
gaoduan peixun	高端培训	high-end training
gonggong guanli	共攻管理	public management

gonggong xingzheng	公共行政	public administration
gongkai faxing	公开发行	publicly available
gongkai xuanba; gongxuan	公开选拔; 公选	open selection
gongwuyuan kaoshi; gongkao	公务员考试; 公考	public servants exams
gongwuyuan peixun bu	公务员培训部	civil servants training department
guazhi	挂职	temporary non-executive appointment
Guojia Xingzheng Xueyuan	国家行政学院	National Academy of Administration
Guowuyuan Fazhan Yanjiu Zhongxin	国务院发展研究中心	Development Research Centre of the State Council
Guowuyuan Xuewei Weiyuanhui	国务院学位委员会	Degree Committee of the State Council
Guoziwei Fenxiao	国资委分校	Branch School for the Commission of State Assets
hexie shehui	和谐社会	harmonious society
houbei ganbu peixun ban	后备干部培训班	reserve cadre training classes
houbei xuanren; houbei ganbu; chubei rencai	后备选人; 后备干部; 储备人才	talent reserve pool
hui dai xun	会代训	meeting instead of training
jiaowuchu	教务处	educational affairs office
jiaoyan bu	教研部	academic department
jiaoyuzhang	教育长	head of education
jibie	级别	grade
jiguan dangwei	机关党委	staff party committee
jihuawai	计划外	outside the plan
jingzheng shanggang	竞争上岗	competitive appointment
jinxiu bu	进修部	advanced study department
jiti xuexi	集体学习	collective study
jiwei	计委	discipline inspection committee
jiyao tongxun ke	机要通讯科	confidential correspondence section
ju(ji)	局级	bureau (level)
Kang-Ri Junzheng Daxue (Kangda)	抗日军政大学 (抗大)	Military and Political University of Resistance against Japan
ke(ji)	科级	section (level)
kexue fazhanguan	科学发展观	concept of scientific development
keyan chu	科研处	research office
keyuan	科员	section member
la piao hui xuan	拉票贿选	election fraud
liang kuai paizi, yi tao banzi	两块牌子, 一套班子	two signs, one group
lianluo ke	联络科	liaison section
lilun gugan	理论骨干	theoretical backbone

(cont.)

lunxun	轮训	periodic retraining
mai guan mai guan	买官卖官	purchase and sale of official positions
Makesi Gongchan Zhuyi Xuexiao	马克思共产主义学校	Marxist Communist School (in Ruijin)
Makesi-Liening Xueyuan	马克思列宁学院	Marx-Lenin Academy
minzhu dangpai	民主党派	democratic party
neibu faxing	内部发行	for internal circulation only
peixun bu	培训部	training department
piaojuezhi	票决制	system of election by formal vote
quandang jiangke	全党讲课	lectures for the whole party
renzhi peixun	任职培训	training for office
ronglu	熔炉	smelting furnace
'Sange Daibiao'	'三个代表'	'Three Represents'
shaoshu minzu weiyuanhui; minwei	少数民族委员会; 民委	minorities committee
shehui zhuyi xueyuan	社会主义学院	academy of socialism
sheng-buji zhuyao lingdao ganbu zhuanti yantaoban	省部级主要领导干部专题研讨班	special discussion class for principal central cadres of provincial-ministerial rank
si(ji)	司级	bureau (level)
suzhi	素质	quality
ting(ji)	厅级	department (level)
tiyanshi jiaoyu	体验式教育	experiental education
tongzhan bu	统战部	united front department
tuochan	脱产	not in employment; full time (of student)
wangshang dangxiao	网上党校	web-based party schools
wenping pifa dian	文凭批发店	diploma wholesale shop
xia hai	下海	to go to sea; to seek employment in the private sector
xiao jinku	小金库	small treasury
xiaowu weiyuanhui	校务委员会	committee for school affairs
xingzheng guanli ganbu xueyuan	行政管理干部学院	academy of administration
xingzheng guanlixue	行政管理学	administrative management
xingzheng xueyuan	行政学院	academy of administration
xingzhengxue	行政学	administrative science
xuanjuzhi	选举制	election system
xueli	学历	non-recognized degree
xueli ban	学历班	degree course or class
xuequ	学区	study districts
xuewei	学位	recognized degree
xuewei dian	学位点	degree point
xueyuan	学员	student

xunshiyuan	巡视员	inspector
yi ba shou	一把手	first in command
yi ren wei ben	以人为本	to take people as the basis
Yintewang Makesi zhuyi	因特网马克思主义	Internet Marxism
youxiu qingnian ganbu peixunban	优秀青年干部培训班	training class for outstanding new leading party cadre recruits
yuancheng jiaoxue wangluo zhongxin	远程教学网络中心	network centre for long-distance education
yuke	预科	remedial course
zaizhi	在职	in employment; part time (of student)
zheng	正	full (of post)
zhishu jiguan gongzuo weiyuanhui; gongwei	直属机关工作委员会; 工委	working committee for directly administered departments
zhiwu	职务	rank, level, post
Zhonggong Zhongyang Zhengce Yanjiushi	中共中央政策研究室	CCP Central Policy Research Office
zhongqing ban	中青班	young and middle aged cadre classes
Zhongyang	中央	centre
Zhongyang Dangxiao	中央党校	Central Party School
Zhongyang Gaoji Dangxiao	中央高级党校	Central High-Level Party School
Zhongyang Guojia Jiguan Fenxiao	中央国家机关分校	Branch School for Central Government Organs
Zhongyang Zhishu Jiguan Fenxiao	中央直属机关分校	Central Party School's Branch School for Central (Party) Organs
zhuanxing fazhan	转型发展	transformational development
zhuguan bumen	主管部门	responsible department
zhuren keyuan	主任科员	chief section member
zhuti ban	主体班	main training course or class
zongyuan	总院	general academy
zuzhi bu	组织部	organization department
zuzhi renshi chu	组织人事处	organization and personnel office

References

Abélès, Marc, 1988. 'Modern Political Ritual', *Current Anthropology* 29(3): 391–404.
Abrams, Philip, 1988. 'Notes on the Difficulty of Studying the State (1977)', *Journal of Historical Sociology* 1(1): 58–89.
Alpermann, Björn, 2001. 'The Post Election Administration of Chinese Villages', *The China Journal* 46: 45–67.
Anagnost, Ann, 1997. *National Past-times: Narrative, Representation, and Power in Modern China*. Durham, NC: Duke University Press.
Anonymous, 2008. 'Rebirth and Secularization of the Central Party School in China'. Unpublished paper.
Apter, David E. and Tony Saich, 1994. *Revolutionary Discourse in Mao's Republic*. Cambridge, MA: Harvard University Press.
Barnett, A. Doak, 1967. *Cadres, Bureaucracy and Political Power in Communist China*. New York: Columbia University Press.
Baum, Richard and Alexei Shevchenko, 1999. 'The "State of the State"', in *The Paradox of China's Post-Mao Reforms*, ed. Merle Goldman and Roderick MacFarquhar. Cambridge, MA: Harvard University Press, 333–360.
Bellah, Robert N., 1967. 'Civil Religion in America', *Daedalus* 96: 1–21.
Bernstein, Thomas P. and Xiaobo Lü, 2000. 'Taxation without Representation: Peasants, the Central and the Local States in Reform China', *The China Quarterly* 163: 742–763.
   2003. *Taxation without Representation in Contemporary Rural China*. Cambridge: Cambridge University Press.
Blecher, Marc and Vivienne Shue, 2001. 'Into Leather: State-led Development and the Private Sector in Xinji', *The China Quarterly* 166: 368–393.
Bo, Zhiyue, 2002. *Chinese Provincial Leaders: Economic Performance and Political Mobility since 1949*. Armonk, NY: M. E. Sharpe.
   2004. 'The Institutionalization of Elite Management in China,' in *Holding China Together: Diversity and National Integration in the Post-Deng Era*, ed. Barry Naughton and Dali Yang. Cambridge: Cambridge University Press 70–100.
   2006. *China's Elite Politics: Political Transition and Power Balancing*. Singapore: World Scientific Publishing.

Brødsgaard, Kjeld Erik, 2003. 'China's Cadres and Cadre Management System,' in *Damage Control: The Chinese Communist Party in the Jiang Zemin Era*, ed. Wang Gungwu and Zheng Yongnian. Singapore: Eastern Universities Press 209–231.
Buck Morsse, Susan, 2000. *Dreamworld and Catastrophe: The Passing of Mass Utopia in East and West*. Cambridge, MA: MIT Press.
Burawoy, Michael and Katherine Verdery, eds., 1999. *Uncertain Transition: Ethnographies of Change in the Postsocialist World*. Lanham, MD: Rowman & Littlefield.
Burns, John P., 1989. *The Chinese Communist Party's Nomenklatura System: A Documentary Study of Party Control of Leadership Selection, 1979–1984*. Armonk, NY: M. E. Sharpe.
  1994. 'Strengthening Central CCP Control of Leadership Selection: The 1990 Nomenklatura', *The China Quarterly* 138: 458–491.
  1999. 'The People's Republic of China at 50: National Political Reform', *The China Quarterly* 159: 580–594.
  2004. 'Governance and Civil Service Reform,' in *Governance in China*, ed. Jude Howell. Lanham: Rowman & Littlefield, 37–57.
  2006. 'The Chinese Communist Party's Nomenklatura System as a Leadership Selection Mechanism: An Evaluation', in *The Chinese Communist Party in Reform*, ed. Kjeld Erik Brodsgaard and Zheng Yongnian. London: Routledge, 33–58.
Carsten, Janet, 1997. *The Heat of the Hearth: The Process of Kinship in a Malay Fishing Community*. Oxford: Clarendon Press.
Castells, Manuel, 1996. *The Rise of the Network Society*. Oxford: Basil Blackwell.
Chan, Anita, 1985. *Children of Mao: Personality Development and Political Activism in the Red Guard Generation*. London: Macmillan.
Chan, Anita, Richard Madsen and Jonathan Unger, 1992. *Chen Village under Mao and Deng*. Berkeley: University of California Press.
Chan, Hon S., ed., 2001. 'Introduction. In Symposium: Administration Transformation in the People's Republic of China', *Public Adminstration Quarterly* 24(4): 401–418.
Chen, Jack, 1973. *A Year in Upper Felicity: Life in a Chinese Village during the Cultural Revolution*. London: Harrap.
Chun, Lin, 2006. *The Transformation of Chinese Socialism*. Durham: Duke University Press.
Cohen, Abner, 1974. *Two-Dimensional Man: An Essay on the Anthropology of Power and Symbolism in Complex Society*. Berkeley: University of California Press.
  1981. *The Politics of Elite Culture: Explorations in the Dramaturgy of Power in a Modern African Society*. Berkeley: University of California Press.
Corrigan, Philip and Derek Sayer, 1985. *The Great Arch: English State Formation as Cultural Revolution*. Oxford: Basil Blackwell.
Crouch, Colin, 2005. *Capitalist Diversity and Change: Recombinant Governance and Institutional Entrepreneurs*. Oxford: Oxford University Press.

Cucco, Ivan, 2008. 'The Professional Middle Classes: Management and Politics', in *The New Rich in China: Future Rulers, Present Lives*, ed. David S. G. Goodman. London: Routledge, 126–147.

Dangxiao jiaoyu shi yanjiu zu (Research group on the history of party school education), 2002. *Yan'an Zhongyang Dangxiao de shen'gan gongzuo (The examination of cadres' personal histories at the Yan'an Central Party School)*. Beijing: Zhongyang Wenxian Chubanshe.

De Soto, Hermine G. and Nora Dudwick, eds. 2000. *Fieldwork Dilemmas: Anthropologists in Postsocialist Societies*. Madison: University of Wisconsin Press.

Deng, Xiaoping, 1984a. 'On the Reform of the System of Party and State Leadership (August 18, 1980)', in *Selected Works of Deng Xiaoping (1975–1982)*. Beijing: Foreign Languages Press, 302–325.

　　1984b. 'Uphold the Four Cardinal Principles (March 30, 1979)', in *Selected Works of Deng Xiaoping (1975–1982)*. Beijing: Foreign Languages Press, 166–191.

　　1990. 'June 9 Speech to Martial Law Units', in *Beijing Spring, 1989: Confrontation and Conflict: The Basic Documents*, ed. Michel Oksenberg, Lawrence R. Sullivan and Marc Lambert. Armonk, NY: M. E. Sharpe, 376–382.

Dickson, Bruce J., 2003. *Red Capitalists in China: The Party, Private Entrepreneurs, and Prospects for Political Change*. Cambridge: Cambridge University Press.

Dickson, Bruce J. and Maria Rost Rublee, 2000. 'Membership Has Its Privileges: The Socioeconomic Characteristics of Communist Party Members in Urban China', *Comparative Political Studies* 33(1): 87–112.

Ding, Xueliang, 1994. 'Institutional Amphibiousness and the Transition from Communism: The Case of China', *British Journal of Political Science* 24(3): 293–318.

Dirlik, Arif, 1989. 'Postsocialism? Reflections on "Socialism with Chinese Characteristics"', in *Marxism and the Chinese Experience: Issues in Contemporary Chinese Socialism*, ed. Arif Dirlik and Maurice Meisner. Armonk, NY: M. E. Sharpe, 362–384.

Domes, Jürgen, 1884. 'Intra-Elite Group Formation and Conflict in the PRC', in *Groups and Politics in the People's Republic of China*, ed. David S. G. Goodman. Armonk, NY: M. E. Sharpe, 26–39.

Dong, Yaming, 2003. 'Dui dangqian xingshi xia jiaqiang he gaijin ganbu peixun wenti de yanjiu' (Research on the problems of strenthening and improving cadre training under the current circumstances), *Yunnan Shengwei Dangxiao xuebao (Journal of the Yunnan Provincial Party School)* 5(2): 72–74.

Duckett, Jane, 1998. *The Entrepreneurial State in China: Real Estate and Commerce Departments in Reform-Era Tianjin*. London: Routledge.

Edin, Maria, 2000. Market Forces and Communist Power: Local Political Institutions and Economic Development in China. PhD thesis, Department of Government, Uppsala University.

　　2003a. 'Remaking the Communist Party-State: The Cadre Responsibility System at the Local Level in China', *China: An International Journal* 1(1): 1–15.

　　2003b. 'State Capacity and Local Agent Control in China: CCP Cadre Management from a Township Perspective', *The China Quarterly* 173: 35–52.

Eyferth, Jacob, 2001. Eating Rice from Bamboo Roots. PhD thesis, Faculty of Letters, University of Leiden.
Ferguson, James, 1990. *The Anti-Politics Machine: "Development," Depoliticization, and Bureaucratic Power in Lesotho*. Minneapolis: University of Minnesota Press.
Ferguson, James and Akhil Gupta, 2002. 'Spatializing States: Toward an Ethnography of Neoliberal Governmentality', *American Ethnologist* 29(4): 981–1002.
Fewsmith, Joseph, 2003. 'Where Do Correct Ideas Come from? The Party School, Key Think Tanks, and the Intellectuals', in *China's Leadership in the 21st Century*, ed. David M. Finkelstein and Maryanne Kivlehan. Armonk, NY: M. E. Sharpe, 152–164.
  2005. 'CCP Launches Campaign to Maintain the Advanced Nature of Party Members', *China Leadership Monitor* 13 (Winter 2005). Online at www.chinaleadershipmonitor.org/20051/jf.html.
Foucault, Michel, 1977. *Discipline and Punish: The Birth of the Prison*. London: Allen Lane.
  1978. *History of Sexuality: An Introduction*, volume 1. New York: Vintage Books.
  1991. 'Governmentality', in *The Foucault Effect: Studies in Governmentality*, ed. Colin Gordon and Peter Miller Graham Burchell. London: Harvester Wheatsheaf, 87–104.
Fu Libai, 2004. *Guojia gongwuyuan zhidu gailun* (*Introduction to the national civil service system*). Jinan: Shandong Daxue Chubanshe.
Gaoji lingdao juece xinxi ziliao bianxie zu (Editing group of the policy making information materials for high-level leaders), ed., 2007. *Zhonggong Zhongyang Zhengzhiju jiti xuexi neirong zhaiyao* (*Excerpts of the contents of the CCP Central Politburo collective study*). [No details available.]
Geertz, Clifford, 1980. *Negara: The Theatre State in Nineteenth-century Bali*. Princeton, NJ: Princeton University Press.
Gold, Thomas B., 1989. 'Guerilla Interviewing among the Getihu', in *Unofficial China: Popular Culture and Thought in the People's Republic*, ed. Perry Link, Richard Madsen and Paul G. Pickowicz. Boulder, CO: Westview Press: 175–192.
Goodman, David S. G., 2001. 'The Interdependence of State and Society: The Political Sociology of Local Leadership', in *Remaking the Chinese State: Strategies, Society, and Security*, ed. Chien-min Chao and Bruce J. Dickson. London: Routledge, 132–156.
  ed., 2008. *The New Rich in China: Future Rulers, Present Lives*. London: Routledge.
Gore, Lance P., 1998. *Market Communism: The Institutional Foundation of China's Post-Mao Hypergrowth*. Hong Kong: Oxford University Press.
  1999. 'The Communist Legacy in Post-Mao Economic Growth', *The China Journal* 41: 25–54.
Greenhalgh, Susan, 2008. *Just One Child: Science and Policy in Deng's China*. Berkeley: University of California Press.

Greenhalgh, Susan and Edwin A. Winckler, 2005. *Governing China's Population: From Leninist to Neoliberal Biopolitics*. Stanford: Stanford University Press.

Gupta, Akhil, 1995. 'Blurred Boundaries: The Discourse of Corruption, the Culture of Politics, and the Imagined State', *American Ethnologist* 22(2): 375–402.

Hall, Peter and David Soskice, eds. 2001. *Varieties of Capitalism: The Institutional Foundations of Comparative Advantage*. Oxford: Oxford University Press.

Hann, C. M., ed., 2002. *Postsocialism: Ideals, Ideologies and Practices in Eurasia*. London: Routledge.

Hannerz, Ulf, 1987. 'The World in Creolisation', *Africa* 57: 546–559.

  1992. *Cultural Complexity: Studies in the Social Organization of Meaning*. New York: Columbia University Press.

  2000. *Flows, Boundaries and Hybrids: Keywords in Transnational Anthropology*. Oxford: Transnational Communities Programme Working Paper WPTC-2K-02.

Harding, Harry, 1981. *Organizing China: The Problem of Bureaucracy, 1949–1976*. Stanford: Stanford University Press.

Harvey, David, 2005. *A Brief History of Neoliberalism*. Oxford: Oxford University Press.

He, Zengke, 2005. 'Chuangxin tizhi cong yuantou shang yufang he zhili fubai' (Innovate the system to prevent and treat corruption from the root), in *Zhongguo zhengzhi tizhi gaige yanjiu (Research on the reform of China's political system)*. Beijing: Zhongyang Bianyi Chubanshe, 356–403.

Herzfeld, Michael, 1992. *The Social Production of Indifference: Exploring the Symbolic Roots of Western Bureaucracy*. Chicago: University of Chicago Press.

Hobsbawm, Eric and Terry Ranger, 1983. *The Invention of Tradition*. Cambridge: Cambridge University Press.

Hoffman, Lisa, 2006. 'Autonomous Choices and Patriotic Professionalism: On Governmentality in Late-Socialist China', *Economy and Society* 35(4): 550–570.

Hsu, Carolyn L., 2001. 'Political Narratives and the Production of Legitimacy: The Case of Corruption in Post-Mao China', *Qualitative Sociology* 24(1): 25–54.

Hu, Jintao, 2003. *Zai 'San ge Daibiao' zhongyao sixiang lilun yantaohui shang de jianghua (Speech at the theoretical discussion meeting on the important thought of the 'Three Represents')*. Beijing, 1 July 2003.

Huai, Yan, 1995a. 'Organizational Hierarchy and the Cadre Management System', in *Decision-making in Deng's China: Perspectives from Insiders*, ed. Carol Lee Hamrin and Suisheng Zhao. Armonk, NY: M. E. Sharpe, 39–50.

  1995b. 'Establishing a Civil Service System', in *Decision-making in Deng's China: Perspectives from Insiders*, ed. Carol Lee Hamrin and Suisheng Zhao. Armonk, NY: M. E. Sharpe, 169–175.

Huang, Da-qiang, 1993. 'Teaching Administrative Science', in *Public Administration in China*, ed. Miriam K. Mills and Stuart S. Nagel. Westport, CT: Greenwood Press, 21–28.

Huang, Shi'an, ed., 2003. *Zhonggong Zhongyang Dangxiao hanshou jiaoyu nianjian (Yearbook for 2002 of Correspondence Education of the Chinese Communist Party Central Party School)*. Beijing: Zhonggong Zhongyang Dangxiao Chubanshe.
Huang, Yasheng, 1996. 'Central–Local Relations in China during the Reform Era: the Economic and Institutional Dimensions', *World Development* 24(4): 655–672.
Humphrey, Caroline, 1998. *Marx Went Away – But Karl Stayed Behind*. Ann Arbor: University of Michigan Press.
Huskey, Eugene, 2004. 'From Higher Party Schools to Academies of State Service: The Marketization of Bureaucratic Training in Russia', *Slavic Review* 63(2): 325–348.
Jakobsen, Linda, 2004. 'Local Governance: Village and Township Direct Elections', in *Governance in China*, ed. Jude Howell. Lanham: Rowman & Littlefield, 97–120.
Jiang, Zemin, 2001. *Lun dang de jianshe (On party building)*. Beijing: Zhongyang Wenxian Chubanshe.
Jowitt, Kenneth, 1974. 'An Organizational Approach to the Study of Political Culture in Marxist-Leninist Regimes', *American Political Science Review* 68: 171–191.
  1992. 'The Leninist Phenomenon', in *New World Disorder: The Leninist Extinction*. Berkeley: University of California Press, 1–49.
Jun, Zeng, 2006. *Gonggong guanli xinlun: tixi, jiazhi yu gongju (New introduction to public management: system, values and tools)*. Beijing: Renmin Chubanshe.
Kertzer, David I., 1988. *Ritual, Politics, and Power*. New Haven, CT: Yale University Press.
Kipnis, Andrew, 2006. '*Suzhi*: A Keyword Approach', *The China Quarterly* 186: 295–313.
  2007. 'Neoliberalism Reified: *Suzhi* Discourse and Tropes of Neoliberalism in the People's Republic of China', *Journal of the Royal Anthropological Institute (N.S.)* 13: 383–400.
Kohrman, Matthew, 2005. *Bodies of Difference: Experiences of Disability and Institutional Advocacy in the Making of Modern China*. Berkeley: University of California Press.
Konrád, George and Ivan Szelenyi, 1979. *The Intellectuals on the Road to Class Power*. Brighton: Harvester Press.
Lam, Tao-Chiu and James L. Perry, 2001. 'Service Organizations in China: Reform and Its Limits', in *Remaking China's Public Management*, ed. Peter Nan-Shong Lee and Carlos Wing-Hung Lo. Westport, CT: Quorum Books, 19–39.
Lee, Charlotte, 2007. Promoting Talent and Central Policies: Institutions of Cadre and Civil Servant Training in China. Unpublished paper.
Lee, Hong Yung, 1991. *From Revolutionary Cadres to Party Technocrats in Socialist China*. Berkeley: University of California Press.
Leonard, Mark, 2008. *What Does China Think?* London: Fourth Estate.
Lewis, John Wilson, 1963. *Leadership in Communist China*. Ithaca, NY: Cornell University Press.

Li, Bobai and Andrew G. Walder, 2001. 'Career Advancement as Party Patronage: Sponsored Mobility into the Chinese Administrative Elite, 1949–1996', *American Journal of Sociology* 106(5): 1371–1408.

Lin, Nan, 1995. 'Local Market Socialism: Local Corporatism in Action in Rural China', *Theory and Society* 24(3): 301–354.

Lin, Nan and Xiaolan Ye, 1998. 'Chinese Rural Enterprises in Transformation: The End of the Beginning', *Issues & Studies* 34(11/12): 1–28.

Liu, Mingxin, Juan Wang, Ran Tao and Rachel Murphy, 2008. 'The Political Economy of Earmarked Transfers in a State-Designated Poor County in Western China: Central Policies and Local Responses.' Conference on 'The Reinvention of the Chinese Party-State: Reflections on the Social Transformation in China.' Shenyang, 5–7 December 2008.

Liu, Xirui, 2002. 'Fazhan gonggong guanli tizhi shi woguo de biran xuanze' (Developing the system for public management is a necessary choice for our country), *Gonggong xingzheng guanli kexue* 2002(3): 32–35.

2004. 'Zhongguo gonggong guanli de xianzheng tizhi yu xianshi jichu' (The system of constitutional government and basis in reality of Chinese public management), in *Zhongguo gonggong guanli (Chinese public management)*. Liu Xirui. Beijing: Zhonggong Zhongyang Chubanshe, chapter 3.

Liu, Yucheng, ed., 1996. *Quanguo dangxiao gailan (General overview of party schools in the whole country)*. Beijing: Hongqi Chubanshe.

Lü, Xiaobo, 2000. *Cadres and Corruption*. Stanford: Stanford University Press.

Madsen, Richard, 1984. *Morality and Power in a Chinese Village*. Berkeley: University of California Press.

Mandel, Ruth Ellen and Caroline Humphrey, 2002. *Markets and Moralities: Ethnographies of Postsocialism*. Oxford: Berg.

Manion, Melanie, 1985. 'The Cadre Management System, Post-Mao: The Appointment, Promotion, Transfer and Removal of Party and State Leaders', *The China Quarterly* 102: 203–233.

1993. *Retirement of Revolutionary Cadres in China: Public Policies, Social Norms, Private Interests*. Princeton: Princeton University Press.

2000. 'Chinese Democratization in Perspective: Electorates and Selectorates at the Township Level', *The China Quarterly* 163: 764–782.

2004. *Corruption by Design: Building Clean Government in Mainland China and Hong Kong*. Cambridge, MA: Harvard University Press.

Mao, Zedong, 1970–1974. 'Guanyu muqian zhengzhi xingshi yu dang de renwu jueyi' (About the resolution on the current political situation and the party's mission), in *Mao Zedong ji (Collected works of Mao Zedong). Ten volumes*, ed. Takuechi Minoru. Tokyo: Hokubu Sha.

Mertha, Andrew C., 2005. 'China's "Soft" Centralization: Shifting *Tiao/Kuai* Authority Relations', *The China Quarterly* 184: 791–810.

Michels, Robert, 1915. *Political Parties: A Sociological Study of the Oligarchical Tendencies of Modern Democracy*. Glencoe, IL: Free Press.

Migdal, Joel S., 1994. 'The State in Society: An Approach to Struggles for Domination', in *State Power and Social Forces: Domination and Transformation in the*

Third World, ed. Joel S. Migdal, Atul Kohli and Vivienne Shue. Cambridge: Cambridge University Press, 7–34.

2001. *State in Society: Studying How States and Societies Transform and Constitute One Another*. Cambridge: Cambridge University Press.

Moore, Sally F. and Barbara G. Myerhoff, eds. 1977. *Secular Ritual*. Assen: Van Gorcum.

Nathan, Andrew, 1973. 'A Factionalism Model for CCP Politics', *The China Quarterly* 53: 34–66.

Nee, Victor, 1989. 'A Theory of Market Transition: From Redistribution to Markets in State Socialism', *American Sociological Review* 54(5): 663–681.

1996. 'The Emergence of a Market Society: Changing Mechanisms of Stratification in China', *American Journal of Sociology* 101(4): 908–949.

Nee, Victor and Sijin Su, 1990. 'Institutional Change and Economic Growth in China: The View from the Villages', *The Journal of Asian Studies* 49(1): 3–25.

O'Brien, Kevin J. and Lianjiang Li, 2006. *Rightful Resistance in Rural China*. Cambridge: Cambridge University Press.

Oi, Jean Chun, 1992. 'Economic Foundations of Local State Corporatism in China', *World Politics* 45: 99–126.

1999. *Rural China Takes Off: Institutional Foundations of Economic Reform*. Berkeley: University of California Press.

Oksenberg, Michel, 1968. 'The Institutionalization of the Chinese Communist Revolution: The Ladder of Success on the Eve of the Cultural Revolution', *The China Quarterly* 36: 61–92.

Ong, Aihwa, 2006. *Neoliberalism as Exception: Mutations in Citizenship and Sovereignty*. Durham: Duke University Press.

Pieke, Frank N., 1995. 'Bureaucracy, Friends, and Money: The Growth of Capital Socialism in China', *Comparative Studies in Society and History* 37(3): 494–518.

1996. *The Ordinary and the Extraordinary: An Anthropological Study of Chinese Reform and the 1989 People's Movement in Beijing*. London: Kegan Paul International.

2004. 'Contours of an Anthropology of the Chinese State: Political Structure, Agency and Economic Development in Rural China', *Journal of the Royal Anthropological Institute (N.S.)* 10(3): 517–538.

Pieke, Frank N., Pál Nyíri, Mette Thunø and Antonella Ceccagno, 2004. *Transnational Chinese: Fujianese Migrants in Europe*. Stanford: Stanford University Press.

Price, Jane L., 1976. *Cadres, Commanders, and Commissars: The Training of the Chinese Communist Leadership, 1920–45*. Folkstone: Wm. Dawson.

Raman, Parvathi and Harry G. West, 2009. 'Introduction: Poetries of the Past in a Socialist World Remade', in *Enduring Socialism: Explorations of Revolution & Transformation, Restoration & Continuation*, ed. Harry G. West and Parvathi Raman. Oxford: Berghahn, 1–28.

Redding, S. Gordon, 1993. *The Spirit of Chinese Capitalism*. Berlin: Walter de Gruyter.

Remick, Elizabeth J., 1999. 'Big Plans, Empty Pockets: Local Exactions in Republican and Post-Mao China', *Twentieth-Century China* 25(1): 43–70.
Rose, Nikolas and Peter Miller, 1992. 'Political Power beyond the State: Problematics of Government', *The British Journal of Sociology* 43(2): 173–205.
Saich, Tony, 2001. *Governance and Politics of China*. Basingstoke: Palgrave.
Schurmann, Franz, 1968. *Ideology and Organization in Communist China*. Second Edition. Berkeley: University of California Press.
Seckington, Ian, 2007. County Leadership in China: A Baseline Survey. Nottingham, China Policy Institute, University of Nottingham, discussion paper 17.
Shambaugh, David, 2008. *China's Communist Party: Atrophy and Adaptation*. Washington, DC and Berkeley: Woodrow Wilson Center Press and University of California Press.
Shevchenko, Alexei, 2004. 'Bringing the Party back in: The CCP and the Trajectory of Market Transition in China', *Communist and Post-Communist Studies* 37: 161–185.
Shirk, Susan L., 1982. *Competitive Comrades: Career Incentives and Student Strategies in China*. Berkeley: University of California Press.
Shue, Vivienne, 1988. *The Reach of the State: Sketches of the Chinese Body Politic*. Stanford: Stanford University Press.
Sigley, Gary, 2006. 'Chinese Governmentalities: Government, Governance and the Socialist Market Economy', *Economy and Society* 35(4): 487–508.
Skocpol, Theda, 1985. 'Bringing the State Back In: Strategies of Analysis in Current Research', in *Bringing the State Back In*, ed. Peter B. Evans, Dietrich Rueschemeyer and Theda Skocpol. Cambridge: Cambridge University Press, 3–37.
Sleeboom, Margaret, 2007. *The Chinese Academy of Social Sciences (CASS): Shaping the Reforms, Academia and China (1977–2003)*. Leiden: Brill.
Teiwes, Frederick C., 1993. *Politics and Purges in China: Rectification and the Decline of Party Norms, 1950–1965*. Armonk, NY: M. E. Sharpe.
Thøgersen, Stig, 2008. 'Frontline Soldiers of the CCP: The Selection of China's Township Leaders', *The China Quarterly* 194: 414–423.
Thøgersen, Stig, Jørgen Elklit and Dong Lishen, 2008. 'Consultative Elections of Chinese Township Leaders', *China Information* 22(1): 67–89.
Thornton, Patricia M., 2007. *Disciplining the State: Virtue, Violence and State-Making in Modern China*. Cambridge, MA: Harvard University Asia Center.
Tomba, Luigi, 2004. 'Creating an Urban Middle Class: Social Engineering in Beijing', *The China Journal* 51: 1–26.
Tong, Caroline Haiyan and Hongying Wang, 2005. 'Sino-American Educational Exchanges and Public Administration Reforms in China: A Study of Norm Diffusion', in *Bridging Minds across the Pacific: US–China Educational Exchanges, 1978–2003*, ed. Cheng Li. Lanham: Lexington Books, 155–175.
Tran, Emilie, 2003. 'From Senior Official to Top Civil Servant: An Enquiry into the Shanghai Party School', *Perspectives chinoises* 46. English translation online at www.cefc.com.hk/uk/pc/articles/art_ligne.php?num_art_ligne=4603.

Trouillot, Michel-Rolph, 2001. 'The Anthropology of the State in the Age of Globalization', *Current Anthropology* 42(1): 125–138.
Tsai, Kellee S., 2007. *Capitalism without Democracy: The Private Sector in Contemporary China.* Ithaca: Cornell University Press.
Turner, Victor W., 1974. *The Ritual Process: Structure and Anti-Structure.* Harmondsworth: Penguin.
U, Eddy, 2007. *Disorganizing China: Counter-Bureaucracy and the Decline of Socialism.* Stanford: Stanford University Press.
Verdery, Katherine, 1996. *What Was Socialism, and What Comes Next?* Princeton: Princeton University Press.
Walder, Andrew G., 1986. *Communist Neo-Traditionalism: Work and Authority in Chinese Industry.* Berkeley: University of California Press.
  1995. 'Local Governments as Industrial Firms: An Organizational Analysis of China's Transitional Economy', *American Journal of Sociology* 101(2): 263–301.
  2004. 'The Party Elite and China's Trajectory of Change', *China: An International Journal* 2(2): 189–209.
Walder, Andrew G., Bobai Li and Donald J. Treiman, 2000. 'Politics and Life Chances in a State Socialist Regime: Dual Career Paths into the Urban Chinese Elite, 1949 to 1996', *American Sociological Review* 65: 191–209.
Wang, Yueping, 2001. 'Inside the Central Party School (Zoujin Zhongyang Dangxiao)', *Shidai chao* (13). Online at www.people.com.cn/GB/paper83/3819/462405.html (checked on 23 June 2008).
Wang, Zhongqing, ed., 1992. *Dangxiao jiaoyu lishi gaishu 1921–1947 nian* (Sketch of the history of party school education 1921–1947). Beijing: Zhonggong Zhongyang Dangxiao Chubanshe.
Wank, David L., 1999. *Commodifying Communism: Business, Trust, and Politics in a Chinese City.* Cambridge: Cambridge University Press.
White, Lynn T. III, 1998. *Unstately Power. Volume II: Local Causes of China's Intellectual, Legal, and Governmental Reforms.* Armonk, NY: M. E. Sharpe.
Whiting, Susan H., 2001. *Power and Wealth in Rural China: The Political Economy of Institutional Change.* Cambridge: Cambridge University Press.
Whyte, Martin King, 1974. *Small Groups and Political Rituals in China.* Berkeley: University of California Press.
Wibowo, Ignatius and Lye Liang Fook, 2006. 'China's Central Party School: A Unique Institution Adapting to Changes', in *The Chinese Communist Party in Reform*, ed. Kjeld Erik Brodsgaard and Zheng Yongnian. London: Routledge, 139–156.
Wong, Christine P. W., 1997. 'Rural Public Finance', in *Financing Local Government in the People's Republic of China*, ed. Christine P. W. Wong. Hong Kong: Oxford University Press, 167–212.
  1998. 'Fiscal Dualism in China: Gradualist Reform and the Growth of Off-Budget Finance', in *Taxation in Modern China*, ed. Donald J. S. Brean. New York: Routledge, 187–208.
  2002. 'China: National Development and Sub-national Finance – A Review of Provincial Expenditures.' Report No. 22951-CHA. Washington, DC: Poverty

Reduction and Economic Management Unit, East Asia and Pacific Region, The World Bank.

2007. 'Fiscal Management for a Harmonious Society: Assessing the Central Government's Capacity to Implement National Policies.' British Interuniversity China Centre working paper no. 4. Oxford.

2008. 'Rebuilding Government for the 21st Century: Can China Incrementally Reform the Public Sector?' Paper presented at the conference on 'The Reinvention of the Chinese Party-State: Reflections on the Social Transformation in China.' Shenyang, 5–7 December 2008.

Woo, Wing Thye, 1999. 'The Real Reasons for China's Growth', *The China Journal* 41: 115–137.

Wylie, Raymond F., 1980. *The Emergence of Maoism: Mao Tse-tung, Ch'en Po-da, and the Search for Chinese Theory 1935–1945*. Stanford: Stanford University Press.

Yang, Chiang, 1986. *Six Chapters of Life in a Cadre School: Memoirs from China's Cultural Revolution*. Boulder: Westview Press.

Yang, Dali, 2001. 'Rationalizing the Chinese State: The Political Economy of Government Reform', in *Remaking the Chinese State: Strategies, Society, and Security*, ed. Chien-min Chao and Bruce J. Dickson. London: Routledge, 19–45.

2004. *Remaking the Chinese Leviathan: Market Transition and the Politics of Governance in China*. Stanford: Stanford University Press.

Yang, Jiang, 1982. *A Cadre School Life: Six Chapters*. Hong Kong: Joint Publishing Co.

1983; 1984. *Six Chapters from My Life 'Downunder.'* Seattle and Hong Kong: University of Washington Press and The Chinese University Press.

Yu, Yunyao and Yang, Chungui, eds. 2002a. *Zhonggong Zhongyang Dangxiao jianggaoxuan: guanyu makesi Zhuyi jiben wenti* (*Selected lectures at the Central Party School: basic issues in Marxism*). Beijing: Zhonggong Zhongyang Dangxiao Chubanshe.

eds. 2002b. *Zhonggong Zhongyang Dangxiao jianggaoxuan: guanyu dangdai shijie zhongda wenti* (*Selected lectures at the Central Party School: major issues in the contemporary world*). Beijing: Zhonggong Zhongyang Dangxiao Chubanshe.

Zang, Xiaowei, 2001a. 'Educational Credentials, Elite Dualism, and Elite Stratification in China,' *Sociological Perspectives* 44(2): 189–205.

2001b. 'University Education, Party Seniority, and Elite Recruitment in China', *Social Sciences Research* 30: 62–75.

Zheng, Shiping, 1997. *Party vs. State in Post-1949 China: The Institutional Dilemma*. Cambridge: Cambridge Univeristy Press.

Zhonggong Baoji Shiwei Dangxiao xiaozhi bianxiezu (Editorial group of the Baoji City Party School gazetteer), 1989. *Zhonggong Baoji Shiwei Dangxiao xiaozhi 1949 nian 6 yue – 1987 nian 12 yue* (*Baoji City Party School gazetteer June 1949 – December 1987*). Baoji.

Zhonggong Fujian Shengwei Zuzhibu ketizu (Research group of the Organization Department of the Fujian Chinese Communist Party committee), 2003.

'Dangyuan ganbu zhi jian shouru chaju kuoda dui dang de sixiang zuofeng jianshe de yinxiang' (The impact of the rise in income difference between party cadres on the building of the Party's work style), in *Zhongguo diaocha baogao: shehui jingji guanxi de xin bianhua yu zhizhengdang de jianshe* (*China research report: the new transformations of social and economic relationships and the building of a ruling party*), ed. Li Huibin and Xue Xiaoyuan. Beijing: Shehui Kexue Wenxian Chubanshe, 73–90.

Zhonggong Yunnan Shengwei Dangxiao jianshi bianxiezu (Editorial group of the brief history of the Yunnan Chinese Communist Party Committee Party School), 2000. *Zhonggong Yunnan Shengwei Dangxiao jianshi* (*Brief history of the Yunnan Chinese Communist Party Committee Party School*). Kunming: Yunnan Renmin Chubanshe.

Zhonggong Zhongyang Dangxiao baogaoxuan bianjibu (Editorial department of the selection of reports at the Chinese Communist Party Central Party School), ed. 2003. *Zhonggong Zhongyang Dangxiao baogao jingxuan* (*Selection of reports at the Central Party School*). Beijing: Zhonggong Zhongyang Dangxiao Chubanshe.

Zhonggong Zhongyang Zuzhi Bu ganbu jiaoyu ju (Cadre education bureau of the Central Organization Department of the Chinese Communist Party), ed., 2001. *Quanmian tuijin xin shiji de ganbu jiaoyu peixun gongzuo* (*Comprehensive promotion of cadre education and training in the new century*). Beijing: Dangjian Duwu Chubanshe.

Zhou Feizhou, 2008. 'Tudi kaifa yu difang zhengfu xingwei: cong Xi'an shi Chang'an qu de caizheng lai fenxi yi zhong daiyou pubianxing de fazhan moshi' (Land development and local government behaviour: from the public finances of Chang'an district in Xi'an city analysing a development model with universal characteristics). Paper presented at the conference on 'The Reinvention of the Chinese Party-State: Reflections on the Social Transformation in China.' Shenyang, 5–7 December 2008.

Zhou, Xueguang, 1995. 'Partial Reform and the Chinese Bureaucracy in the Post-Mao Era', *Comparative Political Studies* 28(3): 440–468.

Index

academic staff of party schools, 79
  publications, 89, 95
  sabbatical leave, 123
  travel for academic exchanges, 123–4
academies for 'experiential learning', 127
academies of administration, 43, 45–6, 57
academies of socialism, 64, 184, 185
  function of, 65
  responsibility for, 64
Academy of Socialism, 46, 58
accountability, 165
administrative elite, composition of, 175–9
administrative management, 91
administrative reform, 32–5
administrative science, 91, 92, 101

Beijing Municipal Party School, 20, 124, 129
birth control, 15
Bo Zhiyue, 178
bureaucracies, 17, 122–3

cadre education and training committee, 56–7, 86
cadre management, 17–20, 32–5, 155–6, 164, 176
cadre positions, buying and selling of, 188
cadre schools, 62
cadre system
  modernization of, 44, 193
  professionalization of, 44
  reform of, 18, 32–5
cadre training, 17–20, 26–55, 29
  'à la carte' education, 75, 184
  categorial training classes, 106, 139
  centralization of, 114–40, 185, 187
  collective study, 69
  commercialization of, 137, 186
  correspondence degree courses, 75–80
  courses for
    civil servants, 71, 107, 139
    female cadres, 106, 139
    the highest cadres, 69–70

    leading cadres, 60, 71, 106
    minority cadres, 67, 72, 103, 106, 140
    non-CCP cadres, 139
    non-leading cadres, 45–6
    non-leading civil servants, 71, 107
    young and middle-aged cadres, 71, 106
  cult of eliteness, 15, 19
  curriculum, 106–7, 127, 133, 143, 150
  degree programmes: *see under* party schools
  design of courses, 74
  diversification of, 48, 126–32, 172
  emphasis on formal education, 172, 176
  emphasis on ideology, 193
  exchanges, 121–6
  executive leadership academies, 51–2
  in higher educational institutions, 42
  for highest cadres, 69–70
  history of
    after 1978, 39–47
    after 1989, 43–4
    after 2000, 47–8
    before 1978, 35–9
    in the 21st century, 56–80
  impact of, 19, 163, 181
  institutional arrangements for, 49–52, 56–65
  inter-regional and international dimensions, 19, 126
  investment in, 193
  in management skills, 42
  marketization of, 55, 114–40, 126–32, 184, 185
  models for, 121–6, 131
  modernization of, 108
  national joint conference on, 53, 54
  national plan for, 47–8, 49, 57–8
  number and variety of courses and students, 65, 104–5
  objectives of, 73–4, 107–8
  off-site training programmes, 131
  openness and international cooperation in, 21
  and party rule, 180–95
  policies and practice of, 19

Index

political training, 59, 150
  at prestigious universities, 127
  privatization of, 185
  professionalization of, 140, 141
  quality, 50, 79, 114–20, 132
  rank, level and jurisdiction in, 121
  recruitment of students, 58, 130
  recruitment of teachers, 80
  reform of, 8–9, 52–5, 184
  relationship between trainees and universities, 128
  ritual aspects of, 14
  and socialization, 150
  specialization of, 42, 184
  spending on, 53
  standardization of, 46–7
  study methods, 106
  study of Marxist classics, 41
  study tours, 131
  systematization of, 46–7
  teaching methods, 146
    case analyses, 146
    lectures and seminars, 109–10, 146
    reading classes, 70
    self-study, 41
  time away from home and work, 84
  travel or temporary residence away from home, 123
  Trial regulation on cadre education and training work, 54
  types of
    'high-end' training, 42, 127
    main courses, 70–2
    non-vocational political training, 150
    novice training, 71–2, 73, 169
    professional courses, 42, 70
    refresher courses, 71, 72–3
    reserve cadre training, 71
    short-term courses, 39, 108
    specialized professional training courses, 70
  unifying theory and practice, 73–4, 108
  unintended effects of, 181–2
cadres, 26–55, 28–32
  ability of, 50
  alternative career opportunities, 157–8
  attitudes to training and education, 76, 176–7, 178
  autonomy and choice of training, 54
  career bureaucrats, 62–4, 161
  careers of, 17, 141–79, 151–63
    impact of education on, 153
    control over careers, 173, 176
    parents' careers and, 157
  commitment to the party, 173–4; *see also* party spirit
  competition among, 55
  cooperation between hierarchical levels, 160
  deployment of, 29
  educational qualifications, 32–3, 114, 141
  expectations and experiences of training and education, 142–51
  formation of networks and communities, 148–9, 182
  grades, ranks and levels, 30–1, 152, 154
  ideology and practice of Leninism, 51, 144–5
  individual training needs, 54
  loyalty to their native location, 159
  meritocratic power elite, 1, 28
  mobility of, 123, 152, 155, 163
  'number one' posts, 154
  opportunity to mix with a variety of other cadres, 147
  professionalization of, 174
  promotion of, 152–153
    importance of education in, 162
  recruitment of, 29, 151, 156, 163–75, 189
  relationship with teachers, 109–10
  requirement to participate in training, 42, 126, 183
  retirement ages, 32–33
  sense of belonging, 149, 158–9, 183
  specialization, 154
  'talent reserve pool' of, 169
  techniques of the self, 18
  technocratization of, 187
  types of
    basic cadres, 28
    expert cadres, 173–5, 178–9
    female cadres, 152–3, 155
    leading cadres, 30–1, 34, 166, 170, 173, 174
    local cadres, 28
    non-CCP, 62–4
    non-leading cadres, 30, 166
    non-local cadres, 159
    non-party members, 62
    regular cadres, 30
    state cadres, 28
  unity of theory and practice, 158
capitalism, 1–25, 187, 193; *see also* market reform
Carsten, Janet, 151
case analyses, 146
Central Party School, 20, 22, 23, 37, 38, 65–68, 184
  after 1977, 40
  agenda of, 118–119
  Branch School for Central Government Organs, 59
  Branch School for Central (Party) Organs, 59
  collective life at, 112
  Correspondence Academy, 78–9, 115, 117, 163

Central Party School (*cont.*)
  curriculum, 67
  'disciplinary construction', 90, 97
  distance learning, 67
  External Training Centre, 129–30
  'four how to understand' research questions, 98
  funding of, 48
  ideological training, 67
  links with foreign institutions, 124
  master's degrees, 117
  non-degree cadre training, 66
  novice training, 73
  number of graduates, 66
  openness in, 112–13
  periodic training classes, 66
  publications, 100
  quality of academic staff, 65
  Regulations for the management of research projects at the Central Party School, 97
  Relevant opinions on further deepening the reform of cadre education in the Central Party School, 52
  research at, 68, 97
  research report on political reform, 98–9
  self-study, 67
  short-term courses, 66
  socialist theory and practice, 97
  special discussion classes, 68
  study of Marxist classics, 67
  'three transformations', 112
  training programmes at foreign universities, 125
  types of classes taught, 38–9
  weekly report sessions, 68
Central Radio and Television University, 120
charisma, 18
  organizational, 18, 41, 191, 192
China
  anti-corruption campaigns, 6
  central and interior parts of, 50, 116, 120, 187
  civilizing project of the state, 19
  economic growth, 4
  entrepreneurial success in, 5
  market economy, 4, 10, 125
  neo-socialist governmental discourse, 9
  political elite in, 141–79
  popular protests in, 189
  private sector, 185
  totalitarianism, 12
China Disabled Persons Federation, 15
Chinese Communist Party
  adaptability, 6
  and the administrative system, 141
  broadening of membership, 190

cadre education department, 57
cadre schools, 62
Central Compilation and Translation Bureau, 188
Central Organization Department, 52
Central Policy Research Office, 99
Central Propaganda Department, 52
Circular regarding the strengthening of the work of party schools, 44
commitment to revolutionary transformation, 190–1
control over the cadre system, 26, 33, 161–2, 189
credibility of, 191
Decision of 2004, 35
democracy in, 35, 164, 190
ethnographic work on, 20–1
legitimacy, 34
Leninist ideology, 4, 6, 11
Leninist organizational principles, 6, 27
management of cadres, 17–20, 32–5, 155–6, 164, 176
nomenklatura system, 161–2
office of the education committee, 57
'opinion' on the development of philosophy and the social sciences, 96
organization department, 57, 63
party discipline, 27
party spirit, 27, 115, 142–3, 182
Politburo, 69
power of, 1, 192
recruitment to, 10, 37, 156
rectification campaigns, 27–8
re-establishment of its leading role, 192
relationship with the government, 26
resilience of, 178
role in examinations, 171–2
role of, 11, 16
socialism and, 3, 9
Temporary Regulations on the Work of the Party Schools of the Chinese Communist Party, 45
transition to a ruling party, 171
United Front Department, 26, 29, 58, 62, 130, 139
willingness to experiment, 192
Circular regarding the strengthening of the work of party schools, 44
Civil Servants Law, 33–4
civil service system, 33, 46
civil society, 92
Cohen, Abner, 14–16
Cold War, 194
competition among training providers, 138, 164
constructivism, 15

correspondence degree courses, 75–80, 114, 163
    curriculum, 76–7
    examinations, 77, 78
    quality of, 114, 116
    recruitment of students, 75
    replacement with recognized degree courses, 119
    requirement for time spent in class, 76
    sale of diplomas, 114, 178
    'sidelines', 75
    teaching materials, 78
    variable quality of, 80
corruption, 5–6, 161, 187–8
counter-bureaucracy, 17
Creation journal, 100–1
Cultural Revolution, 32, 39, 41
culture, 13, 14–16

Decision of the Chinese Communist Party centre on the correct handling of party schools at all levels, 40
Decision of the Chinese Communist Party Centre on the strengthening of the building of the party's ruling capacity building, 35
Decision on the strengthening and improvement of party school work in the twenty-first century, 47, 114–15, 116
degrees, 75, 133, 163
    marketization of, 79, 133
    xueli, 77, 79, 116
    xuewei, 77
democracy, 35, 92, 190
    and capitalism, 2
    and corruption, 6
    depoliticization of, 93
    elections, 164
    and socialism, 4
'democratic parties', 62
Deng Xiaoping, 4, 33
    cadre training, 41
    examinations, 165–6
    'four cardinal principles', 34
    On the reform of the system of party and state leadership, 35, 43–4
    reform of the party, 32
dissidence, 190
distance learning, 77–8, 79
    web-based, 53
dual elite model of political loyalists and professional experts, 175
Duan Eryu, 21, 22, 106

Edin, Maria, 6–7
education *see* cadre training
'educational activities' campaign, 27

elections, 164
eliteness, cult of, 15, 19
Enlightenment, 194
examination system, imperial, 166
examinations, 171–2
    and applicants outside the area, 172
    topics covered, 170
    types of, 167–8
    written and oral, 168
executive leadership academies, 51–2

factionalism, 113, 161
Falungong, 190
favouritism, 161
Ferguson, James, 181
Fewsmith, Joseph, 98
Ford Foundation, 99
Foucault, Michel, 15, 181
Four Modernizations, 41, 42
freedom of expression, 189

Gang of Four, 40, 41
globalization, 131, 194
Gold, Tom, 22
Goodman, David, 160
governance, 5, 10, 92, 187
    centralization, 10, 49, 179
    depoliticization of, 93
    institutions of, 17
    neo-socialist, 23
    party's control of, 156
    socialist, 26–8
government, participation by non-CCP members, 62
government departments, 61, 62
Greenhalgh, Susan, 7, 15

Hainan Provincial Party School, 114
harmonious society, 11, 98
Harvard University, 125
Harvey, David, 7, 191
He Zengke, 188
Herzfeld, Michael, 14
higher education, market in, 79
Honghe Prefectural School, 133, 135, 138
    attitude of students, 149–50
    cadre training plan, 139
    quality of instruction, 149–50
    school of socialism, 139
Hu Jintao, 45, 69, 98
Hubei Provincial Party School, 103
human rights, 2, 190
humanities, degrees in, 178

ideology, 3, 6, 183
  classes on, 108–9
  importance and use of, 18, 142–3, 143–5
Internal Reference for Ideological Theory journal, 100
Internet, use of, 23, 53
Internet Marxism, 114–20

Jiang Zemin, 98
job rotations, 160
Journal of the Central Party School, 100, 102
Journal of the Yunnan Academy of Administration, 100–1
Journal of the Yunnan Provincial Party School, 100–1, 132–3
Jowitt, Kenneth, 18

Kennedy School of Government, 125
Kipnis, Andy, 8
Kohrman, Matthew, 15
Konràd, George, 175

labour market for professionals, 174
law, 109
leadership, 18, 154
lectures, 109–10, 146
Leninism, 6, 9–10, 91, 189, 190, 192
  adherence to, 35, 51
  and neoliberalism, 193
  role of the party, 34
Leninist organizational principles, 6, 27
Li Bobai, 163
Li Yongkang, 21, 22
liberalism, 194–5; *see also* neoliberalism
Liu Shaoqi, 38
Liu Xirui, 92–3
local government
  autonomy of, 50, 186–7
  financial constraints of, 134, 138, 186
  and hierarchical rank, 65
  legitimacy, 165
  and party schools, 138
  role and structure of, 179

Macao Technological University, 120, 124
main courses, 71–5
  categorial training classes, 72, 106, 139
  length and intensity of, 72–4
  novice training, 71–2, 73
  objective of, 70
  reserve cadre training classes, 71
  types of, 71
  young and middle-aged cadre classes, 71
Manion, Melanie, 188

Mao Zedong, 28
  dominance of the party, 37
  power of ideological study in 'correct thinking', 143–4
  Report on the work style of party rectification, 37
Mao Zedong Thought study classes, 39
market for professional talent, 185
market in administrative jobs, 173
market in teachers, 80, 128
market reform, 3, 5, 7, 125, 131, 192
  impact on party schools, 137
Marx–Lenin Academy, 38
  types of classes taught, 38–9
Marxism, 73, 91
  Internet Marxism, 114–20
Marxist classics, study of, 41, 182
Master of Public Administration degree, 93–4
May seventh cadre schools, 39, 40
May Thirtieth Movement, 36
meritocracy, 1, 28, 35
Michels, Robert, 163
Migdal, Joel, 13
Military and Political University of Resistance against Japan, 37
Miller, Peter, 9
minority cadres
  Chinese language proficiency, 104
  remedial semester, 104
  special courses for, 67, 72, 103, 106, 140
models, in Maoist practice, 131
modernization, 49, 131, 180–1, 190

National Academy of Administration, 20, 22, 45–6, 52, 92, 184
  funding of, 48
National Degree Committee, 103
National Minorities University, 103, 120
National Party Schools Work Conference, 108
neoliberalism, 92, 164, 191, 192
  and Leninism, 193
  and neo-socialism, 7–11, 194–5
neo-socialism, 1–25, 93, 164, 185, 187, 189, 190
  and neoliberalism, 7–11
neo-socialist rule in China, anthropology of, 1–25, 180–7
nepotism, 161
New People's Study Society, 36
new socialist countryside, 98

oligarchization, 163
organization departments, 126, 128, 151, 158, 162, 186

party building, 89, 91, 106
party rule, future of, 187–95

party schools, 26–55, 185
  before 1978, 35–9
  academic credibility, 95–6
  academic staff, 85–6, 95
  administration, 85–9
  cadres' attitudes to, 110–11
  centralist agenda, 118
  classes and groups, 147–8
  collective life at, 111–12
  competitiveness in, 113
  conference of heads of provincial schools, 108
  correspondence degree courses, 78, 79, 80, 85
    income stream from, 79, 80
  curricula, 89–94, 107
  degree programmes, 77, 102–4, 114, 119, 185
    xueli degree courses, 103–4
  departments
    academic disciplines, 85, 89–94
    academic services department, 85
    advanced study departments, 72, 88
    civil servants training department, 88
    correspondence course department, 85
    educational affairs office, 87, 88
    research office, 88, 89
    training departments, 72, 88
  'disciplinary construction', 95–6
  discussion sessions, 160
  enrolment procedures, 115
  establishment of, 36
  examination standards, 115
  extracurricular activities, 83, 148, 149, 160
  facilities, 82, 84, 135
  'five old courses', 89
  format of lectures and seminars, 109
  funding of, 42, 48, 133
  governance of, 86
  in government departments, 61
  head of education, 87
  ideological training, 183
  image of, 44
  inspection delegations to foreign countries, 125
  institutional integrity of, 140
  in large service organizations, 61
  levels of, 132–40
    county, 20, 55, 73, 78, 132
    local party schools
    prefectural, 20, 72–3, 78, 132
    provincial schools, 60, 132
    township, 73
  life and work at, 81–113
  linked positions, 122
  and local government, 138
  marketing and design of courses, 128
  merging of institutions, 133–4
  monitoring of staff performance, 86, 88, 112–13, 146
  network of, 57, 78
  non-degree training courses, 70–5, 104–13
  number of students, 104–5
  openness in, 111–12
  part-time courses, 103–4
  personnel management, 88
  quality inspections, 115
  quantitative quotas in teaching and research, 95
  regional model schools, 51
  relationship between teachers and administrators, 122
  in remote and poorer parts of the country, 129, 130–1
  research, 89, 90, 95–102
  rest and relaxation at, 83, 111–12, 182
  role of, 45, 121
  salaries of staff in, 47
  self-generated income, 135–6
  as the 'smelting furnace', 44
  social activities, 148
  specialized professional training courses, 71
  sports activities, 83, 149
  staff publications, 89
  standardization of, 115
  in state-owned enterprises, 61–2
  student accommodation, 81–2, 83
  student–teacher relationships, 110–13, 121–2
  systematization of, 115
  'teacher–student exchange' sessions, 110–11
  teaching in, 115
  teaching plan, 87
  temporary party branches, 148
  'transformational development', 118
  use of the Internet, 23
  use of 'xueyuan' for students, 110
  vertically integrated systems of, 59, 78, 122
  web-based, 118
  websites, 128
party spirit, 115, 142–3, 182
party-state, 180–7
  power cult, 182
  and reform, 5–7
  as society, 12–16
Peking University, 20
  Centre for Continuing Education, 129
People's Political Consultative Conference, 64
philosophy, 89, 91, 96
political economy, 89
political rationalities, 9
political science, 89
political training, 59

power, 19
  abuse of, 178
  of the CCP, 1, 191, 192
  and culture, 14–16
  dramaturgy of, 14–15
  production and distribution of, 12
  of the state, 12
power cult, 19, 182
prefectures, administrative departments, 61
Price, Janet, 36
Programme for educational reform in the Central Party School's Correspondence Academy, 115
promotions, 160, 169, 185
  age restriction on, 153
  public selection and examinations, 162
providers of cadre training, 127, 139, 138
public administration, 91, 101
  master's degrees, 93–4
  study of, 92–3, 128
public administration courses, 91, 92, 93, 128
public management, 91–2
  study of 92–3, 128
public management courses, 91, 92, 93, 127, 128
publications, editorial freedom, 102

Qilin Party School, funding of, 137–8
quality, and modernization, 180–1
Qujing Prefectural School, 124–5, 133, 134
  correspondence degree courses, 80
  funding of, 137

Raman, Parvathi, 2
recruitment of cadres
  competition in, 164–5
  examinations for particular posts, 165–6, 168–9, 176–7
  'expert' mode of appointment, 176
  new avenues for, 185
  open selection, 166–7, 169–70
  public selection and examinations, 171, 189
  regulations on, 166
  transparency in, 164–5, 188
Rectification Campaign of 1942–43, 37
Regulations on the work of selection and appointment of party and government leading cadres, 166
Relevant opinions on further deepening the reform of cadre education in the Central Party School, 52
research
  direction of, 96
  forbidden topics, 102
  'four how to understand' questions, 98

funding for, 99–100
management of, 99
in party schools, 95–102
and policy making, 98
quantitative quotas for, 95
rites of passage, 182
Rose, Nikolas, 9
Ruijin Marxist Communist School, 36
rule of law, 34

SARS, 190
schools of administration, 57, 59
scientific development, 98
scientific socialism, 89, 98
self-study, 41
seminars, 109–10, 146
service organizations, party schools in, 61
Shevchenko, Alexei, 6
Shilin County Party School, 133, 135–7
Sigley, Gary, 7
social engineering, 49, 50
social sciences, 96, 109, 127, 178
socialism, 1–25; *see also* neo-socialism
  and capitalism, 2
  definition of, 2–3
  and democracy, 4
  divergent forms of, 187–95
  and liberalism, 194–5
  and the market, 7
  resilience of, 7
  scientific, 89, 98
  state socialism, 194
Song Renqiong, 42
'special discussion class for principal central cadres of provincial-ministerial rank', 69–70
'spiritual pollution' campaign, 27
state
  anthropology of, 13–14
  mode of reproduction, 16
state-building, 4, 8, 10, 188
State Council
  Degree Office, 94, 95, 116
  Development Research Centre, 99
state-in-society, 13
state-owned enterprises, party schools in, 61–2
Stone Forest, 136
Study Times, 100
survey of students
  interviewees, 196–200
  questionnaire, 201–5
Szelenyi, Ivan, 175

'teacher–student exchange' sessions, 110–11
teachers, markets in, 80, 128

teaching methods
  case analyses, 146
  formal discussions, 147
  lectures, 109–10, 146
  seminars, 109–10, 146
  students' opinions on, 147
Temporary Regulation on National Public Servants, 33, 166
Temporary Regulations on the Work of the Party Schools of the Chinese Communist Party, 45
Tenth National Joint Conference on Cadre Education, 53–4
Theoretical Study journal, 100
Theoretical Trends journal, 100
think tanks, 99
Thøgersen, Stig, 165
'three emphases' campaign, 27
'Three Represents', 11, 47–8, 91, 106
Tibet, 190
transparency, 35, 164
Trial regulation on cadre education and training work, 54
Tsinghua School of Continuing Education, 127, 128
Tsinghua University, 20
Turner, Victor, 182

U, Eddy, 17
United Nations Development Programme, 99

Walder, Andrew, 156, 163, 176
Weber, Max, 17
Wen Jiabao, 69, 98
West, Harry G., 2
Winckler, Edwin, 7
work committees, 60

Yang Dali, 4, 187–8
Yiliang County Party School, 133, 134
Yu Yunyao, 97

Yunnan Normal University, 120
Yunnan Province, 21
  political elite in, 157
Yunnan Provincial Academy of Administration, 43
Yunnan Provincial Academy of Socialism, 64, 70, 81
Yunnan Provincial Party School, 81, 82
  academic credibility, 101
  admissions criteria, 103–4
  annual provincial cadre education and training plan, 105
  autonomy in execution of its tasks, 86
  Centre for Research on Deng Xiaoping Theory, 100
  collaborative master's programmes, 120
  correspondence department, 102
  employees, 90
  examination standards, 103–4
  joint degree programmes, 103
  Journal of the Yunnan Provincial Party School, 132–3
  minority master's programme, 103
  minority students, 103–4, 106
  objectives of cadre training, 73–4
  party building, 106
  publications, 100–1
  recognition of its degrees, 102–3, 116–17
  research at, 21–25, 99–100
  Research Office, 99
  sabbatical leave, 123
  survey of students, 143
  'teacher–student exchange' sessions, 110–11
  training courses for leading cadres, 106, 168
Yunnan Teachers College, 137

Zeng Qinhong, 51
Zhao Ziyang, 33
Zhou Tianyong, 98
Zhu Rongji, 34